BLACK CHILDREN AND UNDERACHIEVEMENT IN SCHOOLS

A Case Study and a Review of the Debate
on the
Issue of Black Underachievement

Frances Benskin

MINERVA PRESS
MONTREUX LONDON WASHINGTON

**BLACK CHILDREN AND
UNDERACHIEVEMENT IN SCHOOLS**

Copyright © Frances Benskin 1994

All Rights Reserved

No part of this book may be reproduced in any form,
by photocopying or by any electronic or mechanical means,
including information storage or retrieval systems,
without permission in writing from both the copyright owner
and the publisher of this book.

ISBN 1 85863 124 6

First Published 1994 by
MINERVA PRESS
10 Cromwell Place
London SW7 2JN.

Printed in Great Britain by
B.W.D. Printers Ltd., Northolt, Middlesex

BLACK CHILDREN
AND
UNDERACHIEVEMENT
IN SCHOOLS

A Case Study and a Review of the Debate
on the
Issue of Black Underachievement

Acknowledgements

I would like to thank all those who contributed to my research and gave their support in making this book possible.

I express my gratitude to the teachers, head teachers, lecturers, pupils and parents who devoted their time to me wholeheartedly and constructively. Without their help and cooperation I could not have proceeded with the study.

I also wish to thank Dr Collis for his advice and help with the computing of the data. I am grateful to Dr Sharma who offered some valuable advice, and to those not mentioned here, but who have contributed to the study.

Contents

Acknowledgements v
Preface ix
Introduction xi

CHAPTER ONE
A Review of the Debate on the Underachievement
of Caribbean Children in Schools 15

CHAPTER TWO
Different Perspectives and Aspirations Among
Students and Parents 70

CHAPTER THREE
Social Disadvantage and Educational Opportunities 101

CHAPTER FOUR
Employment and Migration in the Area 127

CHAPTER FIVE
Methodology 147

CHAPTER SIX
Interviews with Teachers 150

CHAPTER SEVEN
The Children's Experiences and Perceptions of School 179

CHAPTER EIGHT
Summary and Conclusions 223

Bibliography 233

Preface

The study of race and racism in education can be very problematic indeed. This is so because of the intangibility of such variables as race and racism which cannot be quantified in the same way as sexism, and to some extent class. However, the meaning of class has become very problematic over the years compared to the early nineteenth century when class was a quantifiable and observable factor.

Race is even more problematic in that one cannot easily identify race, let alone trying to quantify such a variable. Racism takes different forms and can be interpreted in different ways which further add to the complexity of the issue. For example we may know that racial discrimination has taken place within the workplace, school, or other institutions, but unless the intention of the person making the decision was made clear that the act was discriminatory, then we may probably have to assume that this was the case. Although to some extent, some researchers have tried to quantify discrimination in terms of the number of white applicants who were successful in obtaining employment in certain institutions, compared to the number of black applicants who were successful. But this would still be considered by some critics as an inaccurate way of quantifying racism due to a lack of statistical analysis and concrete proof.

I have attempted to investigate how racism in schools may adversely affect the performance of black children. The area of study is sparsely populated by black settlers who originally came from the Caribbean during the 1950s-60s, as opposed to areas which are more densely populated by Caribbean settlers.

Firstly, there is some difficulty in acquiring data on the issue due to an absence of recorded statistics. Secondly, the number of children of Caribbean origin in the area is very small and therefore could not be quantified statistically. However, an absence of large numbers of black children in the area does not mean that the study cannot yield adequate results. Good research practice can be based on observation, interviews and questionnaires which can be just as accurate as quantitative methods. Hence we could say that any piece of research that has been conducted with careful thought and planning, can be as enlightening and informative as any statistical analysis. As C. Dane

(1990, p208) suggested in Research Methods, something can always be learned from any data collected regardless of the lack of results from statistical analysis.

The research took place in a Midland conurbation which is renowned for its wealth of abundant raw material such as coal, clay, limestone, and quarrying. These raw materials paved the way for the development of industries, hence the area became heavily industrialized and very much working class in origin. It was seen as predominantly a working class area, with the middle class area mainly on the outskirts of the city.

My hypothesis was that black children are no less underachievers than other groups. Previous researchers persistently claimed that black children underachieved when compared with whites and Asians.

Did they have enough experience of the subjects they were studying and applied the right methodology? It is my intention to explore these issues more deeply to see if any further developments can be achieved.

Introduction

To be black and British seems to attract a great deal of attention, but for the wrong reasons. This has been the case since the late 1950s-60s, when black children from the Caribbean first started school in Britain. There seemed to have been confusion from the authorities from the very beginning, as to whether or not these children should be classed as British or should they remain West Indians, a term that I shall facilitate the use of Caribbeans or black children. Even those born in this country are constantly being referred to as West Indians even though their parents were British subjects before migration to Britain. Although many are now British citizens, this does not seem to alter the fact that they are still called West Indians. This seems to be supported by the phrase used by Powell in the 1960s, that the West Indian or Asian being born here does not become an Englishman. This controversy did not seem to have helped their school achievement, because statistics constantly show that Caribbean children underachieve in schools. Whatever the cause or causes of this, no researcher seems to have found the magic answer. But still they continue to focus on a variety of variables such as home background, matriarchal family, one parent family, pathology, and a loose family structure. But from whose perspective? From their own perception of what constitutes the black family. White middle class researchers have located the causes of black children's underachievement in their home background. Have they ever attempted to look closely at the black family structure as a means of ridding themselves of the stereotypes and biases that have influenced the way in which they have conducted their research? It is on those premises that I wish to argue that other factors may have been ignored, and have been substituted with subjective views by many of the previous researchers, who set out to prove their theories based on stereotypes and biased assumptions. Research carried out by Townsend and Brittan (1972), in over 200 schools, showed that although Caribbean children had a high attendance rate, and stayed on at school longer than other groups, they rarely entered for public examinations, and when they did, they sat mainly CSEs as opposed to GCEs. Coard's study in (1971), on Caribbean children in London, caused concern amongst Caribbean parents when they discovered that their children were underachieving at school. They formed parents groups to discuss what should be done to help their children. Not only were their children underachieving, but they were also placed in lower streams, and a vast number were being sent to E.S.N. Schools, (Schools for the Educationally Subnormal). Coard discovered that in some inner city areas, as much as 70% of Caribbean children were in E.S.N. schools. Could this be a true reflection of their abilities, or does the system treat them differently than other children?

Dhondy et al (1982) suggested that Caribbean parents were informed by teachers that their children would be sent to 'Special Schools', because they needed 'special' attention. This the parents thought was a good idea as it would help their children to make better progress. But they later discovered that they were misled by the authorities, and that their children were confined to schools that had a very low ranking, and could not adequately prepare them for later life. According to Coard, once the children went to those 'special schools', they were rarely returned to mainstream education. As a result the bright ones suffered as well as the less bright ones, because there were no facilities nor provision to match their abilities.

D. Holly (1967), and C. Hill 1969), suggested that racism in schools by some teachers was one of the reasons why Caribbean children underachieved at school. D. Milner (1983) suggested that the situation facing Caribbean children was the result of a culture clash on the part of both teachers and pupils who did not understand enough about each others culture. I would point out that prior to the 1950s - 1960s, most teachers had no contact with black children, and could therefore have been governed by previous stereotypes which depicted blacks in derogatory terms. As a result, Caribbean children could have been seen in the same light by teachers, and would not have been recognised by them as intellectually capable. From a sociological perspective, those factors could have contributed to the poor academic performance of Caribbean children in schools, especially if teachers have a low expectation of them and as a result place them in lower streams. By looking at the performance and experience of Caribbean children in Stoke as an area with relatively few black settlers, it is my intention to give a comparison of different types of areas to see if children's attainment and experience of school is determined by the area in which they reside.

Chapter 1 will look at previous theories on the issue of Caribbean children's underachievement and comment on their findings. It will also look at government policies adopted to deal with the pattern of New Commonwealth migration to Britain, and other aspects that are said to cause underachievement, such as IQ, teacher attitudes towards minority children, language and family pathology approach. Chapter 2 will look at the different perspectives which students and parents hold, and multicultural education as an a new approach to the school curriculum.

Chapter 3 will look at social disadvantage in education and how this affects various groups in different ways. It will take into account issues such as housing, occupation, social class, streaming and other issues which account for deprivation in education. Chapter 4 will look at the characteristics of the area under study, and the types of jobs that migrants have access to. Chapter 5 will explain the methodology in terms of how the data was collected and any problems encountered during the research. Chapter 6 will give an account of the interviews with teachers and how they responded to the topic of study. Chapter 7 will give an account of the children's response to the study and what has been discovered, and any possible recommendations or suggestions that may be beneficial in helping the situation facing Caribbean children in schools. Are they really a problem to be tolerated, or do teachers need to change the way they perceive and treat children of Caribbean origin? Chapter 8 will give an overall account of the study in terms of any new discoveries and any possible recommendations.

CHAPTER 1

A Review of the Debate on Caribbean Children's Underachievement in Schools

This book is about the underachievement debate of children of Caribbean origin in schools. Since the late 1960s the education of black children has been widely debated both educationally and politically. At school they are said to underachieve when compared with white children and children of Asian origin. But why should one ethnic group achieve, while the other underachieve when both groups are of Commonwealth immigrant status? The answer to this is still unknown, even though various studies have made different findings. The debate still remains very controversial and conflictual i.e. Caribbean parents are still dissatisfied at the way their children are being educated by an education system that was once the envy of the world, because it was considered to offer the best type of education, and many still consider this to be the case. But still there does not appear to be any early solution.

There has been an enormous amount of research carried out on the underachievement of Caribbean children in schools. Some of these studies began as far back as the late 1960s. But as this was a relatively new approach in this country, sociologists had very little knowledge on the issue to guide them in their approach on the topic of Caribbean underachievement. They were accustomed to using class as a variable, but where race was concerned, they had very little or no knowledge to this concept as a factor for underachievement. Little's study in (1966) for the Inner London Education Authority (ILEA) on the underachievement of Caribbean pupils found that they underachieved when compared with other groups. He had however linked under-performance to the concept of social deprivation theory which was previously used to assess white working class children. This method would be bound to distort the results of the study because by trying to link the performance of two groups of children from two different cultures would not yield an accurate result. Holly (1967) in Education or Domination looked at the problem in terms of educational practices in schools and what was being done to change things educationally. Holly (1974, p148) went on to look at education and race, and gave a critical review of the school curriculum and biases within it. He commented that this bias helped to reinforce prejudice and sustain discrimination which was already deeply embedded within society. He argued that overt racism existed, but far more pervasive was the low expectation which adults and children held of the abilities of black people. Holly (1974, p148) maintained that schools failed to present an adequate perspective on human cultures, and did nothing to combat the crude caricatures which were found in children's books and comics. As he saw it, racism was a fact in Britain, and this was the way in which children were socialized and taught in schools. He suggested that teachers were also subjected to this false representation of blacks which permeated society in every possible way. Hill (1969) looked at the effects of immigration and integration, and how immigrants would eventually settle in their new communities. But these studies were mere trial and errors or a means of paving the way for further studies concerning New Commonwealth immigrants in Britain.

Coard's study in (1971) seemed to have paved the way for racism and underachievement in schools to be taken more seriously. It was at this point that he suggested that racism was a factor which caused Caribbean children to underachieve in schools. This came to light when a black boy in his class refused to colour himself black in an art session. By now it was becoming more apparent that a Eurocentric curriculum incited black children to hate themselves because it related to white values as the norm, and everything black was portrayed as bad or evil. Townsend and Brittan (1972) in Tomlinson (1983, p38) looked at school performance and found that Caribbean children were at the bottom when compared with whites and Asians. They also noted that Caribbean children were clustered in lower streams. The Redbridge Report (1978) in Tomlinson (1983, p39) showed that in one high school it was discovered that 54% of Caribbean children were concentrated in C streams. In an unpublished study of a Midland LEA, (1978) Williams in Tomlinson (1983, p40) reported that throughout their school careers, Caribbean children were continually placed in the lower streams. He suggested that the schools held back black children rather than push them forward. By so doing, black children were made to feel incompetent and incapable, and that very few of them leave school with the qualifications necessary for further education and training. Allen and Smith (1975) in Tomlinson (1983, p39) found that out of 368 school-leavers they interviewed in Bradford, and 300 in Sheffield, no Caribbean leaver in Bradford had reached A level standard, and only 3 boys and seven girls had O levels or CSE equivalent. In Sheffield 7 boys and 15 girls had O level or equivalent. They found that overall white children had mean passes of 2.8, while non-whites had mean passes of 1.9. The authors suggested that while the schools tried to justify this by family background, language, lack of pupil application, an alternative explanation could be that a lack of educational qualifications legitimized the use of black children as unskilled labour. Rex and Tomlinson (1979) in Tomlinson (1983, p39) interviewed 25 Caribbean school-leavers and found that they achieved 63 CSE passes between them. The students were resentful that the teachers had steered them towards CSE rather than towards O level courses. Craft (1983) in (Tomlinson, 1983, p40) found in his London study that the performance of Caribbean children lagged behind that of other pupils in fifth year exams, even when controlled for social class. Caribbean pupils were also more likely to go on to colleges than to move on to fifth form courses.

Rampton (1981) in the Committee of Inquiry found that Caribbean children were disproportionately over-represented in CSE groups. Drawn from a sample of six LEAs, it found that 46% of Caribbean children entered for CSE examinations compared to 33% of a national average. They were also over-represented in ESN schools. ESN, low streams and CSEs are topics that seem to dominate the debate concerning Caribbean underachievement. There are many other studies which showed similar results, but it would be very time consuming and repetitious to discuss all such findings. But this volume of evidence clearly shows that Caribbean children underachieve at schools. Many have also drawn our attention to the fact that they were located in the lower streams at school or placed in ESN schools. This means that there is something seriously wrong with the way they are processed through the school system. But this is a factor that researchers have largely ignored. School processes and decision making within the schools would seem to remain a closed institution to those outside of the educational arena. Therefore precise information as to why Caribbean children underachieve at school remains difficult to extract. One may rely on the good will of teachers who say that they treat all children the same, as several teachers have told me, but in reality the situation may be completely different. If a certain group of pupils are always congregated in lower streams, this is a sign of differential treatment in the classroom. Eggleston and colleagues (1985) found that black children do tend to be treated differently within the same classroom, but they suggested that this may also extend to class differences. These studies would seem sufficient evidence for us to deduce that black children do not have access to equal opportunities within the school system and as a result they fail the system. Taylor (1983, p126) commented on Townsend and Brittan's research (1971) which pointed out that there was a clear indication that there was a disproportionate number of Caribbean children in ESN schools, than would be expected in proportion of Caribbean children in the whole of the population. Taylor stated that the DES figures for 1970 by Townsend and Brittan showed that there were estimated to be 109,580 pupils of Caribbean origin in all primary and secondary schools, of which 2,550 pupils were found in ESN schools. Taylor stated that this was in excess of the ratio of four to one when compared to other immigrant children in ESN schools.

Tomlinson (1983) suggested that Little's research (1966) for ILEA, linked Caribbean children's underachievement to social deprivation theory, and this may have complicated the issue. Rampton (1981) was commissioned by the government to look into the school performance of Caribbean children in schools. This was followed by the Swann Report in (1985) also commissioned by the government. Rampton found that Caribbean children underachieved at school, and suggested that racism could be a factor. Mac an Ghaill (1988) looked at pupil/teacher relations in a comprehensive school, and suggested that teacher attitudes seemed to be a factor that caused underachievement. Likewise Troyna (1977) investigated black children's experiences in schools, and linked underachievement to school factors.

Previously, some researchers had used variables such family background, large families, matriarchal families, which are all mainly stereotypes of black family life. This would mean that such methods would not adequately get to the root of the problem, but would instead, present a distorted view of the issue. As a result they are merely reflecting what the system expects them to find while the main problems remain obscure. Hence the platform is set for the next researcher to divulge similar findings. Did they attempt to look at the culture from which the immigrants came, and the problems they were facing in a white dominated society which they had to adjust to gradually? Caribbean parents had no prior knowledge of the British school system. They first realized that their children were doing badly at school in 1971 when Coard undertook a study on Caribbean's progress in schools. He found that too many were being sent to ESN schools. He questioned the use of IQ tests which were used to measure and assess black children's ability. He suggested that the tests were unfair because black children were not familiar with the type of vocabulary and terminologies used in the tests. He suggested that a child may give a correct answer which is correct in terms of his own culture, but may be wrong in the context of the test prescribed because meanings change from one culture to the next. He argued that the tests were too middle class based, and bore no significance of the abilities and realities of working class children. This brought an awareness to Caribbean parents that the school system was failing their children and something had to be done. They were greatly angered and set out to form parents groups to discuss their children's future within the education system. In other words, if the government was not doing enough to educate their children, they were prepared to find a way of doing so. But what was the government's response to the issue? Did they see this to be a priority, or did they ignore the parents' views? I will look at how government policies may have had an effect on the education of Caribbean children in schools. But how can we measure the effects of the causes of underachievement? We can assume that racism and prejudice may be factors, but assumptions are mere human judgements and cannot present us with proof to this effect. Also, what of teachers' perceptions towards black pupils? Will this be convincing enough for us to draw a conclusion? This will be examined later in the text.

New Commonwealth Migration to Britain

The (1950s-60s) migration of Commonwealth people to Britain was an economic one, due to post war expansion in British industries. Britain as an ex-colonial power had a ready made army of workers in the Caribbean, Asia and Africa, which could be called upon at any time to supply the labour that was needed to meet the demand of industry whenever necessary. Britain was therefore ahead of its other European rivals in terms of manpower, because of the availability of surplus labour that could easily be obtained from the New Commonwealth at any time. Some employers went directly to the Caribbean to recruit workers, while others advertised in the media in those countries. So as we can see, it was a direct invitation at the request of employers why so many New Commonwealth workers took up the offer to come to Britain.

The immigrants went into specific industries such as mining, London Transport, The National Health Service, British Rail, British Steel etc. These jobs were mainly semiskilled or unskilled, low paid, dirty, unsocial hours and shift work. Many of these jobs were made vacant by whites who had become upwardly mobile, and hence, the vacancies were easily filled by immigrant workers. Being British subjects they had no problem of immigration because of the open door policy that had existed since 1948. But they had to pay their own fares, seek jobs, and find their own accommodation when they arrived, although the Labour Exchanges at the time helped many to find jobs. This posed hardship for many, as they had to rely on friends or relatives who were already here to find them accommodation. Some came to Britain during the Second World War and many remained after the war had finished. There was some hostility and resentment towards the settlers, when right wing politicians such as Powell and Osbourne in the 1960s, made political broadcasts that too many immigrants were coming into the country, and that immigration should be stopped before it was too late. This caused anger amongst many of the indigenous people, and as a result some saw black people as a problem that would lower their standards of living and erode their culture. At this point they also saw immigrants as taking up their jobs and creating a housing shortage. As a result of this outcry amongst the indigenous population, we have seen an uprising of the national front who organize marches and protests to send black people back home, and keep Britain white campaigns. This was the result of black people being categorized as trouble makers, noisy, dirty, lazy, and other types of inflated terminologies. These types of controversial arguments and stereotypes may have determined the lifestyle that the migrants would be confined to. They did not have access to good jobs, so they remained in industry, and even then they were allocated to the worst types of jobs that paid less money, and were heavy and dirty. Some black workers have even suggested that this type of behaviour by employers was a direct result of obtaining cheap labour from the Commonwealth, thereby maintaining a colonial image of control over cheap black labour. Sociologists during the 1950s - 60s did not take into account these issues and how blacks were categorized as different and treated differently, in order to locate the causes of underachievement amongst Caribbean children. They viewed the situation from a white middle class perspective, and would have acquired their results accordingly. In the process of their quest to prove that Caribbean children underachieved, they have failed to take into account the fact that there is a diversity between the different Caribbean islands, and that there is also a middle and a working class amongst these people. Although this is not very significant, it cannot be overlooked, because as with the white middle and working class, there is a criteria for differential achievements amongst pupils of different backgrounds, and that not all black children were underachievers. After all, why shouldn't there be a class factor amongst black people? Is it because they are all seen as the same, and none are expected to be intelligent? This mode of thought may have created a situation where it would be impossible for other researchers to be objective, because researchers do draw on previous studies. There was no consensus amongst sociologists, because they entered into their research using different methodologies which would have resulted in different conclusions. Thus, there would have been no comparative methods with which to contrast and compare their findings.

Government Policies

Prior to Coard's study (1971) there has been government debates on the education of immigrant children, but these policies were assimilationist and integrationist, which meant that immigrant children were expected to be absorbed into the British way of life and Britain would become one nation. Roy Jenkins the then Home Secretary's speech was:

"There shall be one British nation. Immigrants would be absorbed within our culture without prejudice, and would take an active part in the direction of society, with equal opportunity, in an atmosphere of mutual tolerance."

But how effective was this statement. All its good intentions seem to have been eroded, with the exception that blacks are merely tolerated in modern Britain. Government policies are not directed towards equal opportunities as such but are vague and ambiguous.

The government did not make any attempt to cater specifically for Caribbean children in schools, because their view was that of assimilationist, in that it was hoped that in time immigrants would become part of the great nation and all would be well catered for. But as it turned out, this did not happen and the government realized that other measures had to be found. Language became an issue, but this was for non-English speakers, so there were widespread debates on this. R. Willey (1984, pp24-76) suggested that as early as 1963 the Department of Education and Science issued a series of pamphlets and circulars offering advice on English for immigrants. It emphasized the need for a carefully planned intensive course making use of modern methods of language teaching at the primary and secondary levels. But this was not in relation to the needs of Caribbean children, but for non-English speakers in particular. The Bullock Report (1975) in Tomlinson (1983,103) suggested that there should be a major appraisal of teachers attitudes and assumptions about language and its uses. It suggested that teachers should accept the language that pupils bring to the school. Willey (1984) argued that throughout the 1960s-70s, the fundamental question of whether or not Caribbean children had particular language needs in relation to the use of Standard

English forms were almost completely ignored by educationists and the DES. Policy makers and resource providers assumed that Caribbean children required no particular attention because they were basically English speakers. The Report urged that any initial difficulty was a temporary one that would go away in time. Tomlinson (1983, p29) suggested that an ILEA research on Caribbean children's performance in school had linked their poorer performance to social deprivation hypothesis. This explanation was seen as contradictory, because it bore no relation to the issue of underachievement. As can be seen, from as early as 1966 when Little carried out the research for ILEA, there has been confusion over the issue of the underachievement of Caribbean children. These surveys may have paved the way for even more complicated explanations. As a result of those studies LEAS continued to use the extra resources under the Section 11 of the 1966 Local Government Act to meet the most obviously apparent needs of E2L learners, i.e. to teach English as a second language to Asian children, the majority of whom spoke their mother tongue. Only a few LAs made any attempt to meet the needs of their Caribbean pupils. This tells us that from the very onset of migration the needs of Caribbean children were largely ignored, but priority was given to the apparent needs of Asian children. This shows that there are regional differences in the way that local authorities catered for their pupils. Most schools made a concerted effort to accommodate Asian pupils, whilst making no attempt to accommodate Caribbean pupils. This could have been one of the reasons why Asian children do well at school because they knew that they were welcomed and accepted by the authorities who did everything in their power to ensure that they were well catered for. This could have constituted a problem for Caribbean children who saw that no attempt was made to cater for their specific needs. If teachers made no attempt to accommodate nor encourage them, this could have created hostility between themselves and their pupils. As many studies have shown, Caribbean pupils are not highly rated by their teachers as academics. Thus, a hostile start between both groups could have implicated the schooling of Caribbean children. This is how it works, if black children have been labelled as failures at the beginning, this would be likely to affect future generations of Caribbean children, because teachers would continue to perceive them in that light. LEAs also faced a staffing problem and a shortage of resources. Jones (1977) outlined that local education authorities adopted different strategies to deal with the problems that were by then becoming acute. Some authorities asked immigration officials to keep a check at their port of entry on the number of immigrant children who were arriving, and to note their destination. This would enable them to identify the areas and schools which could be classed as priority areas in order to make provisions accordingly. But this scheme was ineffective as immigration officials used different strategies to identify groups of children, while others thought it was too difficult a task and refused to help. To help LEAs cope with the staffing problem, some adopted a policy on staffing. There was a problem of training sufficient teachers quickly, so some adopted in-service training for teachers already employed. Out of 71 LEAS, 41 provided this type of training to meet the needs of immigrant children. The duration of the courses varied between full time and part time, and the number of weeks allowed. Between 1967-70, 108 teachers from 23 LEAs received full time training of one term duration, while 34 teachers from 14 LEAs attended part time courses. There was difficulty in attracting secondary teachers on to the scheme, apart from those already engaged in the teaching of remedial work. Jones (1977) suggested that despite the efforts made by local authorities in informing teachers that special instruction was necessary for children from the New Commonwealth, teachers did not recognize this to be an important matter. It would appear that the authorities were in favour of helping to provide special instructions to help the children, but due to the uncooperativeness of teachers, not a great deal was done. Some of the teachers were too busy guarding their positions as professionals, and probably thought that this type of effort would demote them. After all why should they make any special effort to help children who were seen as coming from deprived backgrounds in foreign countries? Thus, teacher attitudes may have contributed to the underachievement of Caribbean children in schools, because they did not attempt to welcome them into the school system.

Another policy adopted by some LEAs was to recruit staff from the New Commonwealth, but this was not without controversy. Some policy makers thought that this would lead to a trend of separate service. Some thought that if Asian teachers were employed, their dialect might not be helpful, and there would be a risk that they might slip into their own language when dealing with Asian children. Some teachers were against the idea of ESL classes being held in schools, because in their opinion Asian children should pick up the English language as they went along. They rejected the idea of mother tongue being taught in schools, as they suggested that this would lead to the children developing a split personality, thus hindering their progress. Jones (1977) outlined that the Caribbean teachers who were employed at the time were not specifically in charge of Caribbean children, and they were seen as less of a threat to the school system. It is ironic that the teachers had no interest in making adjustments to help immigrant children, but at the same time they were against the recruitment of New Commonwealth teachers. Some were more concerned about their status as teachers than their dedication as teachers with a commitment to helping their pupils. Many may have entered the profession for the benefits and rewards which it offered, rather than to have any concern for the well-being of their pupils as caring professionals. It is no wonder that recently the Conservative Government has realized that teaching standards are not what they should be, and have proposed to evaluate and reward teachers on the basis of their school performance.

Another policy was that of dispersal or bussing. Tomlinson (1983, p12) suggested that in 1965 the Department of Education and Science (DES) Circular 7/65 produced a section on spreading the children. It recommended that dispersal should become an official policy. i.e. to send children to school in other areas away from their local environment. But several authorities rejected it because they saw it as illegal. Tomlinson (1983, p12) suggested that ILEA was one of the authorities to reject the policy, because it was deemed unfair to immigrant children. But why was this policy formulated in the first place? This was to prevent a high immigrant population in some schools. The idea was that if the number of immigrant children in a particular school was small, it would account for better race relations, and if the number was too high, it would alter the ethos of the school (Tomlinson 1983, p127). Some white parents in some authorities had also complained that black children were holding their children back. Thus, this policy was given priority in order to convince white parents that their complaints were being taken care of. But when black parents complained that their children were underachieving at school, it took more than a decade for the government to decide to look into the problem, and even then it was not done wholeheartedly, but piecemeal and ad hoc. This type of response would question the purpose of the education system, in terms of inherent biases and inequality within the system. Tomlinson (1983, p18) looked at a list of policy objectives published by the DES which was considered to be beneficial. They were:

1. To help create a climate in schools in which colour and race were not divisive, and which would give all immigrant children opportunities for personal development in their new environment.

2. To ensure that building programmes and teacher quotas reflected the needs of the areas with large numbers of immigrant pupils.

3. To offer practical help and advice to teachers faced with the challenge of teaching immigrant children.

4. To safeguard against any lowering of standards due to the presence of large numbers of non-English speaking children which might adversely affect the progress of other children.

5. To encourage and promote relevant research.

(Tomlinson 1983, p19: DES 1971:15).

It could be argued that the DES in trying to create policies which would enable minority children to benefit, seems to be reinforcing racist overtones which should have been ruled out in the first place. It commented on lowering of standards if there were too many minority children in a particular school, which is the very term white parents had used to complain about their children's education being affected. One could however argue that before the presence of black children in British schools, white working class children were seen as underachievers, but under the guise of social deprivation. But the arrival of a new group of immigrants meant that attention must be focused elsewhere. It was also noticed that teachers faced with the teaching of minority children were supposedly faced with a challenge, and should therefore be advised accordingly. I would suggest that it would have been a better proposal to enlighten teachers about the way in which they teach minority children. They should have been advised about cultural differences, and how to gradually accommodate black children into the schools. Instead, they were probably made to think that they were dealing with a group of alien children who were uneducatable, but they should tolerate them as best as they could. Those non-English speaking children should have been given special instructions by skilled personnel to help them settle into their new environment. But they were thrown in at the deep end and expected to find their own way out. Such policies would only help teachers to reinforce their own prejudices against minority pupils and treat them differently.

The DES has frequently been criticised for its lack of involvement relating to policies for ethnic minority pupils. According to Tomlinson (1983, p25), despite pressures on the DES to produce policies especially related to ethnic minority education during the 1970s, the government's response was to subsume the problems of minority children under those of the disadvantaged. The DES response to the 1974 Select Committee was that while the government believed that it was necessary to make formal arrangements for the development of the education of immigrants, and the education for a multiracial society, there was also a need to provide for those suffering from educational disadvantage. As a result of that debate, there was the setting up a unit for Educational Disadvantage within the Department and one at Manchester. Policies for a Central funding was rejected on the grounds that the Section 11 Grants and Urban Aid funding was sufficient. One could argue that the government seems to be avoiding the responsibility of providing sufficient funding to meet the needs of minorities, because it does not consider those problems to be serious enough to be tackled by government intervention. Minority issues are therefore often overlooked, rather than to take any form of priority. The placing of minority issues with that of the disadvantaged, would seem to imply that they are already a disadvantaged group, so if they are placed alongside the indigenous disadvantaged, there will be no need to provide additional funding specifically for minority issues. Rutter and Madge (1976) in

Tomlinson (1983, p24) pointed out that minority children suffer specific disadvantages over and above that suffered by the indigenous, notably racial discrimination. The authors could have developed this theme further in order to establish the effects of racial discrimination on the education of ethnic minorities. But hardly any emphasis is placed on the racial elements of schooling, and this makes it difficult to investigate the problem of racism suffered by minority children. Tomlinson (1983, p25) suggested that an American scholar Kirp (1979) wrote in a thesis that British Educational Policies during the 1960s-70s, have been characterized by racial inexplicitness, due to its omission of educational programmes specifically for non-whites, and its lack of concern over the possibility of racial discrimination in education. He quoted the following:

"The aim of British policy has been on the one hand, to stress the infinitely diverse needs of individual students, and on the other, to embed race in some broader context such as educational disadvantage."

(Kirp 1979, in Tomlinson 1983, p25).

Kirp is suggesting that racism in Britain is not taken seriously enough by the government for them to take it as a priority issue, but rather, to weave their way around it by including other issues. By listening to various TV programmes on race issues in America, in my view it would appear that government intervention on such issues as race, is more frequently carried out and is more effective than it is in Britain. So why don't the British government do more to combat racism is schools? There is a possibility that it does not want to be seen to interfere by telling the teachers to fight against racism, when it does nothing to curb such measures in society. Racism in Britain is structured and institutionalized, and would require vast measures for any changes to be effective. As a result the government would prefer to pretend that it does not exist, whilst hoping that any individual or group differences will simply go away in time. The government has on several occasions remarked that certain policies do not work, so it is best to leave certain changes to employers or others in charge of certain institutions to implement such changes.

However, due to pressure on the government to investigate the education of Caribbean children, the appointment of Lord Rampton was commissioned in (1979) to look into the issue of Caribbean children's underachievement is schools. The committee's findings showed that black children were at a disadvantage in schools. It cited issues such bad housing, inner city deprivation and lack of political participation for their failure in schools. It also suggested that there was racism in schools, but this was mainly to be found amongst some of the younger teachers. Rampton did not fully commit himself to the issue of racism, but he had paved the way for further research on the issue. It is also the case that the study was conducted in inner city areas which would reflect the findings of inner cities. Taylor (1983, p4) suggested that the research was undertaken on the basis of some previous studies on the same issue, also the time factor dating back from as early as the 1950s could be called into question. The research was also wide ranging so that a complete picture could not be built up. For a study to be valid it must be representative of a national survey, and Rampton's study fell short of this. It has however, touched on the issue of racism which shows that this is an issue that is worth exploring more fully in order to discover the extent to which it affects the abilities of Caribbean children in schools. Such large scale and well funded studies are in a better position to consolidate their efforts on certain issues than smaller scale studies which are more restricted and limited in resource. Swann (1985, p733) was also commissioned by the government to investigate the issue of black children's underachievement. But this report is rather vague, broad and ambiguous. It covered a very broad area which included a variety of ethnic groups of children, with the topic of Caribbean underachievement barely glossed over, with no coherent solution or recommendation. It however suggested that the Select Committee since 1973, had recommended that there was a shortage of black teachers in education, and that those who were already in teaching lacked promotional opportunities, but this was never taken up by the government. Townsend and Brittan according to Swann, had noticed that one in five probationary primary teachers and one in sixteen probationary secondary teachers felt that there had been any specific reference to the education of immigrant children in their initial training. The study in failing to recognize the implications of racism in educational achievement, has recommended that the 1976-77 proposal on the teaching of Caribbean language and culture be taught in the form of black studies in institutions, rather than to suggest a change in the attitudes of teachers. The study has therefore fallen short of its intended purpose, and has instead diverted from the path of the investigation. It looked at the situation facing Liverpool black youths, and noted that the teachers were uncertain about the lack of policy by the authority which did nothing to guide nor direct them, because it did not make any special provisions for its ethnic population. How therefore can it be expected that an adequate answer be found as to the causes of underachievement amongst Caribbean children? In an inner city area such as Liverpool, blacks face severe forms of discrimination and deprivation, and this study could not adequately provide causes nor effects of underachievement amongst Caribbean children. It would be difficult for anyone with no experience of inner city lifestyle to investigate those problems objectively. Again those studies reflected a middle class perspective, and could not adequately account for the specific problems faced by Caribbean children.

Anti-discrimination Legislation

Phizacklea and Miles (1979, p6) argued that prior to the 1958 Noting Hill and Nottingham riots between black and white groups, neither successive Labour nor Conservative governments saw New Commonwealth immigration as a problem. But after the riots the issue of immigration became a major political issue and has continued to remain so ever since. Since those incidents blacks have continued to be seen as a problem in Britain. Thus the first Act to curb immigration was in 1962, which limited the number of New Commonwealth immigrants who could enter Britain. Since then subsequent Acts have been formed which further restrict those who can enter the country. The government believed that if fewer immigrants came to Britain, this would allow for better Race Relations for those who are already settled here. It therefore sets out to formulate laws which aim to protect black immigrants. The Runnymede Trust (1980) looked at various stages of the development of anti-discrimination legislation. It noticed that the Race Relations

Acts of 1965 were a significant step forward which attempted to influence behaviour and attitudes. It was set up to deal with complaints against discrimination on the grounds of race, colour, ethnic or national origin. This was meant to be in places such as hotels, restaurants, entertainment and public transport. Only a few complaints were made because many of the regulations fell outside the scope of the Act.

This Act was followed by the 1968 Race Relations Act which was extended to cover housing, employment, services, and publication of discriminatory advertising. Due to the widening of the Act, in June 1974 Public and Economic Planning (PEP) indicated that discrimination in employment was widespread and was found in recruitment for all manual jobs. It found that Asians and Caribbeans applying for unskilled jobs faced discrimination in at least one third of the cases. In 1975 the Labour Government found a number of weaknesses in both Acts and replaced them with The Commission for Racial Equality in 1976. This gave broader and wider policies to identify and deal with discriminatory practices in industries, firms and institutions. It gave two definitions of discrimination, direct and indirect. The first is when a person is said to treat another less favourably on the grounds of race, colour, nationality, ethnic or national origin. The latter refers to treatment which can be described as being equal in the formal sense as between racial groups, but discriminatory in effect on a particular racial group.

Gaine (1987, p33) looked at whether or not a policy on race would be effective. She suggested that it would help to clarify certain issues, but in white schools it would be more difficult because teachers constantly insist that there is no problem there. An absence of black children does not mean an absence of race related issues to deal with, especially in a multiracial society as Britain today. In her view, we need to look beyond the boundaries of race and racism in order to be able to explain educational achievement and failures in their proper context. I would suggest that because education developed on a white middle and upper class culture it is unlikely to change, due to the established structures and institutions of society which do not allow for any major changes to take place. Hence education remains the privilege of the rich, in that they can afford to buy the type of education that they want for their children. This is why education remains divided by class, because class is a major dominant force within the education system. It is therefore unlikely that the government would intervene by formulating strict educational policies for the benefit of minority children. Education is just as divided by race as it is by class, and perhaps even more by race. The reason why I suggest this is that policies have been reformed slightly to accommodate for the education of the working class. But racism is embedded in the structures of the entire education system, and no amount of reform can change this, and moreover, no attempt has been made to do so on racial grounds. Over four centuries of structured racism in literature which perpetuated in educational institutions and filtered downwards into the rest of society cannot be easily erased. That would be going against the whole structure and purpose of the British education system, as its main function is to maintain the status quo. As Rose's study (1969) in Tomlinson (1983, p24) showed that despite the presence of immigrant children in Britain, the DES as a bureaucratic organization has never played a key role in implementing policies in favour of the education of immigrant children. But as Cashmore and Troyna (1983, p150) suggested how quickly the DES responded to the views of white parents and rushed through Parliament the policy on bussing as a means of dispersing black children from certain areas. They stated that this policy was without foundation, because there was no evidence to suggest that any concentration of immigrant pupils would be of any significance, due to the level of multiple deprivation that already existed in those areas. It would appear that the presence of immigrant pupils came to be significantly linked with disruption and a lowering of educational standards in British schools, even though there already existed deprived and decadent schools in certain areas. Immigrants are always seen as intruders and are likely to be blamed when anything goes amiss. In the 1960s immigrants were blamed for taking jobs which whites should have, even though those jobs were already vacated by whites. They were also blamed for the housing shortage even though there already existed a housing shortage after the war. Then came the latest occurrence, black children were holding back white children, even though some of those schools were already decrepit, ill-equipped, and in run down areas where standards were already low. As Troyna suggested, the presence of immigrants would have made no difference to the already existing standards of multiple deprivation. Those exuding remarks by politicians and parents are quickly picked up and learned by the white indigenous children, who grow up with the same type of attitudes about blacks which they pick up at school and in the home. Most of the white children in my research thought that Pakistani's owned all the corner shops, and were taking up their jobs and should be sent back home. Others thought that in the West Indies, people lay on the beach all day, and this leaves them very little time to work. If West Indians owned the shops I wondered what their views would have been. This shows how racism is perpetuated from one generation to the next. One boy wrote in a short essay that very soon the Queen of England will be a Pakistani. These are the views of white children in schools in the 1980s. This shows that there is a need for vast curricula changes to enable people to modify their views from a Eurocentric to a multicultural view of society.

In the USA the Committee on Race and Education by Swabb (1984) in Mac an Ghaill (1988, p43) looked at neighbourhood school policy in relation to Public Schools, and environments associated with disadvantaged schools. They found that the neighbourhood school policy cause children from one residential area to attend the same school. This is likely to encourage a concentration of black children to attend certain types of school, because their parents tend to live in one particular area of the city. Those families tend to share other common issues relating to educational disadvantages such as low income, low educational level, poor housing, lack of recreational facilities, all of which make those children vulnerable to low standards of achievement in education. The Committee also reported that school is only one factor in influencing success or failure. The other most important factors are to be found in the home environment, the community, and attitudes towards family life. They argued that those factors have important bearings on the child's ability to learn, and the types of relationships they develop with their teachers and colleagues. If their home environments are adverse to that of the school, their school performance can be expected to suffer. Many of the black children in that neighbourhood were found to suffer many of the problems that were typical of underprivileged children. It was found that many were concentrated in certain areas because of historical factors such as them being restricted to well defined and less desirable areas than other minorities. It is a known fact that blacks do not have the same access and privilege as whites to resources that are necessary for their development and well-being. They are mainly always confined to densely populated areas with very little amenities, which restrict them from making any headway in the society to which they belong. They do not have access to good schools to which to send their children. Therefore the very limited education which they receive will not equip them to take up broader challenges in society in general. I would argue that educational policies are therefore dictated by politics, and as can be expected black children will continue to be seen as underachievers. As Bowles and Gintis (1976, pp56-239) argued that the working class in particular are socialized into their roles in society by the schools which teach them to be obedient servants and accept their roles. Sociologists tend to focus on attitudes of children or teacher attitudes or other visible variables when researching disadvantage in education. But have they actually investigated the structures and barriers which act as a safety net to bar undesirable groups from freely gaining access to better and higher standards of education? The education system starts off unequal and this continues to dominate the structure of education throughout Western societies. This is especially so in capitalist societies where education developed on a middle class basis and continues to be dominated by wealth and privilege. This privilege ensures continuity of education in the hands of the middle classes. Educational reforms are therefore not expected to be of any great benefit to the majority of the working classes.

Schooling and IQ

Coard's study (1971) showed that large numbers of children of Caribbean origin were sent to ESN schools. He argued that this was the result of them being wrongly assessed by educational psychologists who had no knowledge of the background or origin of Caribbean children and assessed them wrongly as having low IQs and behavioural problems. Townsend (1971) in Tomlinson (1983, p43) discovered that while 0.68% of all non-immigrant children attended ESN schools, the figure for Caribbeans were 2.33%, while Indians were 0.32% and Pakistani's 0.44%. Townsend explained the findings in terms of a problem of assessment and a lack of culture fair tests. Coard discovered that an ILEA report carried out in 1967 showed that some schools had up to 30% immigrant children, of which three quarters were of Caribbean origin. The report also stated that some headmasters were of the opinion that many Caribbean children were wrongly assessed, but did nothing to help them. The numbers returning to mainstream schools were very low. Edwards (1979, p5) found that whereas assessment procedures were waived for Asian and European immigrants, they were seen as a normal part of the assessment procedures of the evaluation of Caribbean children. This pattern continued despite evidence that those tests had little validity because of inherent cultural biases. Coard found that those children attending ESN schools were considered as having low intelligence, an IQ of between 50-80. I would add, that if the tests were middle class oriented as in fact they were, it is obvious that children who were not accustomed to the British way of life would fail them drastically. So too would a great deal of the white working class children, because they would not have had access to that type of learning. Tomlinson (1983, p33) however, looked at Jensen's work (1969) and suggested that IQ tests were no longer considered as valid for the measuring of intelligence, but other explanations had to be found. This led to alternative methods of explanations such as lower socio-economic status of black families. This led researchers to focus on black children as being socially disadvantaged, and this type of assumption made a suitable platform for their research.

Coard (1971) looked at the class system and commented that it is the white middle class people who construct the IQ tests, therefore it was not surprising that it was the white middle class pupils who passed the examinations by scoring the highest. This type of testing he argued, had nothing to do with real abilities. He also pointed out that an emotionally disturbed child was most likely to do badly on IQ tests. The very fact that the child has to sit in one place for a considerable length of time answering a series of questions, or doing tasks that are foreign to him, is bound to lead to frustrations and uneasiness. He stated that black working class children came from a different background with a different set of life experiences. This meant that they would be bound to have difficulty in understanding and answering those same questions, regardless of how intelligent they may be, because the tests were not culture fair. The type of language used in the tests as Coard saw it, was part of the daily life experiences of middle class children. This gave them confidence when answering the questions and they were bound to feel at ease. Caribbean children are in a worse situation than the white working class because they are at a double disadvantage in terms of race, colour, and class.

Coard (1971) noticed that black children fell behind in their classroom work, and they got low scores in relation to their abilities. He suggested that the ways in which black children were adversely affected by their teachers' attitudes, were prejudice, low expectations and patronizing. He said these attitudes were widespread and had devastating effects on Caribbean children. In one instance one of Coard's colleagues noticed that two white teachers sat in the staff room smoking and had refused to teach 'those niggers' who made up most of the class. When the matter was reported to the headmaster he took no action. Some heads actually persuaded Caribbean children to leave school early on reaching the leaving age. This was so, even though the parents wanted them to stay on at school to continue their education in order to gain some qualifications. Townsend and Brittan (1972) found that of the 40 primary schools they studied, about 30 of the headmasters and headmistresses, and about 20 secondary heads commented that disciplinary problems were frequently identified amongst Caribbean pupils. On the other hand, Caribbean parents were of the opinion that the schools lacked discipline, because in their country of origin, children behaved at school because good behaviour is part of the school's disciplinary practices. Here, the parents suggested that teachers had no control over their classroom, and that was one of the reasons why their children were underachieving. Edwards (1979, p3), noticed that even when black children receive all their education in Britain, their performance was still below that of the white indigenous children. He also commented on the large numbers of Caribbean children in ESN schools, which is an indication that they were unfairly assessed by educationists. He found that there were often four times as many black children in ESN schools, compared to whites. He argued that this would only exacerbate the problem in later years rather than solving it. The decision of the DES in (1973) to cease collecting statistics on ethnic children made it more difficult to monitor the progress of minority children. Edwards argued that even though it appeared that the number of Caribbean children entering ESN schools were decreasing, the overall picture was still depressing, and was likely to remain so for some time yet. Despite the low attainment levels of black children, parental aspiration was still high. Edwards suggested that the problem faced by Caribbean children was the inflexibility of the education system which did not recognize that they were in a special needs category. Pursell (1977, p22) looked at inequality in education and noted how the major structure of dominance enabled certain groups to influence legislation. This enabled them to gain institutionalized force of the state which legitimizes their already structured positions within institutions. He also noticed that economic resource is one of the great influences that differentiates people economically and socially. He looked at the situation where IQ and cultural deprivation factors are used to dominate explanations of differential school achievement. He argued that most social science research is centred around those factors, which set the terms in which questions are posed. They significantly influence educational practices and policies, and pervade almost every school in Britain and the USA. Pursell (1973) in Carvier (1975) stated that IQ tests are designed to differentiate people in that it measures their differences, but not their similarities. The requirement for differentiation is so deeply embedded in the education system that it is built in the structure of the tests themselves. In the process when those tests verify differentiated performance, it is used to justify differentiated selection. This is not to say that individual differences do not exist, but it is how those differences are interpreted, justified, and used as a basis for a differential curricula and rewards.

Halsey (1961, p269) looked at social factors which determine academic success. He found that between 40-60% of the variations amongst students could be accounted for by variation of IQ levels. When IQ is held constant the correlation between IQ and other characteristics are reduced uniformly in size. He also found that apart from IQ, other social factors such as socio-economic status must also be taken into consideration. The higher the occupational status of the breadwinner in the family, the higher the students achievement level. However, this should not be taken as proof of the association between individual's achievement scores and occupational status, as sociologists are still not fully aware of what it is that motivates certain individuals to succeed. We need to take into account the various psychological processes concerned with achievement motivation. Researchers have long sought ways of explaining why some individuals are more inclined to achieve than others. Thus, the study on individual achievement remains a mystery because of the difficulty in piecing together the different factors that might be associated with achievement. It is not all students with a high IQ who will be interested in higher education, although this may be associated with a class factor.

Teacher Attitudes and Expectations

Stone (1981, p251) pointed out that Caribbean parents are eager for their children to acquire a good education. Yet the exact reverse seems to be the case. Where do we look for the answers? There could be a number of interrelated factors such as parental aspiration, economic circumstances, environmental circumstances, the community, teacher expectation, low motivation etc. Of these factors we could refute parental aspiration, as most studies show that black parents encourage their children to get a good education. Some teachers have even remarked that black parents are over ambitious for their children, as Stone (1981, p251) discovered, and that they are of the opinion that they should set their sights on par with white working class parents. This would let us assume that teachers would consequently hold low expectations of Caribbean children, and would not expect them to achieve well at school. From conversations and interviews I had with black and white ex-pupils, many of them have outlined that teachers are poor judges in assessing pupil's competence. They said that teachers always assume that they know best, when very often they are wrong, but will not admit to being wrong. Their training does not provide them with specific knowledge of dealing with specific groups of pupils, and the only knowledge that some teachers may have of black children is based on a stereotype which they acquired from literature and the media. Tomlinson (1983, p80) suggested that teacher attitudes, perceptions and expectations of minority group pupils, will to a large extent depend on the preparation and training they received during their teacher training courses. She argued that many of those teachers although inadequately trained, have gone on to do research on minority pupils. Others, who have remained in the teaching profession, we could assume that when they are faced with the real situation they do not have that specific knowledge to deal with it adequately, and may react instinctively by drawing inferences about black children in order to cope. Teachers have a need to keep control of their classroom, and when faced with situations that seem threatening, may resort to methods that are workable, but at whose expense? Troyna (1987) pointed out that some teachers felt intimidated when faced with a group of Caribbean children who spoke Patois which they could not understand. This shows that anything that seems alien to teachers is immediately outlawed because it is seen as an infringement in their schools.

Milner (1983) looked at the effects of teacher expectations of Caribbean children. He drew from Rosenthal's experiment where the subjects were influenced to produce a certain type of behaviour. The researcher communicated non-verbally to the subjects the kind of responses that were required of them. Several classes of children were given a non-verbal intelligence test, which was intended to measure their intellectual growth. A proportion of each class was designated as academic spurters and their names were given to their new class teachers at the beginning of the next school year. All the classes were re-tested twice more on the same test at four monthly intervals. The spurters showed considerably greater gains in IQ than did the rest of the children who were not chosen. The authors concluded that when teachers expected that certain pupils would do well intellectually, they did remarkably well. The teachers also judged the children as more likely to succeed, more interesting, curious, and less in need for social approval. Conversely, those children who were not judged favourably by their teachers, were destined to fail, because of the pressure directed towards them as potential failures. They were not expected to succeed, and that was exactly the result. Even the high ability pupils who did not attain their teachers approval for success, became academic failures because that is what was expected of them. Very often because of the social backgrounds of certain pupils, teachers took a dim view of them, and even those pupils with the best of intentions can become victims of a vicious circle. In part, Caribbean pupils may have fallen into this category, by underachieving at school. A child's first encounter with school is of crucial importance as to how they fit into the system. They first have to be accepted by their teachers and peers. Any slight misunderstanding of the teacher about certain pupils, in terms of dress, appearance, behaviour or even the area in which they reside, may lead to the teachers drawing inferences about them. Once that happens, those children may be labelled throughout their school life as non-achievers, a label that is always effective. This label has affected Caribbean children for the past three decades, in that they are continuously seen as underachievers within the school system. Brown (1979) argued that very often teachers are not willing to take the time to get to know their pupils background or culture. She spoke of a teacher who had a Caribbean boy in her class at school and said that she had difficulty in dealing with him. Another teacher who had attended a weekend seminar on black culture said that she gained an enormous amount of experience which completely changed her attitude and perception towards black children. Why did the previous teacher have difficulty in dealing with one boy? This shows that a lack of experience amongst some teachers when they have to deal with black children, can have serious consequences for the child concerned. This may be partly because they view them as different and do not make the effort to try to get to know them before drawing conclusions about them. As Holly (1967) pointed out, teachers should try to concentrate on similarities amongst their pupils, rather than on differences.

Eggleston and colleagues (1985) found that black youngsters were more likely to remain in continuing education, as many go on to college. They also found that some teachers may tend to treat black and white children differently within the same classroom, but this also extends to class differences. Tomlinson (1983, pp74-75) also commented that it is logical that if teachers hold stereotyped views of black children, this will lead to differential classroom treatment which will be to the detriment of the children's education. Tomlinson also explained that Giles, a visiting USA professor at the NFER in London, visited fifteen junior and eight secondary schools, and was convinced that there were both subtle and overt forms of discrimination in British schools. He suggested that this was as a result of teachers' attitudes and behaviour towards Caribbean students.

Eggleston and colleagues also discovered that Caribbean children can get labelled by their teachers if they ask too many questions. Conversely, if they do not participate they can also get labelled as lazy or not interested. This puts black children in a dilemma from which they cannot escape. They also found that there was a tendency for careers officers to bring with them preconceptions and stereotypes in the process of training and guidance. Some Caribbean children have suggested to me that some careers officers were of the opinion that they were not capable of pursuing good careers, and tried to steer them into lower type occupations other than what they wanted to do. Eggleston and colleagues (1985) found that black youngsters were less likely to gain early access to employment. The authors explained this by saying that the youths could probably be compensating for their loss of opportunity at school by going to college. This factor is a valid one, because many of the children I interviewed said that because they did not have the opportunity at school to take their O levels, they had to go on to college to take them. Some Caribbean parents were also dissatisfied that the schools had deliberately held back their children. This attitude amongst teachers seem to be widespread. They seem to think that black children are not capable of taking O levels, because that type of knowledge is above their capabilities. So they put them in for the second rate CSEs which they know will not get them very far because of their lower status. Most Caribbean parents are keen for their children to have a good education, (Stone 1981), because they see this as an escape from the manual labour sector to which they have been mainly confined. Therefore when they see that the schools deliberately help their children to underachieve, this causes anger and resentment among them. They see this as blatant racism amongst teachers. This may not be obvious to the teachers themselves that what they are doing to black children is wrong, and even when the parents complain about the injustices of the schools, they are not taken seriously by the teachers. It is no wonder Coard in 1971 wrote: "This is what the British Education System is doing to our Children". It fails them regardless of their abilities. In the Voice newspaper, (9.8.91) Yvonne Taylor spoke to Jack Straw the Shadow Education Minister about the underachievement of Caribbean children. He suggested that one of the critical causes of underachievement is low expectation. He said that "too often he goes into schools and talk about the level of achievement of children, and the teacher may take him aside and say, what do you expect of these children?" He noticed that this attitude was found mainly in inner city areas. He was also concerned about the inability of some parents to speak out about issues which affect them, and that many do not know that they can exercise their rights.

In the USA Schwabb (1964, p49) found that many of the school personnel he studied, had a negative attitude towards the community and its inhabitants which led to a double standard of behaviour and teacher expectation. Some teachers believed that the children of that particular neighbourhood could not learn, and the children were satisfied with their sub-standard performance. Some of the parents adopted the same persuasion and the belief that whether the children were educable or not it was of little importance in view of their probable future opportunities. The parents probably felt that even if they tried to change the situation they would be powerless in their effort to do anything constructive. Even if they succeeded, the opportunities for their children would be limited so they developed a fatalistic attitude. This type of parental attitude was further extended to other agencies in the community such as welfare, health, sanitation, and the police, all of whom were of the opinion that nothing better was expected of these people. These negative images were translated into poor motivation for the children, who had internalized the stereotyped notions of what was expected of them. However, it should not be assumed that all children from disadvantaged homes are underachievers. Some are capable of doing well at school, but this will depend on the attitudes of their teachers toward them and the interactions that take place between pupil and teacher. Schwabb suggested that there is little teachers can do to improve the child's immediate home and environmental situation, but at the same time they can help by offsetting the environmental facts, by opening the doors through which the child can escape. It is quite possible to say that teachers cannot change the child's home environment but they can make the effort to welcome and accommodate their pupils regardless of the areas from which they came. If lower class pupils are aware that they are being thought of as inferior by their teachers, this will be very discouraging for them to want to partake in their school activities. Nash (1973, p123) suggested that teachers often argue that working class children are slower and less interested than middle class children in learning what they teach. But this might be because the teacher goes too fast when transmitting the lessons, that the children cannot take in what is said. This very often happens, because several children whom I interviewed commented on the same topic. They said the teachers do not make the time to explain things to them so that they can understand, and very often this bores them. It is important to explain things to children in order to capture their interest and attention. It is also important to let the children take part in whatever is going on in the classroom so that they will feel at ease and less intimidated by their teachers as some children do. Teachers are supposed to create the right kind of climate where all children will feel confident in an environment where they can be socialized with confidence to meet later challenges when they leave school. If schools deny them that chance, then they are failing in their duties as caring institutions which are there to offer guidance and assistance to the young of society. Nash (1973, p123) argued that if the outcome of interactions between teacher and pupil is seen as a failure on the part of the child, the responsibility is as much a failure of the teacher also.

A study carried out by Krupczak (1972) in the USA, found that black pupils were more affected by teacher expectations than were white pupils. Yee (1968) and Baker (1973) found that lower class students were more vulnerable to teacher expectations than middle class pupils. Rosenthal and Jacobson (1968) in Pursell (1977, p131) found that younger children showed greater expectancy effects than pupils in higher elementary grades. The authors concluded that the consequences for teacher expectations are strongly held, and are related to modified teacher behaviour. They found that students exhibited more cognitive gains if teachers taught more and showed more warmth towards them. Likewise, pupil personality and self-expectations seem to interact with teacher expectations which have consequences for their cognitive gains. Pursell suggested that teachers are more likely to hold negative expectations for lower class and minority children, than for middle class and white children. But why should teachers constantly view working class children as less educable than middle class pupils? It could well be that most teachers hold a middle class perspective and can only see things from their point of view. Their socialization and training would have led them to believe that the working classes have a culture and belief of their own which is contrary to that held by the mainstream culture. According to Nash (1973), teachers would tend to hold one of two types of attitudes, either that nothing can be done to help working class children, or they are in need of pre-school programmes and compensatory education. The above could be accepted as valid, because teachers are more likely to accept middle class pupils as conformists and educable than working class pupils. The powerlessness of lower class and minority children make them more likely to be influenced by teacher expectations. Halsey (1961) looked at how the attitudes of teachers influence their pupils. He found that one type of influence in particular is the extent to which teachers understand the nature of talent in the population, and the extent to which social class barriers hinder educational achievement. He also suggested that the relationships between motivation and family background are important factors. According to Halsey the teacher who is aware of those relationships will be better able to encourage and develop talent than the teacher who cannot recognize those relationships. But are teachers necessarily aware of the talents of their pupils? Talents are wide-ranging, so this would depend on whether or not a teacher is capable of recognizing all those differing talents which pupils have, or are they interested in other variables such as behaviour, personality, dress, area etc. Nash (1973, p121) showed that there was a strong possibility that teachers viewed personality as a very important indicator of a child's self-image and competence. If those facets hold true, one would expect that children of Caribbean origin would actually be non-starters on teachers ratings. My reason for saying this is that several authors have commented that teachers view Caribbean children as boisterous and aggressive, and on that basis they would not be highly rated or assessed by their teachers as potential successes. Hence they are placed in C streams or remedial classes by their teachers as many findings have shown.

At an Education Forum in Birmingham (1985) Simpson, for the Commission for Racial Equality, looked at underachievement amongst Caribbean children in the Birmingham area. Of the nine schools she studied, it was found that teacher attitudes played a key role in helping Caribbean children to underachieve. Caribbean boys especially were always being reprimanded by their teachers and have to spend much of their time explaining themselves to the headmaster. Further punishment also led to more time wasting. Therefore much valuable time that should be spent in the classroom learning, is spent on accountability and detentions. Such harsh measures are bound to have a detrimental effect on the education of Caribbean children, in that instead of being able to fully partake in their lessons, the time is being spent on them being punished. Therefore the whole debate surrounding Caribbean children as underachievers seem unjustified, in that the real causes have not been adequately investigated as to why these children are still underachieving. With their length of stay in Britain, especially those born in this country, it would be expected that their school performance would improve. But even in the 1980s-90s they are still underachieving and there is no clearly defined explanation. This would bring into question whether or not they are intellectually incapable, or the schools are failing in their duties to educate them as a group, as previously mentioned. IQ has proved to be redundant as a valid measure of intelligence in any race, and hence must be discarded. So we could instead look at the school and ask whether or not it is providing adequately for its black pupils. What are the factors which prompt them to underachieve? Many researchers on the subject of underachievement of Caribbean children have so far failed to look at the environment of the school, and how teachers interact with Caribbean children in schools. They may help them to fail the system by putting them in lower streams rather than to help them succeed within the system. Given that this is the case, the real failures are not the children, but those who have failed them by not facilitating them a fair chance to prove their capabilities. (see Nash, 1973, p123). Success at school is determined by the interaction between teacher and pupil. As Nash argued pupils are well aware of their class positions and what is expected of them by their teachers. How they view themselves will be dependent on how strongly they are influenced by their teacher's perceptions of them.

Mac an Ghaill (1988, p38) looked at a comprehensive school which was once in a prosperous residential area, but it had deteriorated into a typical inner city suburb with multiple deprivation problems characterized by a lack of employment, inadequate housing, social amenities, and disillusionment among its young. The white community blamed the black community for the deterioration. During the recession of the 1970s, there was a rapid decline of industries where blacks were employed. The authors used the above criteria to test teacher/student relations. They found that the specific response of the white staff and teachers toward black students were largely one of generally held racist stereotypes, which developed in national and local political circumstances. In other words, although the problems were there before the arrival of blacks, their presence had drawn attention to the already existing deprivation that had accumulated in the area. The school which was previously a secondary modern when it was opened in 1959, had high expectations of being all white, local and new. The perceptions of the white staff had changed when black pupils entered the school. They were seen as creating social problems of all sorts by the teachers. Many of the staff emphasized the superiority of the British culture based on racist images that were historically linked to British imperialism. Black pupils were seen as a threat to civilized standards of British society, said Mr Fleming, a history teacher. The black children were seen as coming from underdeveloped countries and rural backgrounds, which made them unable to cope with the demands of a highly developed industrial society. Some teachers spoke of Caribbeans as belonging to the jungle. The teachers used derogatory labelling, followed by suspensions, corporal punishment and official bullying to deal with black pupils. Mr Fleming's statement suggested that most of the teachers were fascists in those days, and two PE teachers were selected to 'lay in' on the big West Indian lads. In other words, it was only the very fit PE teachers who could discipline these Caribbean lads physically. Some younger members of staff were warned by older members that there were specific problems to be encountered by the black youths. Mr Lyons recalled that as a student teacher at the school on a teaching practice course, the introductory talk by the school management was: 'Look out for the West Indians and what they do. If they went mad, we just have to leave them alone to cool down. There was nothing we could do. If they swore at us in their own language, we must report it. They had a lot of trouble from them in the past'. The above statements would suggest that the teachers viewed Caribbean children as creating multiple problems, from being mad, to having a language problem, and being trouble makers. But if they could not understand their language in the first place, how could they interpret swearing in order to report it? The researchers found that stories were told with racist overtones by the staff, and how older staff had dealt with student confrontations in the past, particularly with the big West Indians. It would appear that these teachers were creating their own sets of problems for the school, by alienating the black pupils instead of accommodating them. They were well aware that it was the children who would get the blame for disorderly conduct, as there would be no repercussions on them. It was common practice for teachers to evaluate Asian students in technical terms and Afro-Caribbeans in behavioural terms. The above statements would seem to suggest that teacher attitudes towards Caribbean children are very negative in most respects. If teachers constantly resort to stereotypes and labelling when dealing with Caribbean children, it is no wonder they are always in conflict with them. This is because the students see this as an insult to their characteristics which can be harmful and dangerous because it creates hostility within the school, between teachers and the pupils concerned.

A group of black youths at the school who called themselves the Rasta Heads created a sub-culture of resistance to schooling to protect themselves against what they saw as teacher aggression against them. The Rastas said that this sub-culture was a means of them surviving the system which they saw as hostile to them. The teachers became even more suspicious when they could not understand the language used by the Rastas, and labelled them as deviants. In Becker's terms, once a label has been applied, it is likely to be successful in its outcome. The teachers constantly complained that Caribbean children refused to be disciplined, even though they had not tried to understand why they were behaving in that way. The students on the other hand had complained that the teachers had acted upon stereotypes by treating them as inferiors, and showing them up in front of their schoolmates by slapping them up and making them feel low, even lower than the other children. This is a situation that will cause Caribbean children to be rebellious. If they feel that their teachers deliberately show them up in front of the class, without good reasons, they are likely to show resistance by being defiant. They view their behaviour as a protection against further intimidation by their teachers. It would be interesting to see the amount of interaction that takes place between these pupils and their teachers, for a better understanding of what actually takes place in the classroom. The Rastas mentioned that the teachers made them feel even lower that the other children. If they felt that they were not accepted as human beings by teachers whom they regarded as guardians, it would be difficult for them to show them the respect that pupils should convey to their teachers. If teachers stopped being indifferent to their pupils, and accept them all as individuals, this would allow for better classroom relationships, interactions and classroom management.

Recent studies such as Rampton (1981) and Swann (1985) were commissioned by the government to look into the situation facing Caribbean children in schools. Rampton suggested that there was some element of racism in some schools, but this was mainly amongst a small minority of teachers, was the view of the Committee. The Committee however, identified racism as a factor of underachievement, although it stressed that this was not the only variable. It suggested that whether racism was intentional or unintentional on the part of teachers, it could pave the way for teachers to use stereotyped, negative or patronizing views in assessing the abilities and potential of Caribbean pupils, and this could lead to them yielding to the self-fulfilling prophesy. It urged teachers to examine and re-appraise their attitudes and behaviour in order to challenge all manifestations of racism and to play a leading role in seeking to change the attitudes of society as a whole towards ethnic communities. Rampton had made some startling discoveries on the issue of Caribbean underachievement, but was replaced by Lord Swann, who had a different perspective on the issue. Rampton quoted the following passages:

"Whilst we cannot accept that racism intentional or unintentional alone accounts for the underachievement of West Indian children in our schools, we believe that when taken together with, for example, negative teacher attitudes and an inappropriate curriculum, racism does play a major part in their underachievement."

A. Rampton, (1981, p66) in Summary.

"There seemed to be a fairly widespread opinion among teachers to whom we spoke, that West Indian children inevitably caused difficulties. These pupils were therefore, seen either as problems to be put up with, or at best, deserving sympathy. Such negative and patronizing attitudes, focusing as they do on West Indian children as problems, cannot lead to a constructive or balanced approach to their education".

A. Rampton (1981, p76) in Summary.

Swann (1985) attempted to locate the causes of the underachievement of Caribbean children by embarking upon a very high profile and comprehensive study on the issue. But the study is so comprehensive, that it has hardly located the causes with a view to suggesting any beneficial recommendations that would help Caribbean children. He has looked at every possible race of children, when in fact more emphasis should have been placed on Caribbean children's underachievement. This is because they were the main subject of investigation, a follow up of The Committee of Enquiry earlier on the same topic. Swann probably saw that there was a need to restructure the entire education system to cater for all children, some of who might otherwise have suffered the consequences of not benefiting from school. He saw that a re-appraisal of teachers performance was necessary, so rather than confine himself to one particular group on the issue of underachievement, he decided to look at all aspects of the education system. This shows that the education system is in need of reorganization in order to accommodate each and every child regardless of their social class background, colour or nationality.

Swann's diversification on the issue of Caribbean children's underachievement has not convincingly dealt with the problems faced by black children in schools. Is it because racism is such a controversial and delicate issue, that those not affected by it, find it difficult to deal with. By prevaricating around the issue, the case remains unsolved, and underachievement continues with no clearly defined explanation. At one point Swann asked why despite the influences of economic and social deprivation, racial prejudice and discrimination in the education system and society at large, do Asians succeed where Caribbeans fail? Though the committee found little objective evidence to this, it put forward the contrived view that there is the possibility that Asians keep a low profile which makes it easier to succeed in a hostile environment, while Caribbeans are given to protest and a high profile which has the reverse effect. He later suggested that this is a stereotype and should be viewed with caution due to exceptions in both groups. He did not explain what the exceptions are. Is it to mean that one group is so vociferous that it acts against them, while the other act passive and thereby succeed? These are merely subjective views, and as the Committee admitted, stereotyped judgements and should be viewed with caution. It is therefore not part of a valid investigation and should be refuted.

One could ask why the need for such a high profile investigation if the findings are going to be made obscure, ambiguous and difficult to decipher. Wouldn't it be a better idea to use the resource to improve the education of children who are already at a disadvantage in the education system including black children?

Again it appears that race as an issue seems to attract attention that warrants investigation, but no sooner the investigation starts, race becomes unpopular amongst investigators and respondents alike, and again fades into the background and paving the way for another topic or another discovery. Underachievement would seem very much to be linked with race, but due to a lack of concrete evidence this has to remain an assumed factor until further proof can be obtained. As previously mentioned on page 26, Kirp suggested that the aim of British policy seemed to embed race in some broader context such as educational disadvantage. This would seem to be a way of perpetuating the legacy of colonialism by deliberately refusing to recognize the fact that Commonwealth citizens are now part of British society, and no longer the ruled by the Great Britannia a few decades ago. Most of those ex-colonial countries now fly their own flags, but in the host society citizens are still seen as a second rate, disadvantaged group required to serve their former masters. Hence the government makes no attempt to recognize their immediate needs and implement policies to help their cause.

Both studies carried out by Rampton (1981) and Swann (1985) were unrepresentative of a national survey, as they were mainly confined to inner city areas, and the findings would have reflected what was expected of inner cities eg. Poor housing, low pay, unemployment, poorly equipped schools, teachers not trained for this type of job, and a lack of provision within the schools would be of a lower standard when compared with the more affluent areas. When class is taken into account, social class ranking for Caribbean parents ranged from manual to unskilled occupations. That is similar to that of working class whites, coupled with vast rates of unemployment. Although a few Caribbean mothers are nurses, and some of the men are now in business or professional occupations, that is not taken into account, probably because they are in a minority, or because the father's occupation is usually used as a criteria in ranking social class status. In those cases almost all Caribbean fathers are classed as manual workers, irrespective of the type of work which they do. Teachers would use these measures to assess the ability of Caribbean children. Under those circumstances, they would be categorized as under-achievers. Genetics is still also used to judge and categorize people, and darker skinned people are still seen as inferior because society continues to treat them differently. Hence, although IQ may no longer be a factor for achievement in its broadest sense, and may have faded slightly into the background, skin colour is still very much in the forefront because it is used daily to assess and categorise people.

A study by the Commission for Racial Equality (1985), showed that on average, Caribbean children enter for two O levels, English and Mathematics. Few go in for science subjects and they are more readily placed in the lower streams than whites and Asians. This could also be linked to a class element where whites and Asians are expected by their teachers to perform better than Caribbeans. The researcher found that streaming was prevalent, and was used to determine the choice of exams that pupils take. With Caribbean children largely confined to the lower streams, this meant that they had little or no chance of taking O levels, let alone passing them. No one knows how teachers derive at these decisions in deciding who takes what type of exam. Why is it that in their judgement Caribbean children are not fit to take O levels based on teachers opinions and assessment of their abilities? I have been told of Caribbean children locally, whose parents were professionals, and the children were made to take CSEs, because the teachers told them that they could not take O levels. After leaving school the children had to go to college to do their O levels in order to pursue their careers. Some white ex-pupils whom I have spoken to have commented on how some teachers are poor judges of pupils' competence. How can Caribbean children be held responsible for their low academic achievement, while such attitudes by teachers go unquestioned? There was also a strong indication that even though the schools were comprehensives, they perpetuated a grammar school tradition. This would seem a way of maintaining the class system which has for centuries dominated the education system.

At a conference on ethnic education in Birmingham in (1985) many black educationists gave their views on the education system and how it caters for black pupils. One of the speakers commented that even after twelve years of compulsory schooling, many black parents were unhappy about their children's progress of schooling in Britain in the (1970s). The children were doing badly in their school work, and when the parents complained to the teachers they got no satisfactory answers. The teachers blamed the background of the children and the lifestyle of their parents ie. one parent families, shift work, harsh discipline in the home, and unrealistic expectations for their children. Some teachers looked at the values held by the white working class for their children and asked why can't black parents set their expectations in line with the white working class. Even if black parents did set their expectations in line with the white working class, their children would still be at the bottom of the scale because of the barriers set by society. Social class is just one of those factors. Black parents have realized that their children are at a double disadvantage, so they encourage them to do well at school with the intention that this will give them a better chance in life. However if they do not get additional support from their teachers, it will be difficult for them to succeed through the school system.

The power and authority that teachers have over their pupils remains unquestioned. I have been told by several pupils that they were afraid of their teachers, especially when they went into a new class and did not know what to expect. The children said that some of this fear only diminished when they later discovered that teachers are humans just like anyone else. This shows that there is a need for teachers to try and be more friendly towards their pupils. They can do this by letting them know that they are not authoritarians to be feared, but that they are there to help them develop their talents and personalities, so that when they leave school and go out into the world outside, those days will be remembered with great pride and affection. Teachers do have a duty to help their pupils in this respect. That is part of the idea of being in a caring profession, or in the role of a second guardian.

This dissatisfaction led to black parents setting up parents groups to discuss their children's future. Hence there was the setting up of supplementary schools or Saturday schools where black children received extra tuition by volunteer staff. Supplementary schools helped to boost their confidence in themselves and to value their culture which the mainstream schools had denied them. Since the (1970s) the introduction of black studies in some educational institutions have given black children a better self-identity. Many began to query issues relating to famous blacks past and present. Stone (1981, p251) argued that compensatory education was seen as a form of re-socialization which is in effect bound up with self-concept and self-image. If black children knew more about their own history this would boost their confidence and enhance their learning abilities. Supplementary schools have proved to be of vital importance to the educational well-being of many black pupils. It provides an atmosphere where pupils and staff support each other, and provide help in whatever subjects pupils require help with. It offers an informal setting where pupils feel at ease with themselves and their tutors. This friendly atmosphere enhances their confidence in their own learning abilities and enables them to partake more fully in mainstream education.

Kelsall and Kelsall (1971, pp46-47) looked at the social and ethnic biases that are built in the techniques that are used for measuring IQ tests. They stated that school policy further exacerbates the educational handicaps of the socially disadvantaged groups. The authors are of the opinion that if different methods of selection were used in schools, rather than that of the conventional IQ type testing, whether or not children from disadvantaged backgrounds would fare better. An alternative suggested by the authors, would be to substitute the opinions of those who have taught the children, or rather the opinions of those who have assessed the children. As we are aware, teachers' opinions of children carry great influence when deciding the positions they should hold within the school. I have been told by two children whom I interviewed that middle class children get preferential treatment within schools, and are more likely than working class children to be placed in upper streams. Therefore, when it comes to assessing Caribbean children, they will be even less favourably placed than white working class children, and are more likely to be placed in the lower streams. Assessment is based on the opinion of the teacher towards a particular child and it is likely that biased assumptions can be made. Who decides whether or not a child should be placed in O level classes or CSE groups prior to the introduction of the GCSE? This type of selection is purely subjective and can have ramifications for the future of the children concerned.

King (1969) suggested that according to social class chances in education, middle class children have a longer educational life than working class children. He quoted from Douglas's study which showed that children of professional and managerial fathers have about nine times more chances of getting a grammar school place than children of semiskilled or unskilled manual workers. Where levels of measured intelligence are concerned, middle class children tend to overachieve relative to working class pupils. Taylor (1983) found that in one high school in the Redbridge enquiry, that although the number of Caribbean children were small, there were 33% of them in remedial class, and the majority were in B and C streams in the second year. By the third year, 54.5% of Caribbean children were concentrated in C stream. This trend appeared to continue throughout the school with only the occasional black pupil in A stream. Was this an act of tokenism, or an effort to show that the black child in A stream was the only one who had reached that stage, and the school was fair to all its pupils? Racism works in such subtle forms that sometimes it cannot be questioned, even though there is sufficient proof. But as long as it cannot be quantified it is likely to remain an insidious or assumed factor in the underachievement of Caribbean children. What else could explain them being placed in C streams or ESN schools other than racism or just sheer teacher attitude if the pupils were capable? It would be far better to use experience and close observation to measure prejudice than to rely on tailor-made statistics which can be distorted anyway. I am not saying that carefully worked out statistics are wrong, but that human error or bias can enter into their work especially if the sample is incomparable or unrepresentative. Why is it that Caribbean boys are said to be picked on by teachers even more than Caribbean girls? This is possibly the result of teacher attitudes, as boys tend to be bigger and more aggressive which is seen as threatening for the teachers as Troyna (1987) and others found.

Williams (1978) in Taylor (1983, p110), reported that on an analysis performance on Caribbean children in a Dudley school, they were continuously placed in the lower streams from infant through to secondary school. When some teachers were asked for their opinions on the willingness of Caribbean children to learn, twice as many were rated below average, and none were thought to be above average. The test also showed that of those Caribbean children in the 4th and 5th years for English and mathematics, almost half were found in the bottom two sets. Out of 82 black pupils, only two were selected for O level English, and six for O level mathematics. This shows that very few pupils would leave the school with any formal qualifications necessary to pursue further education or even skilled jobs. The majority would be destined for unskilled jobs similar to the plight of their parents.

It is debatable why children of Caribbean origin should consistently underachieve as most studies have shown. The answer could lie in them being placed in lower streams throughout their schooling. Children in the lower streams are not expected to do well, and they are well aware of this. They also have less access to good classroom learning material and may not have the best aspiring teachers. Teachers decide on the type of knowledge that pupils should have, and higher status knowledge is conveyed to upper stream pupils. If Caribbean children are constantly being undermined by their teachers, they are likely to do less well than their white and Asian counterparts because they are denied the type of knowledge that is required for them to succeed. This will give their white and Asian counterparts greater confidence in themselves as achievers. Taylor (1983) suggested that Little (1975) warned of the danger of over generalization in regards to the behaviour of black children which can result in a set of contradictions. It is a fact that black children are seen as badly behaved, and this will go against them when there is any slight misunderstanding between themselves and their teachers. An ex-black pupil commented that when she was at school, if black children questioned the teacher they were labelled as aggressive.

Some black children have told me that they have often been blamed by their teachers for some wrong doings by white children. Is it because teachers immediately assume that black children are devious and therefore cannot be trusted? If that is the case, how then are they going believe that they are capable of being educated?

Rubovits and Maehr in Milner (1983) conducted a study consisting of black and white children of comparable ability of whom half was presented to the teachers as gifted, and half as non-gifted. The researchers noticed that the white gifted children were treated best of all, being praised more often, called upon more often, and given more attention. They were also chosen more often, and the most liked or the brightest would often be referred to as the leader of the class. Conversely, the black students were given less attention, praised less, and criticized more often than whites. The authors noticed that in racial terms, the gifted blacks bore the most negative reactions from their teachers, even when compared to the non-gifted blacks. The study has pointed out not only the effects of teacher expectation on learning, but also how it operates in teacher/child interaction. But Milner (1983) pointed out that teacher expectations are not the sole explanations of black children's underachievement, as other factors may be involved. He stated that in the interaction process, both teachers and pupils enter this exchange with expectations and preconceptions on which they structure their perceptions of each other's behaviour. Each may be unaware that they may have little control over their behaviour being seen in that way. But whatever the outcome of the interation between them, it is the teachers who hold the winning cards, because the pupils have very little control over the messages transmitted to them. It is therefore up to the teachers to set the precedence and to communicate effectively with their pupils so that they all can have an equal chance of success.

Of the many factors suggested as being responsible for black children's underachievement, these range from cultural backgrounds, home circumstances, linguistic and cognitive deficits, and behavioural problems. These have been evaluated by various authors such as Taylor (1983), Essen and Ghodsian in Milner (1983), but with no clearly defined explanation as to why this is the case. Taylor's explanation is that it is difficult to prove due partly to the few studies on the issue of teacher expectation of Caribbean children. This makes it difficult for anyone to conclude that underachievement is caused by teacher's low expectation, as this alone is not a good enough explanation. Tomlinson (1983) also suggested that teacher attitudes and expectations of minority groups are difficult to prove empirically. However, a good measure would be close observation over time into the attitudes and actions of the respondents, but this would be very time consuming and expensive, and even then, people under observation can modify their behaviour accordingly. This is why sociology has difficulty in its claim to be scientific, because human attitudes are subjected to change at any time. However, if Caribbean children are continually being placed in lower streams, regardless of their abilities, then there is a good chance that an hypothesised conclusion could be drawn on the basis of racism or teacher attitude. In my opinion, if teachers hold stereotyped views of Caribbean children, this will govern their behaviour and lead to differential treatment in the classroom, to the detriment of black children's education. If they consider the children to be poor achievers, they will not encourage them otherwise nor change the opinions which they hold of them. Prejudice is like an ideology, once it is held it cannot be easily discarded. Tomlinson (1983, p27) suggested that much of the research on ethnic minority education was used to fuel political and ideological debates rather than to initiate strategies to improve minority education. Some of the criticisms of the findings was based on the fact that researchers assumed that the experiences of the different groups of children were similar, and this assumption was considered dubious according to Tomlinson. I have suggested that some of the findings were based on assumptions rather than on fact, because of the different experiences and backgrounds of the researchers and the participants. It would be difficult for white middle class researchers to be objective or sympathetic when studying a group of participants who are culturally and racially different to themselves, and with no experience of their lifestyle or customs. They will be inclined to enter into their study with assumed ideas rather than with a view to being objective.

 Rogers (1981) in Tomlinson (1983, p74, par4) suggested that there is evidence to demonstrate that teacher expectancy effects will sometimes take place. He pointed out that further studies of the sources of those expectancies would be required for a greater understanding of the characteristics of teachers and the sources of their beliefs about their pupils. A few studies have suggested that it is possible that teacher expectation can be effective in causing underachievement, but none has bothered to explore the issue further in order to gain the proof that is required for a firm conclusion. Some of those studies are Taylor (1983), Stone (1981) and Eggleston (1985). This theme would be worthwhile pursuing in order to gain further proof, rather than some researchers merely hypothesising or assuming what the case might be rather than what it actually is. Assumptions can be dangerous because they bear no relation to reality.

Brittan (1970) in Tomlinson (1983, p75) carried out a Department of Education and Science survey in which 510 teachers from 171 primary schools were interviewed. The researcher noticed that there was a willingness amongst teachers to make generalizations about children of Caribbean origin and to produce contradictory stereotypes. The teacher's views suggested that these difficulties facing Caribbean children were to be found in their home environment or in part their genetic characteristics. Here we find issues like genetics, home environment, behavioural traits being brought into play, which are typical labelling theories used by researchers and teachers alike to categorize and judge Caribbean children as underachievers. Brittan (1975) also found that teachers felt threatened by the behaviour of Caribbean adolescents, and linked their behaviour to a militant black response to white society. According to Brittan they did not stop to find out why those children behaved differently, they just formed their own opinions based on past stereotypes. Hill (1974) suggested that teachers should stop looking for differences amongst Caribbean children, and concentrate on their similarities.

Taylor (1983) suggested that some writers have been less circumspect in their view on the underachievement of black children. Taylor (1983, p195) also found that amongst some head teachers, there was a strong feeling that the learning process for Caribbean children was slower than for other groups. They were also of the opinion that Caribbean children would tend to underachieve and be remedial as they lacked the ability to concentrate for any length of time. Teachers were more willing to make generalized statements about Caribbean children as a group with more than two thirds of the 171 primary school teachers and 339 secondary school teachers expressed unfavourable opinions about Caribbean pupils, whilst holding favourable opinions about Asian pupils. Such unsubstantiated opinions by teachers may lead to the fostering of bad relationships between Caribbean pupils and teachers. If pupils are aware that their teachers do not hold favourable opinions of them, they are likely to internalize the idea that they are incapable of succeeding, so they might as well be failures. This is the role of the 'self-fulfilling prophesy', and why so many children fail at school. If they are aware that their teachers hold low expectations of them, they are likely to fulfil that role. This seems to have affected many Caribbean children at school, and has caused them to underachieve. I would argue that although findings suggest that they underachieve, they are not underachievers as such, but the structure of the education system and the unseen barriers that exist within it act as a barrier to keep certain groups at the bottom of the stratification ladder. When they are placed in C streams there is no way in which they can compete on equal terms with other groups. This leaves them vulnerable for the system to categorize them as underachievers.

Rubenstein (1979) looked at the type of work that blacks do and the type of housing in which they reside, and argued that this puts them in social class four and five. Hence, the type of school which black children attend will be mainly State Schools in areas of conservation. He also noticed that in schools, opinions will have already been formed about certain group's ability to succeed via the education system. Brittan in Rubenstein (1979) noticed that two thirds of teachers indicated unfavourable opinions of Caribbean pupils, in comparison to Asian and European pupils. Rubenstein suggested that some of the myths about blacks in Britain arose out of the ethnocentrism of some social and educational research workers and national leaders who view the educational failure of Caribbean children as arising out of their ethnic, social and cultural norms. Such gross misconceptions are bound to have an adverse effect on the true educational performance and capability of Caribbean children. They do not have access to wealth and privilege as do many middle class children, and this puts them at a gross disadvantage educationally. Banks and Finlayson (1973) argued that the relationship between social class and socio-economic status is well established. Therefore, if we take factors like motivation, homework orientation, conformity to parental values and expectations, position of pupils within the school, these factors would raise the expectations of teachers, parents and pupils alike amongst the higher socio-economic groups. Whilst the lower form pupils, had the reputation of being seen as 'dull' according to their teachers, and this lowers their confidence in their own ability and expectation to succeed. If they do not have the confidence in themselves that they need to succeed, it is highly unlikely that they will be high achievers. Teachers can help those children by giving them the confidence they need to help them succeed. Their levels of attainment will to a large extent be based on the level of interaction between pupils and their teachers. If teachers convey the message of failure to their pupils, that is exactly what those pupils will do. This could be one of the reasons why upper stream pupils do well, because they know that it is expected of them to succeed, while it is the opposite for lower class pupils.

Language and Social Deprivation

The debate on language and how it might affect the educational performance of Caribbean children in school is a very complex one, and researchers seem divided on the issue. Many researchers however, are of the opinion that Creole as a substitute language hinders the learning ability of Caribbean children. Tomlinson (1983, p103) looked at the findings of writers such as Jeffcoate (1982), Derrick (1977), in Tomlinson (1983,105) and suggested that the medium of education in British schools is the English language, and any child not speaking English will be at a disadvantage. (Derrick, 1977: 4, in Tomlinson, 1983, p103). Tomlinson suggested that English as a second language (ESL), was on the agenda in the 1970s in relation to the development of multicultural educational policies. Bhatnagar (1981), in Tomlinson (1983, p103), suggested that the retention of minority languages was a crucial factor in maintaining minority cultural identity. The Bullock Report (1975) also persuaded teachers that children should not be required to cast off the language and culture of their home at the school's threshold. Tomlinson also suggested that the language problems of children of Caribbean origin were researched in the 1970s, and there were indications that the use of Creole could be linked to poorer performance at school. But

Caribbean parents rejected this explanation, in that it had nothing to do with their children's poor performance. Bald (1981) in Tomlinson, (1983, p103) suggested that in his view there was sufficient evidence to suggest that dialect speech may have consequences for school achievement. The debate led to a project being funded by the Schools Council at Birmingham University between 1967 and 1970. Wight pointed out that the ability for children in the Caribbean to be bi-dialectical was not uncommon. He suggested that a continuum model illustrating how a child moves from Creole dialect to standard English could be understood in terms of the variety of speech patterns used by Caribbean children. Edwards in Tomlinson, (1983, p109) pointed out that teachers seem to have a particular attitude towards dialect speech, but they could play a role in helping children to acquire English dialect. She also pointed out that by constantly correcting Creole features could have harmful effects on the self-confidence of Caribbean children. She saw these speech features as logical and should not be classed as broken or inferior speech.

The use of Creole by Caribbean children were seen by teachers and researchers as inferior to standard English, and this was assumed to be responsible for their low achievement at school. The language referred to as 'Creole', is a mixture of the English and African languages, and can be understood only by its users. Hence, when Caribbean children used it at school, it was to the annoyance of their teachers, who could not understand what they were saying. As a result they may have reached the conclusion, that Caribbean children had a learning problem. Rather than trying to help the children, teachers immediately placed them into lower streams where there would be no progress for them educationally. The issue surrounding Patois is very controversial. In Jamaica where it is widely used as a local dialect, but it is discouraged by the parents who want their children to succeed educationally. But it is very rural in origin, and is widely used by farmers and some traders, so it is actually part of the Caribbean language that cannot be discarded, and hence it is used by some of the younger Caribbean generations in Britain. Many of the second generation Caribbeans in Britain now take pride in the use of Patois, because they see it as part of the continuation of their roots. But the irony is, Patois does not hinder children's learning ability in the Caribbean, so why should it hinder their learning ability in this country? Is it the fact that teachers and educationists use it to exonerate themselves from the reasons for Caribbean children's underachievement? This is a possibility because although there are many other languages used in this country, the children who use them are not ostracised as underachievers by their teachers. I have therefore concluded that Patois could not be a valid factor for the underachievement of Caribbean children in schools. Taylor (1983) has also suggested that evidence on the dialect issue of Caribbean children seemed divided in importance, and there is insufficient evidence for it to be substantiated. Fagan (1958) in an analysis of some written work by Caribbean children gave an indication of popular prejudice when he described Creole as merely broken English. He suggested that good English had all the charms and expressiveness that good language should be. The only type of language that Fagan considered to be standard was that which was written in proper grammatical form. But we could question who decides what is proper grammatical form of the various different language types which is widely used, or is his interpretation merely reinforcing middle class values on language, whilst denouncing minority languages as inferior?

Family Pathology Approach

To many middle class educationists and professionals the black family is viewed as pathological. They harbour the opinion that the black family structure is lacking in cohesion and is therefore likely to be deficient in providing a positive and stable environment in which to bring up their children. This instability is further linked to their educational performance in schools, which prompts teachers to think black children are uneducatable due to the instability of their home environment. Tomlinson (1983, p46) commented on the Interim Report of the Rampton Committee (1981) which stated that the difference between the average achievement of Asian pupils and Caribbean pupils, was a consequence of a deficiency in the West Indian home in providing the right type of environment. But as Tomlinson suggested, many Asians suffer poverty, overcrowding, and discrimination which is in some ways worse that than that suffered by Caribbeans, together with the handicap of a language problem. Yet society does not classify them as constituting a pathological family. As teachers see it, the father is the strength in the Asian's homes, whereas in the Caribbean's homes, the mother is the strength. Such assumed factors cannot be accurate in deciding that the black family is pathological. We would need to look at a wide range of black family homes before deciding on such unfounded generalizations.

Johnson (1970, pp50-62) looked at the black family in the USA, and explained that the family is the basic social unit of society through which socialization is transmitted. He argued that if the family is ineffective in transmitting those basic tenets, ie. the values held in education, a principle towards education, those doctrines that education is the chief good and can offer great rewards, or if they have different aspirations from that of the curriculum, then the children will have extreme difficulty in achieving at school. They may also suffer other deplorable conditions of family life, such as divorce, desertion, separation, illegitimacy, matriarchal families, and State aid which is part of the sub-culture to which they are accustomed. Those are the views held by many researchers about black children, and this is likely to lead to bias in the way they carry out their research on those children. This, he argued, had eroded the self-concept of black men and boys, and placed a heavy burden on the women who had to act as mothers, fathers, and caretakers. He explained that this pattern derived from the slave plantation era which did not allow family units to develop amongst black families, because very often men, women, and children were split up and sold to different slave owners. Only those children who were too young to be separated, were allowed to remain with their mothers. This structure did not change after the abolition of slavery, so the pattern perpetuated until much later. Although there is now greater stability amongst black families in the USA and elsewhere, the stigma created centuries ago, still has a damaging effect on many black families. Teachers will therefore find it difficult to dismiss those beliefs which they acquired during their own socialization and training. It is very easy for teachers to dwell upon a legacy of misconceptions and perpetuate them to succeeding generations without questioning their beliefs about the validity of such values. The process of depicting black families in such a negative way in textbooks, films and the media, can have implications for the education of black children in schools.

Johnson (1970) suggested that 'ghetto life' in the USA can have a debilitating effect on its youngsters. It portrays a sense of helplessness on those children who unfortunately find themselves in those circumstances where the portrayal of crime, disease, poverty and family breakdown are seen as the norm. The scars of such environments are inescapable, as it portrays a sub-culture which is the only one those children will ever know, "the culmination of a cycle of poverty and crime". Although not all ghetto families fall into this trap, this is the image portrayed to the wider society, and one which filters into structures and institutions where the effects can be devastating. This makes it difficult for black children to be accepted positively into institutions with a view to succeeding on a par with other groups. If they are viewed negatively, it is expected that their performance will be accepted in the same light.

In Britain the notion of 'family pathology' would seem to be adopted by some schools and the social services when dealing with black families. There does not appear to be any studies on the education of black children referring them specifically as pathological, but the term has been used by some teachers to describe Caribbean children as meaning that they are from unstable home backgrounds. It is worth looking at pathology in terms of how the black family is portrayed by the social services, as this also involves how the children are socialized and prepared for their schooling. This is relatively a new research by a group of black professionals and social workers. However, many researchers have so far focused on the victims as being in need of correction, whilst they have ignored the real issues that needs tackling. They have failed to look at structures and institutions and how racism is embedded within the social structures of society. In this case the school could be classed as another facet of the social system in the way that researchers have presented their findings by pointing at the victims. The Association of Black Social Workers and Allied Professions (1983-90) looked at the way many social workers categorize black families as fragmented and unstructured. Founded since 1983, the group is trying to re-evaluate previous meanings that have been used by social workers when dealing with black families. It discovered that many social workers have construed black families as fragmented structures, because they consider their patterns of child rearing to be inadequate. For instance, they consider the involvement of the extended family in child rearing practices to be inadequate and unhealthy for the child. But ABSWAP has outlined that this is normal and healthy amongst black families, and has contributed to the survival of the black family historically. It stated that the meaning of bonding to black families was very different to that held by social services and society in general. It also stated that social work operates within the framework of white middle class values, which is at variance with the experience of the black family. They have very little understanding of the socio-economic conditions of black people, and are therefore far removed from their experiences. In previous years the removal of black children from their real parents who were considered unfit to care for them, and into the care of white foster parents who were seen as fit parents, may have caused an identity crisis amongst many black children. Many black parents were led to believe that their children would be taken into care temporarily by the social services, but when the parents realized, many of those children were being fostered out to white families. Those white families do not possess the appropriate experience to meet the black child's needs, so they are reared with exclusively white values, only to face hostility in society later which they cannot adequately deal with. Now the 1989 Children's Act is committed to giving back the responsibility of black child rearing to black families, who can respond to those children's immediate needs and welfare. Since it appears that there are different meanings and values in the way black families rear their children and the way it is viewed by social services, it cannot be concluded that the agencies have the correct answer as to what constitutes the pathological family. Blacks have had to resort to historical circumstances in the way they care for and rear their children. It would therefore be incorrect to say that the black family is pathological and unstructured, because they are capable of bringing up their children in a hostile society just as any other parents would, regardless of colour or race. We now see in society a spate of single parent families, broken homes, divorces and separations amongst white families and other ethnic groups. Are those parents now seen as unfit to rear their children adequately, or will those children be taken away and placed into the care of the experts? It would appear that the problem of race and colour lies with the agencies who consider themselves to be experts at knowing what is best for everyone else.

The pathology factor amongst Caribbean children in schools could be linked to Coard's study (1971) when large numbers of Caribbean children were placed in ESN schools due to them being wrongly assessed by psychologists and educationists. This would seem to be a common factor amongst professionals when dealing with black people that their whole family structure is fragmented and lacking in organization and ordering. Tomlinson (1983, p75) stated that Townsend and Brittan's research in the 1970s stated that teachers often made generalized statements about Caribbean children and produced contradictory stereotypes. They described the children as lazy, passive, withdrawn, boisterous, aggressive, and disruptive, descriptions which they did not use to describe white or Asian children. The researcher also noticed that the teachers considered that these difficulties were to be found in the child's home environment or genetics. These comments show that although genetics has been disproved as a correct measure for IQ testing, the established theory is still used in everyday practical assessment of black people's capability. During my research some teachers commented that they were of the opinion that in Caribbean families homes the mothers were the strength of the family, while in the Asian home, it was the fathers. Was this a hint that Caribbean children are not from stable homes, therefore they will fail the system regardless of how much help they might be offered? This shows that the perceptions of teachers towards Caribbean children had not altered much since the 1950s-60s when the majority of them categorized Caribbean children as underachievers in schools, and as a result they underachieved. This perception and belief seems to exist nationally amongst teachers and not just regionally. This would imply that embedded in their psyche is the notion that the black family is pathological, and therefore requires differential treatment, a special kind of adjustment programme to make them civilized.

Conclusion

This chapter has looked at factors which have been claimed to be the reasons why Caribbean children fail at school. I have looked at several of those findings, but they do not appear to have drawn any firm conclusions on the issue of underachievement amongst children of Caribbean origin, but have listed a number of possible causes. This would suggest that the causes of underachievement may not be linked to any one factor, but there may be several factors. The difficulty however, is to find the root cause, because it is only then that a solution can be applied. However, the education system is only one aspect of society, but nonetheless, it could play a crucial role in the underachievement of Caribbean children. The way people have been conditioned to think for centuries has been a historical feature which tends to affect people's perception of themselves and others without them being consciously aware of it. In the process they act out stereotypes that are harmful and destructive to others, and hence stereotyping of Caribbean children by teachers could be a factor for their underachievement. If we look at racial stereotypes and the harmful effects which they have had on the black race, there is good reason to believe that this could be the case. Of the various studies which have been carried out, none has been successful in discovering the precise causes of Caribbean children's underachievement in schools. This shows the difficulty faced by social scientists on issues which are sensitive and intangible. Researchers have employed different methods, used different concepts, in which case there is no uniformity on content nor explanation. They set out to look at different causes. Thus the issue of underachievement remains unsolved, and the question of underachievement remains unanswered. Perhaps other methods need to be employed, together with a greater understanding of the issue, and why only certain groups are affected. Or is it the case that greater attention is focused on certain groups because they are more visible and cannot easily escape the stereotypes with which they have been scapegoated? If Caribbean children have been labelled as underachievers, it will be difficult for them to rid themselves of this label. What of those who are now achieving, especially Caribbean girls? Will there be a shift in direction on to another group who will either be at a disadvantage or underachieving in the education system?

Mirza (1992) found that a number of black girls in her study spoke of the school's indifference towards them when they insisted on having a non-traditional career, such as dress design, acting, journalism, creative writing, law, medicine or accountancy. The girls in this category told the researcher that they had no support nor advice from their teachers, who justified their behaviour by saying that the girls would only be disappointed if they strove too high.

On the other hand, Mirza found that the girls who excelled in athletics were not only encouraged and favoured by their teachers, but they were also referred to as being polite, hardworking and talented. However, one of the girls who was very good at tennis and wanted to pursue it as a career, had hardly any support from her teachers who commented that "it is very competitive out there, and however good she is, it might not be the right sport for her." Based on these cases and the teacher's comments and opinions toward the girls, it would appear that in the teachers' views, there is no room in the high status occupations for black girls, and the situation for black boys is even worse because many are not even allowed to reach that level.

Mirza puts it down to luck for those whose determination and hard work helped them through the school system. As she found out, many black pupils are either ill-advised or discouraged by their teachers from pursuing their chosen career.

Keddie (1973) stated that working class children are at a disadvantage from day one at school. The same could be said of Caribbean children who are at a double disadvantage even before they enter the school system, due to the fact that they come from a different culture, and characteristically they are a visible minority, which easily attracts all kinds of unfavourable attention. For the majority of Caribbean children, teachers' immediate perception of them on entering school could be the interaction of failure, partly based on previous stereotypes and preconceptions of black slavery, colonialism, Black Africa and backwardness. This makes it difficult for black children to easily fit into an all white system of education which does nothing to accommodate them, nor to help them overcome any doubt that they may have regarding their own ability. The school merely perpetuates a curriculum which transmits racism, sexism, and classism. It does not seem willing to eradicate those inequalities that are so structured that they cannot be easily addressed nor corrected. Girls are still channelled into the traditional domestic and mundane subjects like typing, needlework and cookery, while boys still follow the traditional male hard core subjects such as maths, physics, chemistry, woodwork etc. As far as race is concerned, the historical myths of inferiority, incompetence, dependency, all serve to alienate black children from fully partaking in their school work.

Racism is a factor that can have devastating effects on its victims and this needs tackling at grass roots level rather than skimming the surface, and hoping the problem will go away. Or is this one of those sociological explanations with no substantial evidence to fit the theories, so social scientists go on prevaricating, and cannot find an adequate explanation? I would suggest that Caribbean children are not underachievers as such, because given the chance they are as capable as any other pupil, but rather, they are victims of an unequal education system that perpetuates inequalities to the detriment of the white working class and Caribbean pupils. The white children whom I interviewed said that Caribbean children are just as capable as anyone else. The teachers also gave similar answers. But my study could not validate this due to an absence of statistics, and reliability on interviews are mere opinions that can distort the facts. But after making deductions from some of the answers given, there is the likelihood that some teachers were subconsciously racist, but their views were carefully controlled. Several studies previously mentioned have stated that Caribbean children were mainly located in the lower streams in schools which meant that they had no chance of successfully making it through the system. Because the education system is so unequal, complex, and class based, there are hidden barriers which serves as a safety valve to ensure that only pupils from certain social class backgrounds succeed within it. Children from lower social class backgrounds are made victims of a system which is very complex and difficult to understand.

Given that this is the case, one could suggest that there is a need for teachers to look more closely at the way in which they interact with their pupils, to see whether or not they are using the right modes of communication which their pupils can understand. Very often the way in which teachers convey messages to their pupils will either enhance or hinder their progress at school. It is therefore of vital importance that teachers try to get to know and understand their pupils feelings, needs, background and culture. It is only then that they will be able to empathise and help their pupils with whatever difficulties they may encounter.

◆

CHAPTER 2

Different Perspectives and Aspirations Among Students and Parents

This section will attempt to look at the differing perspectives of pupils and parents in relation to educational achievement. It will also look at the development of multiracial education as an attempt to reform schools as a means of catering for various groups of pupils which now attend school in a multiracial society. The government has now realized that there is a need to change from a Eurocentric curriculum, to a more liberal type curriculum which will better serve the needs of the many nationalities now residing in Britain. But how will these changes benefit minority children? Will they fare better or worst in the education system? That I will now explore.

Kahl in Halsey (1961, p318) investigated the ambitions of 24 boys from working class families who all had the intelligence to go to college, but over half of which chose not to go further than high school, but instead were content to settle for lesser rewarding jobs. The survey focused on finding out why twelve of the boys were eager to further their education, and twelve were not interested. The project was set up at Harvard University Laboratory of Social Relations, and drawn from a sample of 3,971 boys. The result was as predicted by social class and occupation. Those who had clear occupational aims, also had plans for a career that would prepare them appropriately for the jobs of their choice. About one quarter were definitely planning for a college career. Their IQ scores and the occupation of their fathers turned out to be predictors of their educational ambitions. Most of the boys from high status homes or with high intelligence planned a college career, while those with lower intelligence or from lower status homes, did not aspire to higher education. But we could say that this could have been predicted from a common sense point of view, and did not require statistics to tell us so. However, the matter is not as clearly defined as that. This is because people in higher status positions are assumed to want their children to follow in their footsteps, but very often some of those children are prepared to follow their own careers. Choices are important to individuals and very often children do not want their parents to choose their careers for them, because too much pressure from parents may result in them damaging the students confidence in themselves. The children in my research suggested that they got a great deal of help and encouragement from their parents, but in the end they are allowed to make their own choices. They seemed to choose according to what they thought they are capable of doing, or according to what their examination results would be. It is also the case that some variables such as parental pressure or parental help cannot be quantified, but are observable.

Halsey (1961) found that boys from major white collar families among the quantile of their classmates in intelligence choose college in 89% of the times, compared to those from the lower labour service families. Those from the bottom quantile of intelligence, strove for college only 9% of the time. At the extremes, the prediction was quite good but in the middle range, it was a little less reliable. If a boy was highly intelligent but came from the middle range which was more populous, his aspiration could not well be predicted. For example a boy from this range whose father was a minor white collar worker on skilled labour had an almost fifty-fifty chance of aiming for a college career. As could be expected, it would appear that ability and social class seems to be closely correlated, as those with high intelligence from major white collar workers, were more likely to choose a college career. While those from the lower white collar sector were more likely to opt for a lower type occupation. Economic reward is also another contributable factor, because the higher income families would be in a better position to support their children educationally. The table below shows the percentage of boys who were expected to go to college by IQ and fathers occupation in three thousand three hundred and forty eight cases. (3,348).

Table 1
IQ Quantile

	Low			High	All group
Father's Occupation	1	2	3	4	5
major w.c.	56	72	79	82	89
minor w.c.	12	20	22	29	55
medium w.c.	28	36	47	53	76
skilled	4	15	19	22	40
Other	9	6	10	14	29
All Occupations	11	17	24	30	52

Halsey found that all 24 boys had high IQs enough to go on to college, but 12 aspired not to do so. This tells us that IQ could be ruled out as a deciding factor in pursuing higher education. If we look at their father's occupation as a variable, this ranged from white collar, skilled or semi-skilled. As the differences in the boys aspirations could not be explained demographically nor statistically, interviews were also designed to highlight the situation more clearly. This is because statistics can sometimes omit variables that cannot be accounted for eg. parental pressure or individual motivation which cannot be quantitatively measured, but nonetheless, it sometimes carries a great deal of weight in educational success.

Parental Perspective

It is a known fact that parents play a great part in the education of their children. But to what extent this can influence educational success, is not quite known. At times either one or both parents can put a great deal of pressure on their children to succeed. It is well documented that Caribbean parents want their children to succeed in school, as they have always had a high regard for education. Whether or not the parents themselves are educated, they see this as a chance that they missed out on, so many encourage their children to try hard at school. Taylor (1983, p15) looked at the importance of education for many Caribbean parents. She looked at a Community Relations Council's Report (1977) which covered eight disadvantaged areas across the country. It found that 195 Caribbean parents had higher expectations for their children, compared to the 700 white parents of similarly disadvantaged children. Richmond (1973) in Bristol also found that Caribbean parents were more ambitious for their children than the English parents in the same working class district. Pollak (1979) also found that 66 Caribbean parents were likely to have higher and unrealistic aspirations for their children. Foner's study (1979) showed that the parents were ambitious for their children, but they were apprehensive about racism in Britain, in the sense that, even if they were educated, would they get their desired occupation? Thus, we have a picture where Caribbean parents place a high value on the education of their children, but rarely is this expectation achieved. The parents blame this lack of achievement on racism in society and teacher attitudes towards their children. The parents are perhaps correct in putting this down to racism, due to the fact that racism is institutionalized. This makes it difficult for the teachers to act favourably towards black children. The books which they use in schools constantly remind them that blacks are inferior and less educable than whites. It is also a fact that there is a problem of communication between the school and the home which will add to the existing problem facing Caribbean children.

Halsey's study (1961) showed that within what is called the Common Man's Group, some parents were satisfied with their own position in life, and did not attempt to push their sons up the status ladder. Halsey wanted to see how some families saw themselves as belonging to a particular status group. Some chose the middle section but did not see themselves as belonging to the middle classes, but used phrases like the average sort, ordinary folks, or the common man. Goldthorpe and Lockwood's study of Luton in the 1960s could be associated with the above in that the people under investigation did not see themselves as middle class but said they did their jobs solely for material gains. The fact that they saw a lower class beneath them, people living in slum conditions, did not influence them sufficiently for them to want to seek a better class position. Some said that their way of life was preferred to that of the competitive game of rising higher which they didn't see as worth it due to the responsibility involved. Their attitudes to work were based on things like getting by, balancing the weekly budget, living for the moment, and no concern for the past nor for the future. Having good work mates, a good boss, and a regular pay packet was sufficient for them. Some parents encouraged their children to enjoy themselves while they were young, before the burdens of life bound them to regular work and responsibilities. Others encouraged their children to stay on at school to get certificates which they saw as important in helping them to obtain better jobs. Some of the respondents had vague ideas of what college was about, and some saw it as belonging to the professional people who earned a lot of money. Many felt that the common people like themselves were lucky to have a job on a regular basis and should therefore be satisfied. We could ask if there is a middle and a working class perspective to life, which extends to education. This seems likely in that both groups seem to want different things whether educationally or materialistically. The middle classes have a clear view of what the education system is all about and what they want from education. This enables them to plan their future lifestyle with certainty from an early age based on deferred gratification as the rewards will be achieved later. They are therefore not in a hurry to take the first job that comes their way, but are prepared to make sacrifices in order to achieve their desired effect. This may mean hard and prolonged studying with very little fun, but with the effort and determination of succeeding, they do work hard in order to achieve their objectives (Halsey 1961, p355). On the other hand many working class lifestyles do not dictate this kind of sacrifice. As studies show, many working class children have a view of immediate gratification or the here and now, have fun today while you can as the future is unpredictable. Also many do not want the responsibility of holding high status positions, because they do not think that they belong up there, and would probably not be capable of performing such high ranking jobs. They see many top bosses as belonging to a particular class background, and who have the expertise and knowledge to perform those tasks. As a result many render themselves as unsuitable for those high ranking positions and are prepared to accept the lower ranking jobs with very little reward, though this realization may not manifest itself until years later. Much of this belief could lie in the socialization process which is transmitted during childhood by the parents to their offspring which may have later consequences for their well-being. If a child is made to believe that he or she is incapable of achieving certain standards they are likely to internalize those values.

Another factor as to why many working class children may not take up further education is how useful it is going to be in the long run. During the course of my interviews with students aged 14-16 years, many who were still undecided about what they wanted to do suggested that the length of time for many educational courses seem too much, and in the end it might not be worth a great deal to them. As they saw it, they may not be able to get a job to commensurate with their qualifications, which would be time wasted that could have been spent otherwise. Many suggested that it did not matter what type of occupation they did, as long as they were happy with their choice that's all that mattered. This opinion seemed very much part of a working class philosophy, the uncertainty of where will it all lead to. Middle class students have a positive view that for them education will pay dividends. This gives them the motivation to study hard because of the security it offers them in the end. However, some working class parents significantly encouraged their children to try for a better life which is a chance they never had. But a great deal will depend on the value they place on education and the standard of education they themselves had. But we do not fully know the processes through which those values are transmitted. If some people are satisfied with their positions in life, no amount of high achievement is going to matter to them. Thus, the term achievement may be grossly exaggerated and misused in academic terms, as it may have different meanings to different people. High A level grades and going to university may mean success for academics, while lower grades or none may not matter to others, but depending on what they have achieved, may equally mean success to them.

Caribbean Children's Perspective

For many Caribbean children in Britain a good education is viewed positively. Many parents encourage their children because they want them to succeed. But this view may soon turn into uncertainty when they realize the extent of inequality in education, caused mainly through racism and discrimination against them in the school system. Many realize from an early age that their chances of success in schools are not as good as those of their white counterparts. Thus, many may take a dislike to schools, or pay little attention to their learning. Once their interest in schooling is withdrawn, there is very little chance of them recovering from this traumatic experience. From the studies observed so far, it would appear that teachers do not make a conscious effort to help them either. This may cause many to waste their talents, and as a result get labelled as underachievers. The very fact that they do not get an equal chance in education is very disturbing. They see from statistics, the media, and newspapers that they underachieve, and it is two or three times more difficult for them to obtain jobs when compared to their white counterparts. This may deter them even more from trying hard at school, let alone pursuing further education. They know that they will have to work twice as hard in order to achieve any form of qualifications. Furthermore they are not given the chance to try because for many their first encounter with school provokes such unpleasant experiences that their chances of success are doomed from the start. Many find that teachers do not give them the support and encouragement that they need in order to achieve success, and in the process they are so discouraged that they give up at a very early age. Again, many feel that they are unable to pursue academic work and failing to get help from their teachers, they cannot assess their own capabilities and hence waste a great deal of time and talent. Faced with this handicap and probably insufficient support from their parents who do not have a good deal of knowledge about the workings of the education system, their prospects are unlikely to be improved educationally or otherwise.

Many working class students may prefer not to go on to higher education because of the length of time involved. There may also be an element of uncertainty surrounding their life chances. They are aware that at the end of the course their future will largely depend on employers perception of them, no matter how intelligent they may be. If they feel that they are not from the right background, their chances of getting a god job at the end of their study will be much slimmer than those from privileged backgrounds. Middle class pupils would have already been socialized from an early age about the type of jobs they would be expected to hold in the future. They cherish high expectations of this and many do work hard to achieve their goals because they know that it will pay off in the long run. They are therefore more likely to face the future more positively and with greater certainty than many working class students, who may see themselves as having a handicap and a restricted future.

Some Caribbean children may be even more reluctant about their future, having experienced racism and disadvantage from an early age. Many are deterred from even making it successfully through the school system. They may have already as a result of discrimination, formed their perceptions according to what they see around them. By virtue of their colour and assumed lower working class background by which they are perceived and judged both by schools and society in general, their early perceptions as academic failures may in the end get the better of them, as they may aspire to live up to this expectation. Troyna (1987, p122) looked at student/teacher relations with Caribbean children. Both boys and girls expressed complaints and dissatisfactions regarding their teachers attitudes and behaviour towards them which often led to conflict between pupils and their teachers. Education has for long been divided by sex, class and now race would seem a new dimension not to be ignored. The presence of black children in British schools since the 1960s has brought a new dimension to education. As a result local education authorities and teachers are constantly struggling to find ways of coping with what they see as a new wave of problem children, but to date no solution has been found, and so the debate goes on. However, whatever the outcome, these children are now a part of British society, and it is now up to teachers and educationists to try and remedy the problem.

Multi-Racial Education

A recent government policy on education is the issue of Multicultural Education. The government has finally endorsed it after over a decade of debates and controversies with activists who consider this approach to be beneficial to minority children in schools. I do not mean black minority only, but all minorities, because that is the issue under consideration. It does not concern just helping black children to make it successfully through the education system, but according to the Swann report (1985), to educate all children. This latest acceptance by the government could possibly have a connection with a European view of educational policies and issues as a means of catering for all pupils, as Britain is now part of the European Community. In the 1970s, a European Commission ruled that no pupil should be made to cast off their mother tongue as their first language. During that time multiracial education took a low priority. It has now been replaced by the new accepted version of multicultural education. This new development is to ensure that all cultures are represented in the classroom, and that no culture is devalued. But is multicultural education the answer to race and class inequality in the schools? This seems very doubtful. The reason is that it may only serve to confuse pupils, parents and teachers alike, in making them believe that everyone has equal opportunity within the school, when in fact it may even make education more divided, especially among the working classes who are already at a disadvantage. Tomlinson (1983, p93) looked at some of the arguments surrounding multicultural education. She noted that Jeffcoate's argument suggested that the improving of the positive self-image of black pupils should not be done at the expense of democracy, but that the racist views of white children should be listened to. He suggested that the definitions of multicultural education confounds the needs of black children as a means of combating white racism. He thinks that multicultural education should be seen to reflect multicultural reality by undermining myths and stereotypes, and incorporating minority cultures into the curriculum and promoting equality of opportunity to all groups. This rightly is what multicultural education stands for, but very often the issue is confused to mean making a positive effort to help black children succeed in the school system. But this can only be done when a positive step is taken to combat racism amongst teachers. As the situation is, some teachers seem to think that they are doing a great job to help black children, but this is only a way of pacifying the situation in making black children accept that they are being catered for adequately by the schools.

Downing (1980:3) in Taylor (1983, p95) argued that multicultural education can become an excuse for not providing properly for black children's education, as it lowers their employment prospects and reduces their chances of equality of educational opportunity. Dodgson and Stewart (1981) in Tomlinson (1983, p95) suggested that multicultural education is a policy of containment formulated to defuse threats posed by the second generation blacks. Stone's argument on the issue is that it has become a form of compensatory education based on the 1960s model of compensatory education for the disadvantaged working class. She argued that equality of opportunity for black children would be best served by the traditional formal academic methods. Carby (1980) in Tomlinson (1983, p94) saw multiracial education as a dangerous practice which will encourage black children to discover their culture at the expense of the understanding of the political and economic struggles of being black in Britain. She to, like Stone (1981) argued that the concept developed out of the ideology of the compensatory education ideal to correct working class children. She however went on to concede that the practice is generally accepted as a positive step with which teachers should be committed to work towards an anti-racist society. Although the arguments surrounding multicultural education are manifold, it could be suggested that since the formal methods are highly Eurocentric, it is unlikely that it would work for the benefit of black children. The children in my study said they would welcome a multicultural curriculum because it would cover a variety of cultures, and would give them a better understanding of black history and their ancestral heritage. Some said they had difficulty in coping with things like the Vikings and Napoleonic Wars because they could not relate to them. But they could relate to black heroes and politicians past and present, and the schools did not cater for them in that respect. The image that textbooks offered them of blacks made them feel awfully ashamed and inferior in class. Hence we see that where black studies have been introduced as part of curricula changes, it has proved to be beneficial to black pupils. At least they know that they have a history, one that is different to that which is written in European textbooks that is rigged with biases and prejudices which depicts blacks in derogatory terms. What is required is a balanced curriculum where every child will have an understanding of what is being taught in an unbiased and non-racist form. Not many of the advocates seem to have a clear understanding of what exactly multicultural education means. Although it is said to mean the introduction of a variety of cultures into the curriculum, Kuya (1981) argues that it does not include anti-racist teaching. If this is the case, how then will the aims of equality of opportunity be achieved if those involved have no clear understanding of the issue? This would best be achieved if there was a national or universal agreement on policies and practices surrounding multicultural education.

These changes do not affect private and independent schools, and are therefore not likely to affect the education of those pupils. Halsey (1961) looked at the European class system and noticed how it reflected economic and social development. Education was a corollary of that system which developed to serve the various social classes. He noted that the selective schools are a prime source of recruits for non-manual occupations, and have direct links with universities and the occupational structure. The schools that black children attend are mainly state controlled schools, which means that they are almost totally excluded from higher educational institutions. This means that no matter how many reforms take place in schools, they will not have access to better standards of education.

Stone (1981, p98) looked at the purpose of multicultural education, and argued that it is a form of compensatory education. In her view it is used by teachers to promote their own careers, rather than to be beneficial to black children. She argued that politically, it is seen as convenient as it enables teachers to believe that they are doing something positive for black children. Hence, it serves to further curricula development, but within the scope of compensatory education and cultural deprivation theories. The development of multiracial education movement has been influenced by a claim for social justice and an appropriate education for minority group pupils. Minority group parents have previously claimed that the school system was guilty of misleading and misguiding their children with a curriculum that did not reflect issues of a multiracial society and therefore further put black children at a disadvantage in the school system.

The National Foundation for Educational Research, has played a great part in the sponsoring and promoting of multiracial education. But Stone (1981, p100) has argued that much of the sponsored research lacks a coherent form and is instead bogged down in dispute over details that appears to be irrelevant. She saw multicultural education as unsound because its theoretical and practical implications have not been worked out, and this gives the view that it is merely a way of watering down the curriculum and cooling out black pupils. She suggested that a minority of teachers and practitioners saw themselves as experts within this field trying desperately to pacify waves of racism and prejudice amongst their pupils and colleagues. But she argued that this will not be enough to solve the problem facing black children in schools. Multiracial education will in some way help some practitioners and beneficiaries to develop a better awareness of themselves and others around them in a more positive light, and help to reduce some of the prejudices previously held by teachers about minority groups. It will also help minority groups to be better motivated and promote a positive attitude towards schools and their teachers. But it will not be effective in solving the problems of black children who already start off in a disadvantaged position by virtue of their race, background, and culture.

Stone (1981, p101) argued that multicultural education is seen by its advocates as the great efficator of minority groups problems. But this may not be enough to erase all the disadvantages that black children suffer in society. First and foremost teachers and the rest of society must recognize the fact that black children come from a particular background, one that is perceived to be surrounded with all sorts of damaging stereotypes and illusions. One could suggest that these perceptions must first be regarded as invalid. In the same way that unreliable theories are discarded, those stereotype theories should be rejected and replaced with valid theories. Klein (1987, p92) suggested that the resources in schools often reflect and reconfirm the attitudes of teachers which they acquired in their school days. Unless changes were given to the materials used in schools, it would continue to give children an extremely biased view of the world. She suggested that all the art, music, literature, languages etc. that are taught in schools are exclusively European. While anything that is mentioned about Africa or Asia is done in racist and inferior terms, e.g. the Primitive Art of Ancient Egypt, rituals instead of worship, tribal as opposed to descendants, Dark Africa, meaning the people are backward, savages, wild and uncivilized, and need to be tamed. How could teachers being socialized with centuries of such misconceptions and illusions and a lack of experience about minority children come to view black children as educable? Their Eurocentric education would lead them to draw on stereotypes when dealing with minority children.

Townsend (1971) noticed that due to a dialect difference many Caribbean children were placed alongside retarded indigenous children. Both issues are completely independent of each other. It is about time teachers realize that such falsehoods have been written over three centuries ago by writers who set out to further their own interests by subjugating those people who did not fit their particular image of a superior human race. People believe what they read with the exception of fiction, and that is why there is a need for schools to completely restructure their curriculum and other materials used in schools to give teachers and pupils an accurate reflection of the people's of the world. This is one of the reasons why racism is so institutionalized, because Europeans were socialized into believing that other races of the world were inferior to themselves and such ideas are not easily discarded. But a rethinking on the part of writers and publishers can go a long way in helping to change people's attitudes and way of thinking.

One of the reasons why multicultural education is viewed with suspicion by some critics is that there is no universal agreement or acceptance on the issue. Some teachers may view it as a way of updating the curriculum, but not specifically as providing an education for black pupils. In all white areas it is especially frowned upon as irrelevant because those teachers do not consider that they too have a problem that requires a solution, as they are spared the trauma of not having black pupils in their schools. Those schools will continue to educate their pupils within the conventional norms of a white ethnocentric society without any given knowledge of the changing nature of society from a white dominated to one within a pluralist perspective. Children educated in that manner will have difficulty in facing the realities of the outside world later on.

Teachers as practitioners should be aware that schools should provide equality of educational opportunity for all the children in their care. But unfortunately this is not the case. Schools are unequal in terms of resources, teaching staff, facilities, and location, all of which brings into question the idea of equality of educational opportunity. But teachers can help by distributing those available resources equally amongst the children. Educators have failed to take into account the fact that independent, private, and boarding schools exist alongside the state schools, and these schools have far better facilities than state schools. Private schools are therefore more efficient and provide a far better education in most cases than state schools, partly because they may attract better qualified teachers, and smaller classes, and teachers can afford to spend more time with each individual pupil. Pupils are also viewed in a different light as they will be mainly from middle class backgrounds and are likely to get full cooperation from their teachers with whom they share similar aspirations and values. On the other hand working class pupils are seen as coming from a culture which their values are different from that of mainstream society and need measures of correction before they can fully be accepted into the school system.

Reeves and Chevannes explained that Frazier (1940) in multiracial education (Vol12, no1, p23) suggested that the class structure of the black community provides the most important setting in which to analyse the problem of black children. He suggested that from a very early age the boys especially face a chronic system of unemployment together with the unsuitability of very little education which is offered to them. Granger (1940, p31, V12, N01, Multiracial Education), stated that the problems and needs of black youths were too deeply ingrained in the problems of the national economy to respond to hasty methods of solution. But another article 'Critical Survey of the Black Adolescent and His Education,' indicated that the black educational problem is seen as social and pathological, with family disorientation playing a major part in the outcome. Reeves and Chevannes (1983) however suggested that any pathology is attributed to the restrictions of the economic context both in historical and contemporary terms. The above arguments show that the assumed pathology amongst black families as suggested by white middle class educationists and practitioners, is a product of white society that have been imposed upon them due to restrictions in areas of deprivation and low employment prospects. As a result they are unable to climb the economic ladder of success, and hence remain at the bottom economically and socially. They are then blamed for their own plight, and seen as being unable to advance with the rest of the world. Hence, they acquire another stereotype 'the pathological or disoriented family'.

Historically, the education of blacks have been prohibited and seen as unnecessary, because they did not need to be educated for the type of menial tasks they were expected to do. Hence by keeping them uneducated, white society believed that they would willingly take their place in society without questioning their unequal and disadvantaged positions. Up until the 1960s Black Americans, by not having the right to vote, were not in a position to voice their opinions about their disadvantaged positions in a society which they are rightfully part of. It was not until they started to organize themselves politically and held mass protests and demonstrations that the rest of society was actually prepared to listen to them. The contemporary situation in Britain is very similar in that the education of Caribbean children was not taken seriously by the DES, educationists or teachers who thought that there was no need to formulate policies relating to black children's education. The DES thought their problem was temporary and would be solved as time went by. Instead they embarked on an assimilationist policy, that black people would eventually be absorbed into a British way of life. But when this policy failed, it was realized that other measures had to be found.

Mullard (1984, p16) suggested that historically the first form of racial education or immigrant education can explicitly be reflected as the racism of white society and schools. He suggested that anti-racist education evolved in part as a reaction to both structural and cultural racial forms. As a result immigrant education was already firmly anchored in a structural and explicitly racist definition of the social order, and this reproduces the structural relations of racism as a means of securing an assimilated social order. Mullard (1980-82) in Tomlinson (1983, p94) saw multicultural education as a political response based on racist assumptions which evolved out of a series of political interpretations of the threats which blacks posed to the stability of liberal democratic societies. He saw it as a contradiction, in that it cannot be taken seriously in a society that is already racist. Instead it serves to control black students by directing their political energy and frustrations into what seems like radical studies. In other words, it gives the impression that black pupils are being liberated by being allowed to pursue their own cultural origins, but at the same time they are being coerced by white society into conformity. Mullard's explanation would seem to be a valid one, in that racism is firmly anchored in the structures and institutions of society which makes it difficult for anyone to actually recognize its presence in order to eradicate it. Instead, it reproduces itself in an unrecognizable form while acting as a barrier to the progress of black children. The Voice newspaper, (31.7.91, p2) reported that Esther and Fagbemiro on the topic of better educational standards which is now a priority for the government, some higher and further educational institutions have decided to lower the entrance requirements for black ethnics. They suggested that based on the phenomenon of black underachievement, they were struck by the thought of it. They saw it as an insult that the average black person cannot gain entrance to such institutions on meritocratic principles, or is it the fact that structural racism is so rampant that it distorts the reality. They argued that the dissemination of biased and distorted information via the media about black people, shapes the attitudes, judgements and perceptions of a society, its people and institutions.

This process is self-replicating in that where black people are continually shown in an unfavourable light, they will be underrepresented in higher and further educational institutions. They further argued that the solution is not to recruit token blacks, but rather to question the idea of whether or not these people are failing to reach the required standard for entrance, or are racist attitudes and principles operating against them? In another article in The Voice (9.8.91.) black students who do get the opportunity to enter higher institutions, said they were treated differently to white students, and many of them have put this down to racism. Many said that they felt that they were harshly treated, especially in the marking of exams. I have been told of many bright and hardworking black students, especially male students who the universities fail in their first or second years. This means that they were unable to proceed on to the third year, and hence, had to leave without graduating. Such drastic measures by institutions to discredit black students is unwarrantable and futile. Rather than encouraging talents, they set out to annihilate it, and as a result cause disillusionment amongst the black youths of society.

Multiracial education will not eliminate inequalities due to factors that are both ideological and structural which tend to govern teachers attitudes and actions into how knowledge is used and distributed in the classroom. Lynch (1986, p11) suggested that the practical tasks faced by teachers in a multicultural society and the education system as a whole, is to recognize tensions between goals and social cohesion, and those of cultural diversity, and weld them with a commitment towards greater equality of educational opportunity. But he further suggested that the problem is a very complex one and would require careful planning. He declared that the gap between multicultural objectives and educational practice in Britain was very wide. Would schools readily abandon conventional practice for an alternative one that is relatively new and untried and viewed with caution? Teachers have a way of holding on to old customs and traditions as long as it works for them, and as a way of keeping control in the classroom.

Multiracial education was not actually introduced into schools to meet the needs of black pupils. Lynch (1986, p62) outlined that it was the EEC Directive and Circular 6/81 that requested local education authorities to review their school arrangements for the school curriculum. It stated that it was the view of the Secretary of State that schools should have written aims which should be reviewed two years later. Lynch argued that such a response may have been initiated by the Brixton riots and the publication of the Scarman Report of 1981, which looked at criticisms made by Caribbean parents about educational provisions for their children. Some of these criticisms were as follows:

1. Lack of discipline in schools.
2. The alleged failure of teachers to motivate Caribbean pupils sufficiently.
3. Lack of sufficient contact between parents and schools.
4. Lack of understanding by teachers of the cultural backgrounds of black pupils.
5. Failure of the curriculum to sufficiently recognize the value of the distinctive traditions of the various ethnic minorities.

ILEA had begun to review some of the issues concerning multiracial education since the later part of the 1970s, and had drawn up policies to that effect, though Bradford had previously pioneered the issue of multiracial education. Rampton (1981) had recommended that the DES as part of its review on curriculum arrangement should invite all LEAS, to define their policy and commitment to multicultural education in schools. The response from the DES stated that the Secretary of State recognizes that there are certain broad constraints on the issue of detailed guidance on the curriculum. This statement may have prompted more LEAs to appoint more specialist advisers for multicultural education to support the initiative being taken by teachers at that time. However, despite various surveys being carried out in secondary, primary and middle schools education between 1978-83, only a few bore reference to a multiethnic society, and no reference to multiracial education which is what the main topic was about. The multicultural character of the curriculum was not a major dimension of the investigation, nor the schedule used by the Inspectorate to collect the information. It reported that reading specifically selected for ethnic minorities should reflect the fact that ours is a multicultural society and was seen only in a small proportion of schools. The inspectors did report that those areas of education that were particularly at risk were language development, reading skills at all levels of ability, health education, careers education, social and moral education, and lastly, at a more general level, the preparation of all pupils for life in a multiracial society. Lynch (1986, p65) suggested that after teachers had scrutinized the documents, they may well have thought that there was no major commitment on the part of national government on implementing a multiracial and a multicultural society. Neither for education to reflect multiculturalism, due in part to its vagueness and lack of emphasis and commitment.

The awareness of schools on the educational implications of a multi-ethnic school population varied greatly, and only a minority of schools had examined any changes which they thought necessary in their approaches to pastoral care. Between 1970s-1980s, some LEAS developed policy statements which would provide a framework for teachers in state schools to develop multiracial education. But by 1984 a survey carried out on some LEAS in London showed that there still remained a large number of LEAS who had not yet worked out nor issued a policy statement on either multicultural education or anti-racist education. Independent and private schools were also uninterested in the multiracial issue, as many still had ideas about cultural assimilation. Lynch (1986, p70) suggested that ILEA Inspectorate produced a document on education in a multicultural society which raised a series of questions which derived out of concern that all children should be offered equal opportunities for educational achievement and that children should be prepared for a positive role in a multi-ethnic society. The document stated the following points:

1. There should be a commitment to an overall holistic school policy.
2. A commitment to equality of educational opportunity for all children.
3. The development of strategies to correct racism.
4. A whole curriculum approach.
5. The need for teachers to know pupils linguistic repertories.
6. The importance of classroom strategies and resources to support the learning needs of pupils in a multi-ethnic society.
7. An acceptance of the importance of ethos and atmosphere in the schools commitment to multicultural education.

As it happened, some of the more recent documents have tended to focus more sharply on a multicultural curriculum linked with broader issues such as sexism and classism in education. Thus, by linking other issues it would seem a way of pacifying the term racism as it is such a controversial topic it may not have enough weight on its own to warrant challenging inequality in education. It also affects only a small minority of people and would therefore not be seen as a priority issue. But the inclusion of sexism and classism affects a whole spectrum, and would be seen as appropriate enough an issue to be tackled, hence a multidisciplinary approach towards educational reforms.

Lynch (1986, p75) explained that an overview of LEA policies in multiracial education drawn up by the Commission for Racial Equality indicated that LEAs saw their policies as responses to pluralism and cultural diversity, but also deriving directly from their responsibilities for compliance with the 1976 Race Relations Act. However, there are variations in a range of issues in LEA policy statements which depend on local characteristics such as English as a Second Language (ESL), mother tongue, curriculum development, Section 11 funding, teacher training, in-service training, and ethnic statistics. It would appear that owing to the fact that there was no clearly defined policy statement from the DES on how multicultural education should be approached, each LEA may have tended to develop their own policies based on local issues and the availability of resources. By 1985 there was a great variety of practices across the country, and this was not always in areas of high ethnic composition. Some authorities with a low level of ethnics are now adopting a more balanced policy with a view to helping to eliminate inequalities. But the problem of racism may still be a topic of little or no importance to teachers in those areas, mainly because it is not seen as a major problem. By resorting to a multicultural curriculum they will be seen as doing their best to comply with DES recommendations.

The USA Proposals for Multi-racial Education

Lynch (1986, p146) looked at some of the approaches taken by the USA for multiracial education. Some of their proposals are as follows:

1. Basic information about ethnic and cultural pluralism.
2. Knowledge acquisition and values clarification about ethnic group and their cultures.
3. How to combat racism.
4. Linguistic knowledge of black students in its historic, economic, cultural and political contextuality.
5. Competence for perceiving, believing, evaluating and behaving in different cultural contexts.
6. Skill development in translating multicultural knowledge into programmes, practices, habits and behaviour of classroom instruction.
7. Competences in making educational objectives meaningful to the experiential backgrounds and frames of reference to all students.
8. Skill in achieving learning and teaching style congruency.
9. Psychology and Sociology of ethnicity, including human behaviour and learning.

The USA debate on multicultural education would seem to have adopted far more strategies than in Britain. It could well be that this is because the USA is a far more open society than Britain and is more prepared to tackle and challenge issues however controversial they may be. It could also be the case that they have a far longer history of racial issues and a wider variety of racial groups who put greater demand on the system for something to be done about their plight. Great emphasis is placed on ethnicity and linguistic values of the different ethnic groups and black students, and an acceptance of cultural pluralism.

Canadian Approach to Multiracial Education

Lynch (1986, p168) argues that the Canadian approach to multicultural education sets out to look at causes of racism, and how they can be tackled or combated. They set out to provide an input from everyday experiences, and encouraging and equipping participants to observe aspects of race relations in their schools. They also expect the participants to plan out the professional development for staff in their schools for one academic year. Their list of proposals are as follows:
1. Racist behaviour is learned.
2. Racism is produced by both belief systems and social structures.
3. Racist behaviour has both a cognitive and effective dimension.
4. Educators respond best to initiatives in race relations when they are directly applied to classroom practice.
5. Educators find in-service programmes most rewarding when their experience as practitioners are taken into account and not trivialized.
6. Educators are likely to make changes when the support system within the school provides encouragement and feedback.

The Canadians have a belief that there must first be a recognition between attitudes and social structures, then a look at the relationship between both the knowledge which racism serves, and practices by both institutions and individuals to promote equality. This can be done by first recognizing the fact that racism does exist, and by employing some of those methods, so that a process of equality can be brought about. The Canadians also have a system of pluralism, one which allows for many cultures to coexist, but overall a support for one Canadian nation.

The British Debate on Multicultural Education

It would appear that so far the issue surrounding multicultural education in Britain is still in a state of controversy and uncertainty, due in part to ad hoc policies and lack of intervention on the part of the government to formulate strict policies on the issue of racism in education. Reeves and Chevannes (1983, V12, No.1, p33) looked at research carried out during the 1970s and the outcome of the findings. They noted that Wedge and Prosser (1973) used anti-theoretical traditions like family size, single parents, low income, and poor housing to explain educational underachievement amongst Caribbean children. Fontani and Weinstein (1968, p216) asked who are the disadvantaged and suggested that most of us are. They explained that the meaning of the disadvantaged must be broadened to include all those who are blocked in any way from fulfilling their human potential. They argued that this blocking can take place anywhere whether it be in a slum area, or an affluent suburb, where children also may be neglected, overprotected, ruled by iron-handed parents or guided by no rule at all. He claims that the school has failed the middle class child, as it has done to those from low income families. This statement sums up the fact that the broad view held by society that only certain groups of pupils are disadvantaged, is in some ways a misleading concept. But the term disadvantaged seems to conveniently serve the purpose of shielding schools and institutions from taking the blame of failing in their duties to the less well off members of society, in educating them to the best of their abilities.

Cole (1989, p144) looked at the traditional approach to multicultural education, and noted a number of unchanging attributes which teachers are expected to teach were in themselves problematic. He saw culture as heterogeneous and differentiated by such factors as class, gender and age. Curriculum material have tended to limit black culture, to reduce it to artefacts within a specified number of cultural sites such as art, religion, food, dress etc. He suggested that this approach aims to increase respect for minority cultures and to improve self-concept. But the belief that teachers are morally equipped to enhance black self-concept could mean that there are dangerous assumptions made about the capacity of white middle class teachers to do good for young blacks. Cole saw this approach as patronizing, as it allowed teachers to avoid examining their own racism. It also allows an aura of cultural superiority in that teachers will see themselves as civilizing and righting black students.

Bhavani and Bhavani in Cole (1989, p144) explained that multiculturalism and a tolerant approach are felt by many blacks as patronizing and offensive because it does not confront the basic power relationships which perpetuate racism as in the economic, social and political institutions. By allowing a few black projects on food, clothes, maps, etc it has ignored the racist education system, and racism amongst teachers and students alike. As Cole (1989) suggested, multicultural education is essentially a white approach to education in a multicultural society. The attitude behind much of the work taken on by schools in displaying maps of the Caribbean, food products of those regions, and dress, is done so that racism within the education system can be ignored, thus maintaining the status quo. Cole is correct in pointing out the biases found in the schools and their attitudes towards multicultural education, in that teachers may see themselves as doing something positively for the good of Caribbean pupils. It could be argued that they are only trying to maintain stability within those institutions of power where only those who are chosen to succeed will actually achieve anything from the system. Teachers are expected to uphold the dominant values set by white society, and by being part of that society, they transmit only those values which will be beneficial to the stability of society on the whole. This is done by denying black children the true acceptance of themselves as capable individuals. Instead they instil in them white values of mainstream culture, and no historical achievement of black people, except that they are failures. This message is communicated to the children themselves in their daily encounters with the schools, and can be seen in the places which they occupy in schools.

Foster (1990, p63) in his study at Milltown High looked at issues relating to multicultural and anti-racist education. He found that the school had adopted a policy of multicultural education. Assigned to the department, there was a newly appointed member of staff dealing with multicultural literature, and advising other members on how such material should be incorporated into the curriculum. This led to several teachers beginning to explore the issue and hence, the multicultural and anti-racist approach became the central theme to the departments working philosophy.

This approach had four main meanings:

1. To value and not denigrate the backgrounds and cultures of students.
2. Promoting the value of anti-racism in their teaching.
3. Adopting a non-racist approach in their interaction with students.
4. Teaching about social and political issues and orienting teaching to political aims.

Despite this commitment by some of the staff, Foster noticed that there where others who felt that the existence of racism in the educational system was much exaggerated. This made them resentful and they viewed such aspects of school and LEA policies with hostility, because in their view, they did not accept that any of the normal workings of the school might operate to the disadvantage of minority pupils. Some teachers also felt that there was little evidence of racism in education. Others said they had insufficient guidance in how to incorporate multicultural and anti-racist education into their departmental practices. Some of the staff believed that all white teachers were invariably racist as a result of their mono-cultural upbringing and education. This could possibly cause them to be unconsciously racist and thereby inadvertently favour or foster their relationships with white students. Others argued that broader institutional practices and the workings of the educational system were racist. Others suggested that institutions that are dominated and run by white people in society are racist, because minority people are denied access to power, and important decisions which affect the lives of their children.

Prior to this approach, Foster suggested that black students faced social and educational problems due to the discrimination and disadvantage experienced by their parents. As a result, a sub-culture developed which was reflected and reproduced in the school. As a result, he suggested that many of the students became hostile and ambivalent towards schooling. In response to this hostility, teachers were forced to adapt in order to survive. This in turn had implications for the educational experience teachers made available to students. Foster suggested that conditions created within the school were not necessarily the result of racist teachers but by the structure and organisation of the wider educational system which permits those with greater economic and cultural resources to place their children on more favourable routes in the educational race. He further argued that within school processes were likely to disadvantage black children, and this could explain their relative underachievement. Foster gave the following explanations about school processes:

1. There is the theory that teachers tend to have negative views and low expectations of Afro-Caribbean students, that such students receive inferior treatment in schools, that their educational self-esteem and motivation are reduced, and so they consequently underachieve.
2. There is the associated theory that the curriculum of schools neglect or denigrates the culture of Afro-Caribbean students. As a result they suffer lowered self-esteem and academic motivation, become hostile to their teachers and underachieve.
3. Driver's (1979) suggestion that teachers lack the cultural competence to deal confidently and adequately with black children.
4. There is the view that the definitions of ability and worth that are routinely used by teachers are based on the cultural forms of the dominant groups. In Foster's view all those factors would make it difficult for working class and minority students to perform successfully in the school system, because evaluation criteria are culturally biased, and they lack the appropriate cultural capital.

Foster's study has thrown some light on the fact that although some schools are now adopting a policy of multicultural education there are still some teachers who do not consider this to be a very important issue because they do not think racism exists in school practices. Although materials and books prominently used in schools are very racist in content there is still the notion that "there is no racism" in my school. Foster would seem to exonerate teachers for the failure of Caribbean children in schools. In his view the curriculum at Milltown High now included substantial and positive references to the history and culture of black people and therefore could not contribute to the lowering of black children's self-esteem, but places emphasis on the wider educational, cultural and economic factors.

In my view this would seem to be shifting the blame from schools and on to somewhere else. Aren't teachers part of the whole establishment that makes up the totality of the system from which their beliefs and perceptions of others are developed. Why should they therefore not be racist if they were socialised in a racist society?

The perpetuation of racism in schools has for a long time done enormous damage to the well-being of Caribbean children over the years, and this now requires every effort and help on the part of teachers to improve the plight of those children. The topic of investigation is why so many black children fail in the school system. This could not be purely coincidental. We need to look at a range of issues, but mainly the establishments in which they have been taught, and by whom. It is needless blaming their backgrounds or culture because most black children are eager to learn, and given the chance, they can achieve.

Burgess (1986, p115) looked at patterns of inequality in education between the social classes, and suggested that we should question the interrelationships between class, gender and race in attempting to understand patterns of social inequality. There is relatively little evidence of the experiences of Caribbean children within the school and the interaction processes that take place in the classroom. Cole argued that sociologists have been unable to explain how the relationships between class and race interact and cause black children to underachieve. But perhaps we could assume that people who are already categorised as being in subordinate positions are at a greater disadvantage, because the schools tend to discredit their capabilities. As a result they underachieve, due to the fact that they are seen as belonging to certain groups that do not seem to fit in with the conventions of the school. In certain cases minority groups tend to be in isolation from the school system, because their class background does not allow them to become fully integrated within the school system. Do teachers take them seriously as having academic potential? In Pursell (1977, p131) Rosenthal (1974) identified two types of instrumental teacher behaviour, (1) the amount of material taught, (2) the type of pupil/teacher interaction. Kohn (1973) suggested that students response to teacher expectations varied in extent, and that they either yield to or resist the teachers message.

Differential Life Chances

Lynch (1986, p169) suggested that even where qualifications are similar amongst ethnic groups, evidence shows a more causal relationship between race and unemployment, than between success in public examinations and employment. The Commission for Racial Equality (1982) found that the rate for Asian and white youths was 40%, and qualifications did not appear to be an adequate explanation. Smith, Campbell and Jones suggested that qualifications are irrelevant to some types of jobs. They found that those with qualifications consisted of 9% of white males with O levels, 18% Asians, and 25% Afro Caribbeans unemployment rate. A study carried out by a Social Policy Research Unit in 1984 found that the job positions of blacks in Britain is little or no different from that of the first arrivals in the 1950s -1960s. The disparity between black and white Council tenants had actually grown between 1974-1984. It found that racial inequality had become entrenched and self-sustaining, deriving partly from direct discrimination and partly from disadvantage, because institutions took no account of cultural differences. Lynch suggested that white advocates of multicultural education asserts that curriculum reform and increased support for minority achievement will result in better life chances for black children. But critics argued against such a causality. The reason for this criticism could perhaps be located in the existing unequal distribution of wealth and power that is held by a few in society, and hence, education alone could not put this to right. Lynch puts such differentials for race inequality down to racial prejudice and discrimination, and not just educational failure of minority pupils as the reason why in disproportionate numbers some groups fail to achieve employment. Hence they suffer disproportionately poorer life chances than their white counterparts. If we look at Merton's Social Structure and Anomie, where goals are set but certain groups cannot achieve them due to the complexity of the system. Black groups are excluded from certain institutions though indirectly, and this makes it difficult for them to achieve on par with their white counterparts.

Conclusion

This section has looked at a number of issues relating to attitudes and educational aspirations amongst pupils and parents. It has also looked at multicultural education as a government proposal towards educational policies. It would appear that there is no clearly defined explanation as to why some pupils aspire to high levels of achievement and others do not. It would also seem that a great deal depends on the pupils' own motivation and perceptions of success. But this is just an assumption as educational achievement is still a mystery to social scientists. No one quite knows how this occurs. However, with regards to pupils of Caribbean descent, although they are eager to do well at school, there are barriers which prevent them from reaching the standards of education to which they aspire. Several studies show that they are eager to achieve educationally, but for some unknown reasons they are not allowed to do so. In my judgement it appears that as a group they tend to be viewed negatively by teachers who expect very little of them, and hence communicate this message to them. Although this cannot be statistically proven, sufficient findings have suggested that teacher attitudes towards Caribbean children would seem to treat them differently to other groups, and this could be a factor for their underachievement. I have also looked at some of the literature used in schools, and for teachers to impart that type of knowledge to their pupils, can't leave them any other option than to be racist themselves whether subconsciously or otherwise. Studies show that black parents encourage their children to pursue education as a means of getting a good occupation. They also stay on longer at school and are more likely to go on to college. These are good enough reasons for them to succeed at school. But statistics still show that they underachieve. This could mean that they are not given a fair chance in schools to prove their competence, and this is an area that needs looking into.

According to the responses of some of the students involved in the surveys, racism would seem to be a factor that should not be ignored. Although this is a topic that is not highly rated amongst teachers and educationists, it is also a topic that should not to be ignored amongst researchers, but very often this is the case. Researchers seem to be preoccupied with preconceived stereotypes, which they seem to conveniently use to construct their hypothesis. With this in mind their findings will reflect that view. Until researchers dispose of the biases, prejudices, and stereotypes which they hold of Caribbean children and their family backgrounds, their studies will continually be influenced by those views.

Based on evidence supplied by various authors, and the statements made by the students themselves and some of the teachers reactions to the researchers, racism would seem a factor which cause Caribbean children to underachieve in schools. But as racism cannot be quantified it has to remain an assumed factor until it can be further justified. If teachers see Caribbean children as boisterous, noisy and badly behaved, this will determine how they are categorized and treated by teachers as uneducatable and unstable. If their perceptions of them are as such, then they will not try to educate them, as they will think that it is a waste of their time which could be used elsewhere. Black children's entry into schools could have triggered the impression in the minds of teachers that they are only there to cause disruption to the stability of the schools and creating a problem for teachers and staff, as Mac an Ghaill found. To prove themselves right, teachers may over-react against any slight adverse behaviour portrayed by Caribbean children, and dismiss them as academic failures. Once this happens, it becomes standard practice amongst teachers that all Caribbean children are failures. So hence we have a situation where they are allocated into lower streams, because that is where teachers seem to think they belong. Mac an Ghaill noted that Asian boys were treated better than the Caribbean boys even though they formed a group called the Warriors. But their behaviour attracted less of the teachers attention, as they were seen as conformists and possessing technical qualities. Stereotyping would seem to be a factor that is highlighted here in the way teachers treat both groups. Teachers have a duty to be impartial and non-judgmental towards their pupils, and if they cannot do so, then perhaps many are in the wrong profession. There is the possibility that some chose the profession because of the rewards it offers, and not because they particularly want to help their pupils. But, if it gave them status and power over their pupils, many may have thought that to be rewarding in itself, as they will also gain respect and reverence from them.

The government has however recently admitted that many teachers were below the recognized standards, and should be re-graded and paid according to their performance. This is a failing on the part of the government in not recognizing this much sooner. After so many children have failed in the education system because of the uncaring attitude of some teachers, the government has now decided to act. It has now realized that many children may have been neglected because some teachers were not equipped with the type of knowledge and tact that is required to deal with children in their pastoral care. The USA System of Education has a policy of re-examining teachers competence at intervals to decide their suitability to remain in the teaching profession. How about such a policy in Britain? After all, the good teachers would have nothing to fear, but it would at least give a much fairer chance to those children who want to succeed but are unable to do so because of their teacher's uncaring attitude. If Caribbean children are seen to be displaying what the teachers see as bad behaviour, they will be made to occupy the lower streams regardless of their capabilities and abilities. But why should this be so? If they are capable then they should be placed in the streams conducive to their capabilities. In order to maintain power and control of the classroom, teachers will use their authority to subjugate those pupils who do not conform to the established principles of the school, even if it is to the detriment of their learning.

Foner (1977) was told by some dissatisfied Caribbean parents that their children could have done better at school but their teachers held them back so that they could not make any progress. Also, by denying them a good quality education, the schools prepared them for the menial, and unrewarding tasks which they would eventually hold in society according to Bowles and Gintis. This ensures that they are kept at the bottom of the economic ladder, where this cycle is likely to be perpetuated, in a 'cycle of poverty and deprivation'. Teachers frequently use the term, 'we treat all children alike'. But this would appear to be a misleading statement, one that needs examining and clarifying. Perhaps teachers need to be more aware of their own attitudes and prejudices, and be prepared to treat all children alike regardless of their colour, background, race, ethnic origin or nationality. This in turn, may account for better relationships between teachers and their pupils, and less or no conflict within the schools. The next chapter will look at how aspects of social deprivation may affect educational achievement among minority and other groups.

◆

CHAPTER 3

Social Disadvantage and Educational Opportunities

This chapter will look at some of the problems that may implicitly or explicitly affect the performance of children in schools. This does not affect only minority children, but also a wide section of the white working class. This is because social deprivation is prevalent amongst various groups who will be affected in the same way, and this will in turn affect their education. I will look at some of the previous studies which have been carried out during the 1960s to the present, to see how Caribbean children and other groups have been affected within the education system. The following table shows the achievement of ethnic children in average percentage scores for both sexes in New Society (21.8.87) for ILEA.

Table 2
Differences in attainment levels between ethnic and indigenous pupils in public examinations showing average performance scores in %.

Group	Boys	Girls
Indians	22.5	26.3
Pakistanis	20.8	21.8
Bangladeshis	7.6	15.1
Caribbeans	11.2	15.9
Africans	15.3	18.8
Whites	13.6	16.9

Parekh in New Society: (21.8.87 for ILEA)

The table showed that when boys and girls in each group were compared, girls scored higher in all groups. It also stated that there have been some improvements in the examination pass rates of Caribbean children, but their average scores were still below that of other groups, with the exception of Bangladeshi children. Parekh's explanation in New Society (21.8.87), seems to lie in class and national culture. These are just two of the variables which social scientists tend to use regularly as an explanation for academic success or failure. But there may also be other factors involved such as parental level of education and their involvement in their children's education. Equally important is individual ambition and motivation, because if any of these factors are lacking, no amount of parental encouragement will be persuasive enough. It could therefore be suggested that whatever it is that enables individual pupils to succeed at school is still not quite known, though to some extent, teacher expectation has been found to be successful. Is success to do with the school's environment which sociologists have not yet fully explored? What we do know is that if the right environment is provided, that in itself can be a motivating factor in educational success regardless of class, race or culture. It would appear that children learn through active participation and cooperation of their teachers, parents and peers, and what the individual wants out of education. The children in my study suggested that the schools could provide a better environment and teachers should be more caring and pay more attention to their views and needs rather than to be there just to tell them what to do. This would greatly enhance their learning ability because they would feel more involved. Parekh also stated that the performance of white pupils had not improved, but had deteriorated since 1976. The percentage of Caribbean children taking O levels and CSE examinations had increased from 2% to 4% between (1976) and (1986). This was not significantly high but encouraging according to Parehk in New Society (21.8.87,ILEA). He stated that group differences and different belief systems amongst Asians may help to alleviate some of the conflicting pressures, and make them feel less isolated from the mainstream education system. It could however be argued that even though group solidarity may be important in educational success, it also requires active participation from the schools. There is the possibility that if Asian children were seen in the same light as Caribbean children by their teachers, they could have been categorized as underachievers. But they were seen by their teachers as being technical, and this could have encouraged them to play by the rules of the schools in order to succeed. I am not saying that Caribbean children diverted from these rules, but they seemed to have acquired a label which suggested that their behaviour was different, and so they were treated differently by the system.

Social disadvantage can be seen in a variety of ways. For example, if the home backgrounds of particular pupils are seen to be of a lower standard than that of other children, this is sometimes classed as social disadvantage because those children may not have the same amount of material wealth as other children do. Income could also be another factor which determines people's social status, and how they perceive themselves in society. Those who earn a high wage, may see themselves as different and leading a better lifestyle than many who are either unemployed or are on a low wage. The latter could be classed as being disadvantaged, because their children would not have access to some of the material goods that the former could afford. In such circumstances, some theorists would argue that educational performance depends upon conditions in the home. This could have some validity, because the first stage of socialization begins in the home, and this to a large extent can have a bearing on educational success or failure. For instance, if at an early age the children find that there is an absence of books, toys, and other learning materials in the home, those children will be at a disadvantage when they start school, because children from more affluent homes will have a headstart over them. On a recent TVAM education programme (1991) a professor of education suggested that the first five years of a child's learning experience is crucial, because during those early years the knowledge that is acquired paves the way for later years. It seems that brighter children who are able to demonstrate their abilities and a willingness to learn will be better accepted by their teachers, and this will account for better cooperation and interaction between them, and put the less bright ones at a disadvantage. Many teachers have told me that the children who come to school with certain skills and are able to demonstrate them, will be at an advantage over the rest of the class. This would suggest that from day one, these children are more likely to be accepted by their teachers as future capable scholars, and may at all times be able to capture the teacher's attention over and above the rest of the class.

Other factors accounting for social disadvantage may include racism which may specifically affect certain groups of pupils. Poor blacks in the USA are said to be racially disadvantaged, because they do not have access to the same type of material goods as do whites. The case is very similar in Britain, where blacks are located in the lower paid jobs which makes it difficult for them to achieve good living standards. This tends to adversely affect their children's performance at school. They may be seen by some teachers as coming from homes where proper amenities are lacking, therefore living standards are poor. Tomlinson (1983, p60) suggested that it is well documented that family background and educational success are closely related. This would cause some teachers to have a low expectation of children from lower class backgrounds, as the typical cliché amongst some teachers are, 'what else can you expect of these children?' Dhondy et al (1982, p9) found that at a London school where the researcher taught, many teachers in the staffroom constantly talked about West Indian children. No one knew how to deal with them. Lessons were constantly disrupted, especially in the lower forms where the majority of Caribbean children were placed. This created frustration and problems for the teachers who had no specialist knowledge of dealing with black pupils. By congregating them in the lower streams, teachers may have made the matter worse because lower stream pupils are aware of the fact that not much is expected of them and may think that this gives them the impetus to misbehave. They know that they are denied a place amongst those chosen to receive specialist knowledge, and this is one way of relegating them to the lower end of the scale. Although they may not accept this, they act out the part of being deviants or non-conformists. Faced with this type of situation teachers will have difficulty in finding a solution, due in part to their training procedures, and on the other hand a failure to recognize their own prejudice and racism when dealing with black pupils. Dhondy recalled that during the time spent at university, some of the students who were considering going into teaching as a career, were mainly concerned about class, and how they would try to change things when they were on the other side of the desk, but race had not entered the discussion. Teacher training facilities do not provide instructions on how to deal with pupils who may display some degree of difficulty due to differences in culture and origin, and this needs to be taken into account when training programmes are being planned. To make matters worse, the children may have seen the teachers as hostile to them and in turn redirected the hostility. Dhondy managed to calm the children by threats and entreaties, and by getting them to talk about themselves, and giving them tape recorders and cameras to record their opinions and images, and by story telling. Children sometimes may want their own opinions to be heard, and not just what the teachers have to tell them. Some children may find this a monotony and may act aggressively to appease their boredom.

Lacey (1977, p30) examined the training that teachers undergo and some of the values they held prior to training. He suggested that they adapt certain strategies to enable them to cope in certain situations. Their values and interests differ according to their social class origin, but in the end the values of the dominant classes strive to promote cohesion and agreement. This he suggested, may create stresses within the socialization process, which in turn become an area for conflict and competition. Lacey also saw teaching as a divided profession, one divided by expertise and understanding which professionals bring to the classroom. They may have certain perceptions of particular groups of pupils, even before they enter the classroom eg. the type of area from which they came. In particular, some Caribbean children may fit into this category, and become targets for stereotyping.

Other Factors Relating to Social Deprivation

It is generally believed that the circumstances under which people live can cause social deprivation. It is often suggested that immigrants live and work below the standards of the white population, which cause many to suffer aspects of deprivation. This may be so in many cases, because as studies show blacks earn far lower wages, and often occupy overcrowded conditions in slum areas. Taylor (1983, p27) suggested that according to the 1971 Census, a disproportionate number of Caribbeans were in the lowest status and least desirable jobs. Richmond (1973) in Taylor (1983, p29) discovered that 24 percent of Caribbean males were in nonmanual occupation before migration, compared to 6 percent in this country. Although Caribbean men worked longer hours, their wages were not higher than for whites. This means that even when they worked overtime they still earned less for the long hours worked. The Political and Economic Planning survey by Smith (1974) in Taylor (1983, p29) showed that

Caribbean men tend to have jobs at substantially lower levels than white men with equivalent qualifications. 28 percent of Caribbean men claimed to have experienced discrimination in 1979, compared to 16 percent in 1974, and 25 percent of Caribbean women in the same period, compared to 15 percent five years previously. Eighty two percent of Caribbean men in 1974 thought some employers discriminate. Discrimination in housing and how it affects black families will be discussed later in more detail.

It is obvious that low wages do affect the educational chances of children. As we have seen education is divided by class, race, and gender and this may account for success or failure in the education system. The low income group is at a disadvantage because they will be denied access to prestigious schools. The schools which their children attend will be far less equipped to offer a good quality education, as can be seen in many inner city schools. From the earliest days of the establishment of education, there has been divisions and conflict within the system. Though several Education Acts have been implemented to bring about equality of opportunity for those with equal talent, critics have argued that those policies have failed. Comprehensive Schools were designed in the 1970s to give children from various backgrounds an equal chance, thus bridging the gap that was caused by the tripartite system. But advocates for equality of educational opportunity have argued that this system only reinforces the status quo. As long as there are still fee paying schools and private boarding schools, inequalities in education will remain a dominant feature in society.

Douglas (1964, p84) linked school performance with circumstances in the home, by suggesting that where there are large families, the younger ones are likely to do better, because the older ones are more likely to go out to work earlier. Keddie (1973) suggested that to blame the home is merely taking the blame away from the school, and pointing to the home instead. Labov and Rosen (1970s) in the USA, on cultural deprivation theory, have suggested that urban poverty is not the real cause of underachievement at school. The school is seen as a middle class institution with middle class values which is considered to be the norm for everyone. Thus, children who live in slum areas are seen as failures, because they have not internalized those values set by the dominant white society. Those children are said to have lower IQ than white children in the more prosperous middle class areas. This was the explanation in the 1960s, when theorists such as Eyzenck sought explanations for poorer performance in genetics. Some of those findings have since been ruled out by contemporary psychologists who consider that it is no longer valid to use genetics as a factor for measuring IQ. Nonetheless, the stigma has remained and may have had a damaging effect on many black youths both in the USA and in Britain. Genetically, dark skin still seems to carry the stigma of inferiority and lower intelligence, and this is still used sub-consciously by some teachers and other members of society to judge the competence of black people. This can be very misleading and damaging to black pupils in schools, and the way they are perceived by society at large.

In Britain the situation is classed as different in that there are no significantly large inner city areas that are predominantly black. This to a certain extent will make it more difficult to assess the situation in Britain on a par the USA. But on the whole there are some similarities, in that theorists have argued that blacks are concentrated in the low income group. If occupational status determine one's educational prospects, then it could be seen that black children would be expected to encounter barriers in the education system, and thereby underachieve at school. Because of their parents' class position in society, they would be seen as occupying a working class position or according to Rex, an underclass. But this is not necessarily the case, because many blacks are now moving up the economic ladder by either going into business or moving into white collar occupations. This is however a small percentage, which means that such improvements will still remain hidden.

It has been suggested by theorists such as Stone (1981), Taylor (1983) and many others that Caribbean parents value education and want their children to succeed at school. Many of those parents are of the opinion that being black in a white society can only be compensated for by having good educational qualifications. But the question remains, do parents have enough knowledge about the workings of the education system, and how to use it to their advantage? This seems highly unlikely. Several Caribbean parents whom I interviewed said they were not members of the PTA, none were on school governing bodies, but they did visit the school on open evenings which is once a year to discuss their children's progress with the teachers. They are probably not aware that they could arrange to see the teachers by appointment if they are dissatisfied about their children's education. However, it should be remembered that during the 1960s-70s some teachers were inflexible, and may not have encouraged Caribbean parents to attend schools at unsociable hours. Thus, one visit a year seems hardly sufficient if parents are desirous for their children to do well at school. However, many were of the opinion that when they sent their children to school, it was the duty of the teachers to educate them accordingly, as they were accustomed to in the Caribbean. This led them to believe that their children were doing well at school, and as a result they kept a low profile whilst relying on teachers to educate their children, but unfortunately for many this was not the case.

Migrant Labour

Miles and Phizacklea (1979, p77) looked at migrant labour in Britain and suggested that despite the fact that there is anti-discriminatory legislation by the government, there is still conflict in the low wage sector of the economy. Due to an absence of a minimum wage Act, employers can still exploit employees to a certain extent. The authors noted that when Commonwealth workers entered Britain in the post war period, there were existing structures of wealth and power which determined where black workers were located in the job market. Taylor (1983, p27) suggested that they were allocated to undesirable jobs primarily as replacement workers, to fill those vacancies that were made available by whites who had become upwardly mobile. This meant that there were no hope of them becoming upwardly mobile through promotional prospects. Hence, we have a situation where the pattern has been perpetuated until the present, and exhibiting a wide variety of deprivation amongst many Caribbean families. Edwards observed that many employers still hold the view that young blacks should occupy the same type of jobs as their parents did in the 1950s-60s, and still do today.

This pattern of social deprivation is also prevalent amongst many white working class, but more focus tends to be placed on Caribbeans as a deprived group due partly because of the type of jobs which they hold in society. This could be due to the fact that they are more visible as a group, and their position within the labour market makes them even more vulnerable and identifiable as a deprived group. Castles and Kosack (1973) in Phizacklea and Miles (1979, p77) argued that migrant labour is based on exploitation, and that it is a structured feature that the jobs which Caribbeans obtain are at the bottom of the economic order, and are inferior, dirty and low paid. They suggested that migrant workers in Germany are placed in similar positions as in Britain and other European countries. The only difference is that as soon as the jobs are completed they are sent back to their country of origin, or they might be further contracted. Britain did not have a contractual arrangement with New Commonwealth workers, because being British subjects, they were allowed to enter the country without any such restrictions.

In 1971, when Britain changed its laws on migrant working conditions, the situation was altered. The 1971 Immigration Act virtually reduced the number of New Commonwealth workers who could enter the country to work, yet according to critics, there were no restrictions placed on members from the Old Commonwealth. According to Phizacklea, if Britain's economy had expanded beyond the 1960s, there is the possibility that many Caribbeans would have become upwardly mobile and their place would have been filled by another set of migrant workers. But due to the rapid economic decline, and competition from abroad, this did not occur. According to Steuart Hall, black labour is associated with three main types of industry, viz. sweat shop type, service and catering, and assembly line. He suggested that these are highly capitalized, using low level skills and a great deal of shift work. Over one third of black workers were engaged in shift work, which is twice the figure for whites. The Department of Employment showed that between 1973-75, unemployment figures reached one million for the first time since the Second World War. Of these there were four times as many blacks unemployed compared to the period before 1973. The survey also showed that in some areas the national figure for black school leavers were as high as 60%, which was four times the national average. The figure for 1979-80 rose by 38%, but for minority workers it was 48%. Many Pakistanis and Bangladeshi's were concentrated in the manual labour sector which was exceptionally vulnerable to economic recession.

Housing

It would seem pertinent to look at housing as an issue that is closely tied in with education. The reason is that it is one of those scarce resources that affect immigrant families and may have an effect on the type of education that their children acquire. Many migrant workers live in inner city areas, where housing conditions are usually poor, and job opportunities are subjected to rapid decline. This will have an adverse effect on black children's education. Not only is it difficult to maintain good standards of teaching and learning in dilapidated school buildings, but there will also be difficulty in attracting good teachers to those areas. The 1971 census showed that 4% of all households in Britain, lived in shared accommodation. The figure for people born in the New Commonwealth was 21%. Smith found that 32% of Asians and 30% of Caribbeans lived in shared dwellings. Caribbeans were also over-represented in old terraced type properties, which re-affirmed their status as inferior citizens in a dominant white society. The Runnymede Trust 1975, examined council estates in some inner London boroughs, and found that black tenants were over-represented in pre-war high density dwellings. The figure for white tenants on those estates were 22%, compared to 52% for Caribbeans and Asians. Only 0.6% of suburban cottage estates were tenanted by black families. The author commented that current legislation to sell Council property would exacerbate the problems of inequality in Council Housing.

Rex and Moore (1963-67) also looked at housing problems facing people from the New Commonwealth in Sparkbrook, Birmingham. They found that there were widespread differences between the people of Birmingham due to the presence of over 50,000 black immigrants in their midst. This discontent was not a result of unemployment, as the city was very affluent in those days due to full employment. The housing situation was the cause of the problem because there was a housing shortage, and a waiting list of around 30,000. There was also the belief that some reasonable residential areas were fast deteriorating due to the presence of black residents. Thus, the housing shortage became linked with colour, and the development of a Twilight Zone. In areas where houses were considered too good to be demolished, or were classified as slums, they were converted into multi-storey lodging houses.

Rex and Moore did not perceive the housing problem to be sparked off by the presence of black immigrants. But they noted that there was a process of discriminatory practices that compelled Commonwealth settlers to occupy certain types of houses that was typically expected of them. Even though 30,000 houses were estimated to be necessary to solve the housing shortage, there was no projection for those living with relatives and therefore even if the total number of houses were built, there would still have been a shortage of accommodation. Thus, a waiting list category was devised from A to D. Category A specified the degree to which other social priorities emerged as a direct demand on the availability of housing surplus. B reflected the rate at which the Council moved families from houses defined as unfit. Newcomers to the area would not qualify under A nor B, therefore the researchers concentrated on C and D categories where tenants would be more likely to qualify under the points scheme. On that basis, applicants would have lived and worked in the city for at least five years. Additional points were allocated for shared accommodation, lack of proper facilities, broken families, general health, war service etc. Although the researchers were assured that blacks would be treated the same as whites, they found that there were criteria for excluding certain immigrants from qualifying on the same basis as whites. Any tenant who was regarded as undesirable by housing officials would be placed in a slum area or low density pre-war house. They found that there were few Caribbeans on the modern Council estates, as they were mainly concentrated in the pre-war low density areas, or 'patched houses' in the slum areas. Yet the Council claims not to operate in a biased manner. But in effect, the researchers found this to be so. Caribbean applicants would be seen as rating low in housing category under those schemes.

Building societies also discriminated against black applicants who applied for mortgages. Whether or not this was overt discrimination or an uncertainty of blacks being unable to meet their repayment on loans is not quite known. But there was some discrimination on the issue. Rex outlined that Caribbeans who managed to obtain a mortgage through building societies, had to pay higher interest rates and exorbitant fees to estate agents. Some Caribbeans did manage to obtain bank loans but this was on a short term basis, and they had to provide the banks with between five hundred pounds to one thousand pounds as a deposit to convince the bank manager of their ability to repay the loan. In order to meet the repayment, many Caribbean landlords had to let out some of the rooms in order to meet the financial burden placed on them as immigrants. Then they were accused by the indigenous people of living in overcrowded conditions. But this was something forced on them due to society's discriminatory practices in dealing with people of different races. Once this scheme started there was a huge demand from other immigrants including whites for accommodation especially those at the back of the council housing queue. In some cases white residents left the area for fear of a decline in house prices. Once such multi-occupation started, whole blocks of streets became converted into lodging houses which were once smart dwelling houses. In time the 'Twilight Zone' became an area of immigrants. Thus, it could be said that society creates its own problems, then transfer the blame on to immigrants for creating slums. The view which leads us to believe that Caribbeans create slums, have failed to qualify, because they are placed into impossible situations which they have to deal with in the best possible way. As more Caribbeans now own their homes, there is now no overcrowding among them, as there is no need for them to let out rooms as they did in the 1950s-1960s to help other immigrants who could not get accommodation from white landlords due to prejudice.

Social Class and Social Deprivation

Theorists have argued that social class deprivation is one of the main criteria which accounts for inequality in education. This can be measured by several factors such as wealth, income, occupation, type of parents' education, housing types etc. Douglas (1964, p84) used home background as a variable for measuring educational achievement. He suggested that the larger the family size, the more likely children were to do badly at school. He outlined that there was likely to be a lack of study material in the home such as books, adequate study space, and a deficiency of parental care. H.R. Simpson's analysis on the lack of influence of family size, showed that such influences are fully exerted on test scores by the time a child is 8 years of age. Children in large families tend to suffer more deficiencies of care during infancy and childhood. According to Simpson, when statistical allowances are made for environmental deficiencies, the influence of family size is reduced but not significantly. Douglas also discovered that those children who were encouraged by their parents in their studies, did better in each type of test in reading, picture intelligence, vocabulary and arithmetic.

Foner (1977) interviewed several Caribbean parents in London to discover their social class position, their status in Britain and their educational aspirations for their children in Britain as opposed to the Caribbean. She found that their motives varied, though not tremendously. In Jamaica most villagers associated education with status and privilege and high ranking within the island's class structure. In the Caribbean those parents whose children were at high school or college, could claim status and prestige because their children were bright, over and above those parents who did not have children at high school. Foner noted that education carries status in the Caribbean, and as result some parents will go to great lengths to send their children to high school or college. Conversely, in England she found that for some Caribbean parents' education did not seem to be a major criteria, partly because of the limited opportunities open to blacks in this country. Also, there is a general view amongst them that they would not be looked upon more favourably here no matter how highly educated they were. But she did find that around 14 of her respondents had acquired some form of advanced educational qualifications which had enhanced their occupational status and their income in this country.

Foner (1977) discovered that most of the parents in her sample wanted their children to have a good education, and many said if they had extra funds they would use them to improve their children's education. There was also some ambivalence as to whether some wanted to remain in Britain or should they return to Jamaica. Owing to the fact that secondary education here is free, but they would have to pay for it in the Caribbean which poses some difficulty if the parents do not have good jobs to support the children educationally.

This was the view of the majority of Foner's respondents. For those reasons education was not a high priority here. She found that consumer goods rated high on the agenda for some Caribbean residents. But why should consumer goods take priority over their children's education? This uncertainty could be put down to racism experienced by the parents. They may not want to disappoint their children by pushing them into education only to face further disappointment at the end of it all, when they have to compete for jobs on the market where the competition gets even tougher. This however has not deterred all parents from encouraging their children to get a good education. Many still think that despite all the odds, it is still the only chance that their children will have if they are to make any headway in society.

Foner tried to explain why this might be the case, and why such attitudes differed amongst black parents in England compared to the rural Jamaicans she interviewed in Jamaica. She found that in Jamaica not only was education a symbol of success, but it was also an avenue to upward mobility or the 'good life'. In England education was not seen in the same light. Although many were from prosperous working class families, they had occupied manual jobs in London. They worked overtime in order to increase their wages with the hope of returning to the Caribbean in due course. Foner also found that despite the fact that education is free here and equal opportunities policies exist, the children of Caribbean migrants have very limited access to elite British educational institutions. She found that it is so limited that it is not a realistic goal for the majority to pursue. In contrast, in the Caribbean, the child of a farmer had a better chance of entering an elite secondary school or the University of the West Indies, than the child of a Caribbean migrant with comparable status in England. In (1979) she found that only one Jamaican had succeeded in sending his child to grammar school and none had gone to university.

Owing to those circumstances, and the difficulties involved in obtaining a place at a good school many Caribbean parents were reluctant to focus on education in Britain as a priority for their children. Instead, many settled for what they saw as good jobs, such as nursing, secretarial, clerical, skilled technical or manual work.

Some boys will join the army or navy only to discover that they are not given the chance to do the type of job they enlisted for. Some black parents suggested that racial discrimination in Britain is an impediment to their children's educational advancement. One parent said to Foner (1977) "You'll hardly find a black kid going to university here. But in the West Indies if they have the brain they can get a place without any bother". She said her daughter was recommended for grammar school by her form teacher, but the headmistress prevented her from going. "This is what they do to black kids," was the mother's reply. Another parent said that her child tried to get into a good comprehensive school but was turned down and had to attend a low grade school. Other parents had similar experiences of their children being prevented from attending good schools. These studies show that black children are either prevented from entering good schools, or are kept in lower streams in other cases, which leave them no choice but to underachieve. As Coard rightly said, "This is what the British School system is doing to our children." It sends them to ESN schools, low grade schools, and lower streams. Under those circumstances, how can they be expected to compete on par with other groups? Any improvement on their performance will require a complete change of attitude on the part of teachers to help them overcome this dilemma.

Based on my own experience and from the point of view of several Caribbean mothers, in the Caribbean educational achievement is not governed by skin colour nor social class but by talent or what is regarded as having good brains, regardless of one's origin. If children show a willingness to learn, they are given every opportunity and encouragement by their teachers to do so. No attempt is made to hold children back or to discourage them by race, class or colour. As a matter of fact, some teachers even smack children to encourage them to learn. Children are given a fair and equal chance to learn without bias or prejudice, and if they show a willingness to learn, they are often given extra help by their teachers as long as their parents encourage them. In the Caribbean the parents knew that their children were in the capable hands of their teachers so they did not have a need to interfere with school processes. The only problem that can sometimes hinder success at school, is where the parents lack the financial support to help their children to pursue further education.

Those who are in a less favourable position may find it difficult to achieve the same results, partly because their parents cannot afford to pay high school or college fees. Some scholarships are available, but on a small scale, so only a few children are able to take up the offer. Class is not an important issue which dictates success or failure, because people respect each other regardless of their origin, colour, religion or creed. But the unequal distribution of wealth makes it difficult for the poorer groups to compete on equal terms with those who are well off. So the situation is that people remain divided by economic circumstances, rather than by class or race divisions. People who are wealthy no matter how dark the colour of their skin can join the highest ranks of individuals without any form of prejudice. Even the lighter skinned syndrome that used to be thought of as a status symbol has to some extent declined in importance. It is being brainy that has always carried a high status in Jamaica, or the amount of economic wealth that one has, though colour still have some significance.

Foner (1977) suggested that if migrants attend lower grade schools as is usually the case in inner city areas, they are at a disadvantage. Rutter and colleagues (1975) argued that Caribbean children were more likely to attend schools with high rates of absenteeism, high rates of pupil turnover and free school meals, which could prejudice the teachers perception of them. But it is possible that if the teachers were not already prejudiced, no matter what schools black children attended they would not become victims of racism based on stereotyping. Driver (1977) pointed out that even some teachers with the best intentions often find it difficult to deal with the needs of Caribbean pupils. For this we need to look at their class background, training procedures and what is being done to help them have a better understanding of the culture and needs of black pupils, and the problems they face in a white dominated society. If teachers are not aware of the problems that black pupils face, neither will they be in a position to help them. They must first recognize the fact that Caribbean children do suffer adverse effects of racism in society, in the same way that they accept that some white working class children are at a disadvantage in the education system.

As Foner (1977) argued, second generation blacks may not share the same perspectives as their parents. Being born and brought up in a white dominated society, they are aware of the pressures that may affect them from an early age. They may be exposed to greater disappointments than their parents, having experienced racism either before or soon after starting school. They are in constant contact with the media and television which transmits certain images of black people in derogatory terms which may affect their way of thinking. It may also internalize in them feelings of despair and resentment in a society which denies them the recognition that they deserve. Unlike their parents who were not brought up in a racist society, their upbringing has given them a greater degree of tolerance and overbearing to deal with racism in this country. Many parents also have the advantage of thinking of returning to their homeland one day if things get too difficult for them. But their children cannot even begin to have the same mode of thought, because for them Britain is their home. So it is possible that racism does affect the children more than the parents, because to grow up fighting racism from an early age can harbour resentment and bitterness. Some of the children in my survey have expressed this feeling to me. One boy said to me, "you don't know what it does to you, having to fight racism from the infant school." For any child to grow up with such harsh experience, it can have a devastating effect on their attitudes and behaviour to others. One could not necessarily refer to this as 'having a chip on the shoulder', but rather the result of racism and indifference towards black children.

Self-Esteem

It was previously assumed by some teachers and practitioners that Caribbean children suffered low self-esteem, and this was one of the reasons why they underachieved at school. However, Stone (1981, p56) suggested that findings on self-esteem may sometimes be contradictory, as it could be dependent on the different methods used. Louden in Stone (1981, p56) found that self-esteem was highest where there were large numbers of black children. Other factors he suggested could be the degree to which minority groups are insulated from white racism. Taylor (1983, p161) suggested that self-esteem amongst Caribbean children will be dependent on how they are perceived by others. She suggested that this must be seen in the context of life in Britain generally, where factors such as housing, unemployment, prejudice and discrimination are taken into account. She also suggested that other factors such as neighbourhood, curriculum, classroom, teachers and pupils may also serve to alienate black children from their true potential. She looked at Milner's study (1983) on the dolls test, where 52% of Caribbean children chose dolls that looked like them, and 48% chose white dolls. This was in comparison to 100% of white children who chose dolls that matched their own colour. Milner suggested that many black children were in conflict with their own identity, but that would be expected if white society constantly portray whiteness as good, and blackness as bad in every possible way. Coard (1971) noticed that a black boy had refused to colour himself black, because he thought that to be white was better. Even textbooks which children read constantly reflected those views. Rampton (1981) remarked on a quote in a textbook which read:

"Perhaps she could finish her father's work. He had been interested in savages and backward races. Africa was the place to find such people, Mary would go to Africa. She would go amongst the wildest savages she could find. She would spend her time studying cannibals."
(A. Rampton, 1981, HMSO).

The above quote has categorized black people as savages. This is a term that is well documented in European literature and accepted as correct, in that black people are of a lower genetic pedigree, and therefore are of an inferior status. These negative descriptions served to subjugate the black races throughout history. In Tjfel's term, this is the result of the "word conditioning effect", and how it affects people's way of thinking. This mode of thought has affected both whites and blacks, because it has successfully led many blacks to think of themselves as inferior. Rampton argued that such inferences and illustrations could have damaging effects on black children by such mis-presentations and inaccuracies.

If black pupils are denied their self-esteem, it can lead to a cult following like the Rastafarian Movement which developed in the late (1970s) by black youths who were of the opinion that society had been unfair to them. The movement became very popular and attracted many young black followers. It gave them a high self-esteem, and a belief in themselves as individuals capable of directing their own lives. (Cashmore, 1979). It also gave them fulfilment and an understanding of the real world and their place and purpose within it. In part, this Movement could be viewed as a form of social disadvantage because it has not benefited them as they probably expected. In fact, they were viewed by many people as rebellious and anti-social because they deviated from the norms and values of the host society. But it could be viewed as a form of youth culture among young blacks. Like the skin heads of the 1960s and the punk rockers of the 1970s, who felt that they were being neglected by society, they adopted an alternative lifestyle to suit their own tastes, one which also acted as a protest to voice their opinions to political parties and decision makers whom they hoped would do something about their plight. It would appear that at various times some form of youth culture develops as a means of a "cry for help" amongst the young of society. These movements mainly always develop amongst working class males who see themselves as deprived and disadvantaged in a society where there is much affluence and wealth which is out of their reach. According to Cashmore (1979) it is mainly those men who find themselves at the bottom of the occupational ladder of society and are engaged in menial tasks that carry very little or no reward by way of progress, who are more likely to be engaged in protests. This is a Marxist approach where the masses sell their labour to the owners of capital for very little reward. Even though they are dissatisfied about their work and conditions, they have no other option but to sell their labour for low wages because they do not own the means of production. This creates resentment and can lead to rebellion or protests. We have seen the 1981 riots of Brixton, Nottingham and Liverpool, where dissatisfied black and white youths rioted as a means of protest. This did cause the government to take notice, as it did appoint the Scarman Committee to look into the problem. But that is all that seems to happen. Whenever problems occur, the government seems to appoint these investigators to find out what is wrong on the other side of the fence, but very rarely is it mended. When the next wave of trouble occurs, another Committee is appointed but with the same result.

Troyna and Smith (1983) argued that Rastafarians are not essentially anti-white in their attitude towards whites, but they are anti-exploitation in their views. They see whites as the main exploiters, and recommend that anti-discriminatory laws be implemented to put pressure on employers to eliminate biases in their recruitment practices. The authors suggested that many of the disadvantages faced by young blacks are part of a class structure which divide the races and put people into groups. Similar experiences are shared by some whites who also suffer poverty and deprivation in certain areas. For any changes to be brought about they suggested that there would have to be a re-evaluation in class relations, and a redistribution of privileges between the working class and the white collar sector. However, such notions would seem impossible. This is because people with wealth do not re-distribute it except among their own offspring who in turn perpetuate the same cycle of re-distribution. Only in this case it is a re-distribution of wealth, and not the perpetuation of a cycle of poverty that many working class children inherit. The second generation Caribbeans, though many received all or some of their schooling here have realized that they too face difficulty in competing on the job market, even though some have acquired qualifications. They saw their white school mates attain prestigious jobs even without formal qualifications, while they cannot compete on the same basis. Although some white working class do suffer some disadvantage, black youths do suffer a double disadvantage, because several studies show that they are treated unfairly in the job market at a much higher rate than whites.

Roberts et al suggested that many young blacks are no longer seeking to be assimilated into what they regard as an alien culture, in that they are excluded from participating into mainstream culture. But instead they are forming their own community organizations and are getting more involved in politics. This is not to say that they have always remained outside the political sphere, but until recently they were invisible as a group politically. Powell (1968) in his "River of Blood Speech", did a great deal to raise black consciousness and their political awareness, whilst at the same time, enabled himself to gain widespread support from the white indigenous population. These types of attitudes show that Britain is a racist country, and how entrenched racism is amongst the population. It was during that period that many blacks became aware of their position in society and were determined to change their state of affairs. They began to demand a better deal for themselves and their children's future. In larger cities they began to form groups to question and discuss their position in society.

Caribbean and Asian children are seen to suffer shared problems as victims of racism, which invariably affects both groups differently, in terms of education, jobs, housing, and societal attitudes towards them. But the schools seem to be making a distinction between both groups by saying that one group is more capable than the other academically. According to Straker-Welds (1984) in case studies at ILEA on multicultural education and the effects of racism, he emphasized that societal racism feeds on the historical legacy of colonialism and imperialism. It presents a view which seems natural that certain ethnic groups are biologically different from others, a view which presents the notion of inferiority and superiority of different races. Internationally, this became a structural concept, and at home institutionalized. Once racism became institutionalized, it serves to perpetuate social disadvantage through processes and procedures which place certain ethnic groups at the bottom of the stratification ladder. This has social implications for those who find themselves in this category. Some authors argued that this low position will continue to govern the life chances of those groups.

Racism in the Curriculum

The historical conception of the inferiority of the African races as being intellectually incapable would adversely affect black children in education, housing and jobs because of its effects on people's psyche. According Tjfel in National Association for Remedial Education, (V18: Nov 1983), once people are taught to think in a certain way, it continues to have a conditioning effect on their perception of themselves and others around them. This he called the "word conditioning effect", or "word association", as it leads people to successfully think and act in racist terms which they regard as natural and normal. This type of racism would appear to unconsciously affect Caribbean children more so than it affects Asian children in schools.

Green (1982) in Tomlinson (1983, p77) in his study of classroom interaction in 70 multicultural schools, related teaching styles to pupils self-concepts. He found that where teachers are highly intolerant they direct less individual attention towards Caribbean children, while the tolerant ones divide their time equally between ethnic groups. Those who received a certain amount of individual attention were found to have more positive self-concepts than those who received less individual attention. The result of the study shows that ethnocentricism is an influential factor in pupil achievement. Riley interviewed some black girls in a London school and described how they felt about their teachers' attitudes. The following quotations were made by the pupils as Riley suggested.

1st pupil:
"Its who she likes. If you are a big mouth who likes to answer back, or back chat, she chucks you in the CSE. If you are a softie, listen and don't talk a lot, she puts you in the O level group."

2nd pupil:
"Every time you talked you know, "Hey so and so," we were split up, CSE group couldn't talk to O level group."

A pupil in Rampton's study (1981) commented:
"They always try and put the black kids in for CSE. I wanted to do English O level, and when the head saw me she said, 'What are you doing here? She then said to the class teacher, any trouble from her, send her straight to me. So I left the course, because people were looking at me as if to say, what is she doing here? Teachers didn't ask me anything about what I wanted to do. It put me right off."

(A. Rampton, 1981, HMSO).

Conclusion

Education is now a political issue with constant government intervention on what should be taught in schools eg. There is now the national curriculum which specifies the types of subjects that children should be taught in schools, such as English, maths and science as the major subjects. Yet the government has constantly failed to make any firm policies regarding anti-racist education. Tierney (1982, p32) has however suggested that there is a fundamental contradiction lying at the core of government policies, even though they are oriented around the idea of equality of opportunity. Recent reforms have completely ignored racism as a problem which requires government intervention to encourage educationists, teachers, and the media to develop liberal approaches in order to eradicate racist ideas, beliefs, ideologies and practices. Caribbean children may be dissuaded from trying hard at school if they see that the system operates to constantly label them as failures. What is required is a complete restructuring of the curriculum in order to reflect and value other cultures in the same light as that of European cultures. Even though there are now educational reforms such as the National Curriculum and regular testing for children at certain ages, to what extent these changes will benefit children who are already at a disadvantage in the education system, remains to be seen. Very rarely do working class children benefit from educational reforms. This has been seen in previous other reforms, such as the 1944 Education Act which abolished fees in elementary schools to enable children from poorer families to benefit from education, but the tripartite system did not actually benefit working class children who attended lower status schools. Only a few children who attended these schools, would succeed in the education system. A change from grammar schools to comprehensives in the 1970s, but which critics have argued, has hardly addressed the problem of working class children not benefiting from the education system.

Educationists and political parties should cooperate more fully in trying to find ways of eliminating racist biases and ideologies amongst teachers. This could be done through the provision of race awareness courses, and the elimination of racist textbooks that are still found in some schools. Several black children have told me that they have found these books to be offensive and distasteful, and yet some teachers have said that it is only when certain things are pointed out to children that they will take any notice. It is therefore best not to draw their attention to something that they may not have thought about. How could teachers give such little credit to their pupils? This is underestimating their intelligence, whilst covertly encouraging them to think in racist terms. Mosaic Educational Programme on BBCTV (24.3.91), stressed the importance of presenting positive images in the early years of children's learning. This is the starting point at which their ideas of others around them are developed. Therefore there is a need for them to have good books and good materials with positive images on which to build their experience for later life and how they perceive others around them. The portrayal of negative stereotyping of blacks should be addressed and eliminated. The problem of racism amongst teachers should be one of priority that should be tackled in the best possible way so as not to cause too much resentment, but to make them more responsible for their attitudes and the way they treat their pupils. If this is not done racism will continue to be treated as a topic of no importance, and if allowed to go unchallenged, it will continue to cause a great deal of harm to the learning ability of black children. If they are denied the help they need to help them to overcome any self-doubt that they may have regarding their learning ability, it is likely that they will continue to underachieve at school, by accepting the popular myths that they are academically incapable. Placing them in C streams will not help the situation either. Teachers should make the effort to assess and treat them fairly on the basis of their ability and not by their colour, to enable them to have a fair chance of proving their capabilities. However, the unequal distribution of wealth in society which determines class, status, power and privilege, only serves to maintain the status quo. This will make it difficult for the underprivileged groups to succeed educationally, unless drastic measures are taken to reduce inequalities in the school system. Recently TVAM (1991) ran a series on education in Britain, and commented on the low quality of education that some schools now provide for their pupils. Sir Claus Moser (14.5.91) on breakfast TV spoke of the waste of talent amongst many working class pupils, and the low number of students who pursue further and higher education. He suggested that 16 year olds are getting a raw deal out of the education system and that radical reforms were required to change this discrepancy, which would enable them to view education more favourably. He commented that traditionally education was geared towards a small elite with the masses not feeling that they are part of the system. He emphasized that the attitudes of educationists and employers should be completely changed, also the attitude of people in general in how they see education. Ethnic minorities are especially prone to the concept of social deprivation, and they are more likely to be at risk where educational reforms are concerned, unless they are specifically included and catered for in those reforms. This process of inequality also extends to the job market where they cannot make any progress due in part to their colour and also the lack of a good education. Until researchers take an interest in looking at the social structure and its hierarchy of dominance and power which excludes certain groups from entering traditional institutional establishments, Caribbean pupils will continually be labelled as underachievers, even though they are the innocent victims of a class dominated society. This division also includes race which is now a prominent feature in society. The next chapter will look at the area of study, and the role of Caribbean settlers within it, and how this may implicitly or explicitly determine educational success amongst Caribbean children.

◆

Map showing the six towns of the Potteries.
Source: Ordnance Survey Map, Univ. of Keele.

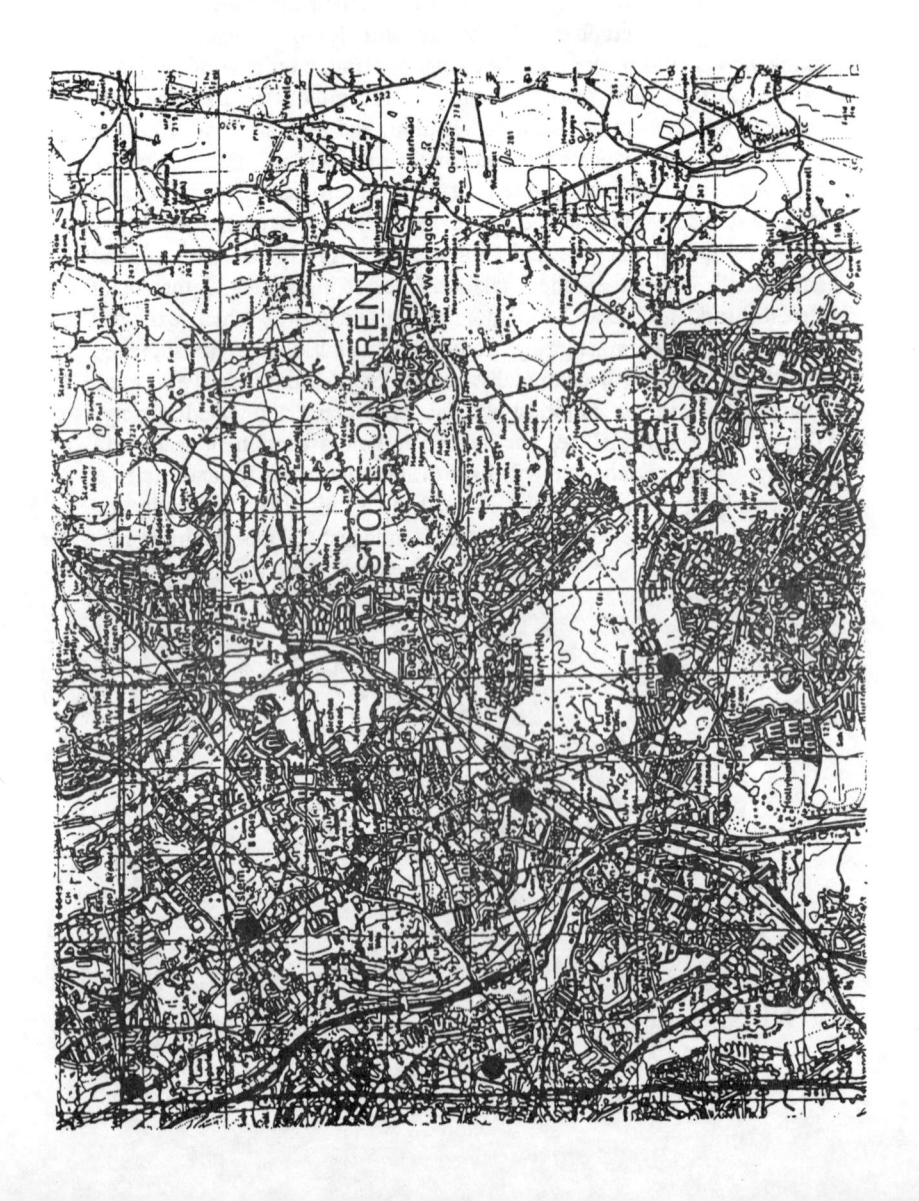

CHAPTER 4

Employment and Migration in the Area

The area of study is situated to the West of the Midlands. It has a unique physical characteristic which distinguishes it from inner city density or slum areas. This can be explained more fully as an absence of vast overcrowding where people live in densely populated and overcrowded conditions. Due to its uniqueness, the local residents seem to have pride in the Potteries as an area of great beauty. Recently the City Council has embarked on schemes to promote the area to make it into a tourist attraction, in order to boost its image from that of a typical industrial setting, to one of expansion and progress. This new approach seems to be gradually paying off with the city acquiring some status, as in 1990 according to the local Evening Newspaper, it was voted the most attractive city in the country.

Stoke-on-Trent is made up of six towns which makes it unique from other cities. In the 1890s these towns were independent of each other, and each was surrounded by its own green fields and pastureland which formed beautiful scenery. Perhaps this is one of the traditions which the locals prefer to hold on to, rather than to drastically change the area for a more modern outlook. But these small towns may have caused outsiders to be confused about the real identity of the city. This is because despite the six towns, which are Tunstall, Burslem, Hanley, Fenton, Stoke and Longton, the city has not got a principal town that can be called its capital, though the main shopping centre is Hanley, where the major department stores are to be found. The National Garden Festival of 1986, highlighted the area, and brought to light the fact that it could be developed more fully, and in the process creating hundreds of jobs which are much needed to help reduce unemployment which began to escalate since the recession in the (1970s) and many firms began to close down.

The area is very rich in natural resources. Coal was the main source of natural raw material. A study of the County of Staffordshire in (1967) by the University of London (Institute of Historical Research) showed that the development of the first canals and railways in the 18th century, made a complete transformation of the West Midlands area. It was able to make better use of its commodities with the advent of better communication and transportation due to the network of roads and rail which are ideally suitable for service facilities. But the area is still not highly rated by people living in other parts of the country who still seem to think that Stoke is still underdeveloped in terms of modernization when compared to other parts of the country. It could well be that many traditional industrial areas such as cotton mill, coal, textiles and quarrying are still viewed with a poor image as the opposed to light industrial areas which are viewed as being progressive. Other sources of raw materials are local clay, iron and limestone which helped in the County's economic development and the formation of the pottery industry. North Staffordshire was also sparsely populated, and as a result, seemed to have suffered a population problem. This meant that it was unable to make use of its abundant raw material until during the 19th century. According to a report in the local Evening Sentinel, (29.8.87) another drop in population seemed to have re-appeared to haunt the county, as during the last five years, 9,000 residents had left the county in search of jobs. Stoke-on-Trent was very badly affected in this exodus, with a drop in population of 5,400. The report also stated that population growth had plunged from 2.2% to 0.2% in the preceeding five years leaving a total of 1,020,400 inhabitants.

These six towns form part of the vast coalfield of Staffordshire. This coalfield is said to be nearly three times as large as the other coalfields in the area, viz Goldsitch Moss, Shaffalong, and Cheadle. These together cover an area of 30 square miles, part of which is found in the Pennine fold. It is part of a great Row Seam which helps to determine the location of the six towns which is the last of the exposed field in the area. The expansion of Staffordshire Coalfield led to the building of many short rail lines for the purposes of transportation for the pottery industry, iron works, and quarrying. The latter part of the 18th century saw a great expansion in the pottery industry in terms of factories, production, export and employment. This expansion was associated with a variety of characteristics, such as the division of labour, which is noticeable in the pottery industry in terms of men's work and women's work, but predominantly women's work. This may have been one of the reasons why wages in the area are so much lower than elsewhere, because the pottery industry attracted more women workers than men.

The Pottery Industry

Pottery making is one of the main sources of manual labour in Stoke on Trent. The industry flourished in the 1950s-60s, when over 40,000 workers were employed in the industry. Recently, since the recession began in the late 1970s, that figure has been reduced by half. The industry experienced a decline in orders, due to foreign competition, and competition at home. During the 18th century, the industry began on a small scale basis, using coal fired kilns to 'bake' the raw product before it could be used. Workers were drawn from the local surroundings, as they lived close to their workplace. According to census reports, in 1851, 37% of family head of households were employed in the pottery industry.

The industry attracted such names as Wedgewood and Bentley who went into partnership. Bentley was said to have had a superior type education, good taste and polished manners which attracted business from the rich and fashionable sectors of society. This led the way for the product being commanded abroad by diplomats in places such as Stockholm, Madrid, St. Petersburgh and the USA. From the 1850s onwards there was an expansion of markets at home and abroad. Some firms went into partnership in order to pool their resources and guard the industry against competition. Wedgewood was also commissioned to design services for the Royal family. But despite such distinctions, the Potteries is still underrated in terms of popularity by many outsiders. But why should this be the case after gaining such national and international status remains a puzzle. It has two museums and three theatres, and other places of interest which are highly commendable, and is also very accessible. One answer could possibly be that it is not a very large and highly populated conurbation, and its division into small towns did not allow it to develop a major capital city which could highlight its popularity. Hence, this low profile may have accounted for its unpopular image, despite its previously high production as a manufacturing area.

However this poor image will change in time, as it gains more publicity in terms of its production, output, and tourism, as there is now a concerted drive by the Council to attract tourists to the area.

The table below shows the huge differences in weekly wages for males and females during the early decades of the 19th century: (in £s).

Table 3

Year	Men	Women	Boys	Girls
1938	4.52	2.21	2.02	1.07
1947	6.16	3.12	2.27	2.11
1963	15.43	7.37	7.40	5.12

Source: Ministry of Labour Gazette, 1948 (London Univ. Study, 1967).

There has been a vast improvement in pay and conditions since the early periods of the industry. This has been the result of modern technology and improved production. But this has not been without loss of jobs. Since the mid 1970s nearly half the jobs in the pottery industry disappeared due to loss in orders and foreign competition. Workers were invited from the British colonies of the Caribbean and South Asia to fill vacancies due to post war expansion. Stoke was one of the areas where jobs were plentiful, so many Caribbean workers came to Stoke due to the abundance of coalfields in the area. Many also had relatives here who had served in the Second World War, and such connections could secure accommodation for them.

The Pottery industry also flourished, but much of the jobs were defined as women's work, so did not attract many male workers who came from the Caribbean. It was also low paid and this may have prevented black male workers from taking up work in the industry. But pay in the mining industry was very good, and many immigrant workers opted for this, even though working conditions were considered dangerous. Workers also came from other areas to seek jobs in the potteries and were successful in doing so due to economic prosperity in post war Britain at the time. Working overtime was part of a process that dominated the 1950s and 1960s, due to the availability of jobs and the post war expansion of industry and services.

Discrimination in Jobs Locally

From interviews with ten male workers from the Caribbean, they claimed that there was racial discrimination by some employers in Stoke since the 1950s, and this does not seem to have changed very much. Some skilled drivers from the Caribbean said they were refused driving jobs by the bus company in Stoke. The men said they were told that it was in the Company's Policy not to employ black drivers. It was about fifteen years later that they employed one Caribbean driver, and later two conductors. The local Railway also refused to employ black drivers at that time. Such forms of discrimination are still prevalent in the 1990s, where blacks still do not have access to certain types of jobs. This is particularly noticeable in all the major institutions, such as banks, building societies, insurance companies and service enterprises such as supermarkets, shops, stores etc. The City Council as a major employer should play a leading role in ensuring that its Equal Opportunity Policy is effective, in that Caribbeans and Asians are treated fairly in the job market. Several black parents have spoken of their discontent that their children are unable to obtain suitable jobs in the area. Many are either unemployed or are employed in manual work. Many of the second generation Caribbeans who want to improve their life chances have to leave the area in order to improve their prospects.

Caribbean men obtained jobs mainly in the coal mines where they worked a two shift system and very often weekends. This demonstrates the kind of jobs they acquired on coming to Britain. Many black people from outside the area mainly from larger cities have frequently commented on the low wages in Stoke compared to elsewhere. Because of this, many who came with the intention of staying to work there, went back to the more prosperous areas. Some Caribbeans have also left because of lack of opportunities and low pay. The Potteries has great reserves of resources, but many Caribbeans found it lacking in opportunities for black people, probably because of the subtle racism that operates to keep them in the unskilled jobs which they were offered. The Sentinel report of (20.4.90) by K. Evans, suggested that Stoke was below the national norm for spending pattern. The report stated that Mr. Connor of the Potteries Shopping Centre blamed the low level of spending on poorly paid jobs in the area. He stated that Stoke is an industrial area where new technology is not in abundance, and high technology jobs are the ones that pays well. The report also stated that Mr. F. Lipp of the City's Chamber of Trade said that Stoke is an 'unusual City', based on craft and industry, and not many Commercial Developments. The city is slower to change and is well behind many of the major cities in terms of development and modernization, but this may be expected of smaller cities with less resources. However, vast changes are now taking place in the area in terms of re-building schemes and development which will enable the city to be recognized as a tourist attraction for its beautiful landscape and uniqueness.

The recession that began in the late 1970s, had its toll in this part of the country. During the past eight years or so, about half the pottery industry has closed down making thousands of people redundant. The Shelton Iron and Steel Works that employed thousands of workers also closed in the 1970s, and many small firms have also closed due to intense competition and loss of trade. The Michelin Tyre Company made two and a half thousand workers redundant in 1985. Such mass redundancies have been very grim for a small city like Stoke with a quarter of a million people. Many coal mines have also closed or reduced their workforce, which has imposed hardships on families who were dependent on industry for their livelihood.

School-leavers and Work

The Evening Sentinel (16.11.89) reported that due to a decline in youth employment in the area, more youngsters are now opting to stay on in further education, with an increase of 16 year olds choosing to continue their schooling. This has meant that there was more pressure on universities and polytechnics to cater for even higher numbers than in previous years. These students are now realizing that qualifications are important in their search for employment. This is a complete reversal compared to the 1960s when jobs were so plentiful that many school leavers had jobs lined up for them even before they left school. However, some children still want to leave school as soon as they reach the qualifying age of sixteen, because they said that by that time they just want to do something different to the repetitive routine work which school provides. Some of the children whom I interviewed said it was not a question of money why they want to go to work, but it is because they wanted a change from school life. Some said they have been at school long enough, so they wanted to do something different. It could be assumed that in the 1950s-60s, many working class children may have been pressurized by their parents to leave school early, due in part to a shortage of money amongst many large families, and also because education was not seen as a priority for many working class parents. But today we could suppose that children are much freer to choose whether they want to pursue further education or not. Those who wanted to leave school said they were not under parental pressure to leave school nor to stay on. In most cases they were given the choice of choosing what suited their capabilities best by their parents. This shows that the children do not seem to be overtly pressured by their parents in their choice of occupation or education, but there is a certain degree of flexibility between themselves and their parents, and their views are taken into consideration.

The total population in the area according to the local Sentinel is just over a quarter of a million, of which Caribbeans and Asians are said to be 1 in 10 to 1 in 15 in some areas. It is estimated that the majority of Caribbeans own their own homes. This is because when many acquired their homes, it was relatively cheaper to buy than renting property which was difficult to find anyway, and there was a problem of racism with many white landlords. This prompted many Caribbeans to buy their own homes. As their circumstances improved, many left the density of the city and settled in the outskirts, which offered a better environment and quality of life. The number of black settlers in the Potteries is very small when compared to black settlement in other parts of the country. This gives an indication of the difficulty involved when doing research on children from Caribbean origin in the area.

Table 4 shows the number of private households in specific districts, and the number of heads of households who were born in the New Commonwealth and Pakistan.

Table 4

The table shows the number of householders in the Potteries, including New Commonwealth Immigrants and Pakistanis.

Each district is numbered from 1 to 8 listing the number of householders in each district.

District	No. of House holders	NCW & Pakistanis
1	12956	42
2	13200	46
3	12189	221
4	10952	563
5	12662	73
6	11616	1194
7	10921	239
8	13519	66

(Source: 1981 Census)

Table 5

Number of immigrants whose head of household was born in the New Commonwealth and Pakistan.

Heads of Households	Children	Total
3902	1215	5115

(Source: 1981 Census)

Table 6

The table shows the number of pre-secondary children in schools in the districts shown.

District	Pakistani	Caribbean	Indian	Bangladeshi	Chinese	European
Tunstall	111	2	1	1	-	-
Burslem	147	11	6	18	5	6
Hanley	323	16	19	9	17	11
Stoke	29	19	29	5	13	14
Longton	218	4	13	7	10	16
Total	828	52	68	40	45	47

(Source: Alcock, (1985) unpub. M. Ed. thesis, Keele Univ.)

The above table shows a vast reduction in the number of Caribbean children in the area, which is now overtaken by another ethnic group, viz, Pakistani. According to the table, they seem to be the fastest growing immigrant population in the Potteries, now that the first cohort of Caribbeans which settled in the 1950s-60s have now left school.

Caribbean Families in the Area

Prior to the 1950s and 1960s New Commonwealth Immigration, there were only a few black residents in Stoke, some of whom have remained after the Second World War. Those war heroes did not form a central part of British society. Even though they were few in numbers, they did not have the same type of access to jobs as whites did, no matter what type of occupation they held in their country of origin. Many of the skilled who came had to settle for unskilled jobs, as those were the only options opened to them.

From my own observation and experience of dealing with Caribbean migrants, migration to this country could be seen partly through the availability of jobs, and partly as a trend. The reason for this is that it was a time when many young people were migrating, and those who did not want to feel left behind, also came as a means of maintaining friendship and family ties. It was also an opportunity for many to come to the mother country which they had learned so much about at school. It was not as a result of overpopulation or mass unemployment as many researchers seem to hypothesize, as the population of Jamaica was only one million in the 1950s when migration to Britain actually began. Many of the migrants were however dismayed at the conditions which they encountered, and wished they had not left their homeland. Prior to migration to Britain, a few Jamaicans used to go to work in the USA, but this was mainly men on a quota system which was very strictly controlled. The majority returned home when their contract was finished. Many of those who came to Britain thought that they could do the same as going to the USA to earn some money quickly and then return home. But for many this was an illusion. They had sold their possessions or left their jobs to come to Britain, and could not envisage an early return as many had hoped due to the circumstances at the time. Many were disillusioned and disappointed when they discovered that their dreams would not be realized. Equally disappointing were the low wages and menial jobs which they had to do. But this was reality for the new arrivals, and a new beginning for many.

Social Activities

Entertainment and other social activities for Caribbean people were lacking in the Potteries, especially for those who arrived in the late 1950s to early 1960s. They found that racism operated in the local dance halls and some clubs, as they were not admitted. But they were allowed in most pubs locally. This for a while formed their main source of entertainment, but it did not suit everyone. A few people held house parties at weekends, but was criticised by their neighbours for being noisy. As Caribbeans became more settled, house parties began to diminish as it was only a temporary pastime to help the new comers settle into their respective surroundings. It would not also be viable to use their houses regularly for parties, so this era was gradually phased out as people became more settled and adapted to a British way of life.

Church Worship

Caribbean people have always been strongly attached to Church worship. They have always belonged to one form of church or another, due to the different types of worship found in the Caribbean. These churches range from Church of England, Roman Catholic, Baptist, Presbyterian, Methodist, Church of Christ, Seven Day Adventist, and some smaller religious sects. The major types of worship in many Caribbean islands are Anglican, Roman Catholic, Baptist and Methodist due mainly to European influences which dominated the islands. On arriving in Britain many worshippers continued the type of worship to which they were accustomed at home. However, many were met with hostility from British worshippers. Some Caribbeans have commented that even some Reverends told them that they ought not to come to their church too regularly. They were amazed at such unwelcomeness, knowing that in the Caribbean people worship together regardless of colour, creed, or sectarian beliefs. This type of behaviour was seen as insulting and unchristian by Caribbeans. Because they found that they were not free to worship wherever they felt like worshipping, many left the established British churches to form their own church.

Hill (1970) looked at the role of the church in the lives of Caribbeans in Britain. He suggested that about 75% of them are Christians, and are regular church goers, and belonged to one of the six major denominations in the Caribbean. But in (1963) he noted that a survey carried out in London showed that only about 4% of Caribbeans were regular church goers. He argued that the reason for the decline in attendance was that Caribbean members became dissatisfied because of the unwelcomeness they received in many white churches, and as a result they turned to other sectarian organisations. In (1964), Calley found that the New Testament Church of God had 23 congregations throughout the country, of which many were centred in London and Birmingham where there were large numbers of Caribbeans. Two years later, there were 61 such denominations, with a membership of 10,500. In Hill's terms, the traditional British churches had failed to hold the allegiance of those immigrants, who were already established Christians in their country of origin, but had been disappointed by the rejection of the British Church to recognise them as members.

Rex, (1970s) in his study of Caribbeans and religion in Sparkbrook, suggested that religion is largely a middle class institution. Hill suggested that the modern British church thrives only in middle class residential areas, whilst experiencing a decline in urban working class areas where church goers are usually drawn from the lesser middle class respectable suburbs. For Caribbeans the church is not seen as class based. Anyone is free to worship in whichever church they may choose, because they know that they will be made welcome. Black churches are seen as a very important part of the black community, and some services are now being televised. In a universal prayer group mission on Channel 4 TV (4.10.90), Stuart Hall commented on the importance of black churches as giving the people pride in themselves, because previously Christianity had denied them some of that pride. He suggested that solidarity is expressed in meetings where people can vent their expressions and feelings and worship in a free spirit. He argued that what is different about these types of worship is that part of the Black Theological teaching states that all people are equal in the eyes of God. There is less emphasis on a white image of God and Christ, and instead God is seen as an omnipotent figure who is everywhere. Hall sees this as a means of breaking down some of the power relationships that was created during colonialism in terms of white values, traditions, and cosmologies etc. The Methodist Church is seen as a non-racial institution. It extended a welcome to black women and girls during the early years of migration to this country, when black people had difficulty in finding accommodation. Most Caribbean parents are strict disciplinarians who try to bring up their children in a Christian manner. Being brought up themselves in a Christian way they try to instil the same in their children. But sometimes when the children experience racism from an early age, they may later detach themselves from the church and form friendship groups as a form of solidarity.

Rastafarianism

Rastafarianism of the 1970s may have developed on the basis of their dissatisfaction of how they were being treated by society. The term Rastafarianism could be seen partly as religious and partly as a youth culture that was adopted by many young black Britons during the 1970s as a means of asserting their true identity, due to disillusionment in society. As they saw it, they were being treated as inferior citizens in a society to which they belong. But such attitudes did not help their situation, because they were seen by many as nonconformists who set out to make matters worse for blacks in general. Society also saw them as subversives or rebels. But this gave them confidence and a belief in themselves, as it helped them to be able to deal with racism better, by viewing themselves more positively. Initially, when they rebelled by taking on their own identity, many parents were annoyed at the idea. But eventually the parents could see their point of view, and knowing that they could not prevent them, many came to terms with the idea. Taylor (1983) suggested that it is very confusing for them because they cannot call any one place specifically their home. It is this feeling of uncertainty that can lead to rebellion and the adapting of an alternative type of youth culture such as Rastafarianism.

M Brakes (1985) looks at youth culture and youth sub-culture in Britain, U.S.A. and Canada. He argues that youth subcultures arise as an attempt to resolve collectively, problems experienced as a result of contradictions in the social structure. They generate a form collective identity which enables those individuals to achieve an identity outside that of the mainstream of society by class, education and occupation. Brakes sees this as a temporary solution with no material gains, but it enables the youths to feel good about themselves by airing their views, so that others can take notice of their protest, dissatisfaction and marginalization in society. Brakes suggests that it is also a form of exploration of masculinity, and is therefore masculinist. He explains that the economic situation of society develops an oppressive culture which alienates large sections of society, of which racial minorities are especially prone. This type of alienation may have prompted black youths to develop an alternative culture, hence Rastafarianism.

Race Relations in the Area

Racism in the area operates very covertly and is difficult to recognize. Although attempts have been made by organisations such as the Community Relations Council, now the Race Equality Council to integrate people from various walks of life such attempts can be very problematic. The reasons are that each group has different needs, and any attempt to change certain aspects of one group to suit other groups would not necessarily help the situation. The provision of a multicultural community centre can ensure that various types of activities are carried out which will enable both the indigenous and immigrant population to try and understand each others cultural habits and customs. Such provisions in the Potteries have been slow to emerge. But on the whole people seem to be adapting to the idea of multiculturalism, which is expected to bring some changes to the Potteries in the near future. Issues relating to social change and discrimination in Stoke is over 10 years behind larger cities. On the one hand people may resist change, and on the other hand covert racism and how it operates, undetected will make it difficult for any major change to be effective. For instance, The Evening Sentinel (15.3.88) reported that the City Council and Staffordshire County Council were urged by the Community Relations Council now the Race Equality Council, to earmark 10% of jobs for ethnics in an equal opportunities drive. But after talks with council chiefs and unions, the unions rejected the proposals, because they said that this would discriminate against whites in favour of minorities. The Council is already devoid of black workers, so how could this be discriminating against whites? Arshad the then Community Relations Officer at the time, was angry at both the council and the union for failing to end discrimination. He suggested that the area is one of the worst in the country for harbouring racial discrimination. This statement would seem to be correct, because if we look in the local high street stores and banks, enterprises and services there are hardly any black workers. The same can be said for the local schools, colleges, and universities which make no attempt to redress the balance. In such cases, how can black children be expected to be high achievers when they realise that they have no role models in those institutions. An absence of black teachers is an indication of racist practices and institutionalised racism being practiced and perpetuated.

The Potteries could be seen as relatively stable in terms of racial harmony, in the sense that no major disturbances have taken place, as have occurred in larger cities. The only disturbance so far has been the Shelton riot of 1985, which could hardly be described as a riot, but a party that got out of hand. A few shop windows were broken during the incident. In the process there was looting in the shops but this was soon contained and quietened down by the police. It was not specifically race related, as white youths were also involved. It is also the case that ethnics in Stoke do not complain to the press about racism, and this projects an image that Race Relations are good, but that is not the case. The type of racism that operates in Stoke is very covert in nature, whilst at the same time very damaging to good Race Relations. Due to an absence of a distinctive pattern of Caribbean settlement, this may have coloured the views of the black residents and given them a misrepresentation of their own needs and values, with the exception of their own reformed Churches. Hence, social integration for Caribbeans in the Potteries was not seen as a major problem, and may not have warranted special government funding for Caribbean residents. As far as employment is concerned locally, discrimination is rampant, and this has disastrous consequences for both the older and younger generation Caribbeans. Many of the older ones remain in whatever type of unrewarding occupation that they can find, or are made redundant as industries close down. On the other hand, the younger upwardly mobile have to vacate the area to find worthwhile jobs, because they are denied this opportunity locally, with the exception of a few who manage to find white collar jobs. Many of those who came as immigrants are still disappointed and dismayed that there does not seem to be any attempt by employers to change the situation. Here are a few case histories of some of the resident migrants in the area, many of whom are now British citizens.

Case Histories:

Of those Caribbean families who came to the Potteries in the 1950s-60s, some have migrated to North America, some have returned to the Caribbean, some went to other parts of the country and others have remained in Stoke. Those who have left did so because they said they were dissatisfied with the limited opportunities and low wages. By immigrating to the USA and Canada, they explained that their chances of a better lifestyle were greatly improved, due to the much higher wages and improved living conditions that they enjoyed. Many of those who have remained, are not entirely satisfied with what the area has to offer, but as is the case, once some people have settled in a particular location, they find it difficult to move to somewhere else. Many have secured their own homes in the area, and this would probably deter them from moving to other areas, because houses are relatively cheaper to buy in the Potteries than elsewhere such as the South and other larger cities. This makes it difficult for them to uproot themselves, only to be faced with greater expenses. On the other hand some are quite accustomed to the relatively quiet surroundings which the Potteries has to offer, and would not now consider moving elsewhere unless it was a real necessity.

No 1.
(The names used are pseudonyms).

Mrs Parks came to England from Jamaica in the late 1950s. She had joined her husband who came nearly a year previously. She left her two children with relatives, with the intention of sending for them when they had settled and saved enough money for their fares. They did so within two years when the children were ten and twelve years old, which meant that they continued their schooling here. Both left school with no formal qualifications but one went to college at nights to further her education, and later went into nursing. Both children later got married and had families of their own. Due to the importance of the extended family for many Caribbeans, Mrs Parks wanted to return home but was reluctant to do so, because as she saw it, her grand children meant a great deal to her. Both she and her husband had the opportunity of going to Canada during the mid 1960s when many Caribbeans were migrating, but she did not want to disrupt her family life again, so they stayed here. Both have some regrets and disappointments caused by migration and racial discrimination in Britain, but suggested that you cannot change the past but you can try and change the future.

No 2.

Mr Logan came to Stoke in the late 1950s and was later joined by his wife. They both worked in industry, the husband in the mines and the wife at a manufacturing firm. They later sent for their daughter, who was age 14 at the time. After completing her schooling here, she also worked in industry. She did not want to continue her education as she did not find school particularly interesting, especially after her upheaval from one country to another. She is now married with a young son. Although Mr and Mrs Logan would like to return the Caribbean, they are somewhat reluctant to break up the family again. On the one hand they are desperate to return, but to them family ties are of extreme importance, and if they went back they would miss the particular relationship that exists within the family. This clearly shows that Caribbean family life is not as fragmented and unstructured as many sociologists claim to be the case. There has always been in existence single parent families, broken homes, divorced families, and the very strict family households. But many researchers on the issue of family background, tend to focus on particular races as being without a rigid family structure.

No 3.

Mr. Barnes came to Stoke in the early 1960s and sent for his wife around twelve months later. They later sent for their three children two girls and a boy aged between ten and fourteen. The children did not do as well as their parents expected them to do at school. But at the time underachievement amongst Caribbean children was not a factor, so whether this could be related to racism as is the case today, is not known. They went on to college to try to acquire some O level qualifications in order to improve their job prospects. One of the daughters wanted to go on to higher education, but did not acquire the A levels she needed. She however went on to do secretarial work and one went into nursing, while the son went into manual work. The couple migrated to the Caribbean a few years ago but later returned due to missing the family and friends they left behind in this country. This shows that when people have migrated for a number of years, their circumstances change, and this makes it difficult for them to return and settle in their original homeland. By then they have lost contact with many of the friends they knew and families may have moved elsewhere or migrated too. It would not therefore be the same for them to try and make new friends in the same manner as they did before migration.

No 4.
Mr Bates came to Britain in the late 1950s. He was single at the time but later met a woman whom he married. She had a son and a daughter by a previous marriage, both of whom she left with their grand parents in Jamaica. They later joined their parents in Stoke. Both parents worked in industry. They earned a good wage at the time. The husband earning between fifteen to eighteen pounds per week and the wife around eight to ten pounds per week. This enabled them to buy their own home quickly and later a car. When the children left school they left the area in search of better jobs. The couple then sold their house, and bought a smaller one in a residential area with a garden and garage, to get away from the density of inner city terraced dwellings. This shows that if black people had the opportunity to earn good wages, they could improve their standards of living enormously. But instead, due to low wages, and probably low morale, many are forced to occupy the cheaper types of terraced dwellings. Many are however now modernizing their terraced houses with the availability of improvement grants from the council, and an improvement in wages.

No 5.
This is the case of Mrs James who came to Stoke in the early 1960s. She was single at the time but later got married. They have two sons and a daughter. Both husband and wife worked in industry. Their children did very well at school and left with O levels and CSE qualifications. Both boys went on to college to do A levels, and one went on to higher education, while the daughter did a secretarial course. The boys had difficulty in finding jobs comparable with their qualifications, while the girl left the area to find work. Though the couple have no direct plans to return to the Caribbean, the thought of returning is never far from their minds. They said that they still miss the land of sunshine which they left behind, and a country where racism is not an issue, and you can get by whatever the conditions, compared to this country. As they see it, one day they probably will

return for good. But it is difficult to leave the children behind even though they are now adults. Re-migration is now a huge problem for many Caribbeans who would like to return to their country of origin but find it difficult to make a decision because they do not want to break up their family structure again. Many would feel lonely without their children and grandchildren, and this is one factor that will inhibit many who would like to return to their homelands. Hence, the stress of migration reappears when it is least expected, on retirement or redundancy, when the migrants are once again haunted by the upheavals of the past.

Conclusion

The small number of Caribbean families in the Potteries seem to have taken a low priority where government planning and policies are concerned with regards to making special provisions for Caribbean children in schools. Stoke also lags behind other cities where any such changes are concerned, because planners and policy makers may not see the need for large scale changes or they may not have the funding to do so. However, during the past ten years or so, the City Council has embarked on planning and refurbishing the city. The Race Equality Council is trying to implement ways of eliminating racism, which is a huge problem for the city. But as previously mentioned, it is a very covert form of racism which hardly attracts any large scale attention, but remains insidious and works beneath the surface to the detriment of blacks in the area. Why should so many Caribbean school-leavers after going to college, have to leave the area in order to try and find suitable employment? I have spoken to many of the parents who are very disturbed at such attitudes of employers in the Potteries and the way racism operates to keep back their children.

The case histories clearly show the difficulties Caribbean families experience as a result of migration. Not only are they parted from their families and friends, but they also have to make new adjustments to their lives, such as making new friends, adapting to new environments, coping with racism which they did not encounter in the Caribbean. Those who have a a desire to return home are very often faced with the difficulty of leaving their children behind and the friends they have made, in order to re-establish new friendships all over again. As a result many may choose to remain here due to the difficulty in re-establishing themselves and setting up home again. We could say that the process of migration is often very problematic, though there are some advantages. But sometimes the experiences encountered do have a lasting effect on individual's lives and well-being. Having stated some of the difficulties which many Caribbean families face in the host country, I will attempt to examine the effects which this might have on the education of their children in schools. Could it be that the type of lifestyle which they experience and the types of jobs which they do may have affected their children's education? After all, children from underprivileged backgrounds are not expected to do well educationally. As we have seen, many studies have shown that some white working class children do suffer a educational handicap, due mainly to the structure of the education system. The next chapter will explain the methodology and the problems encountered during the data collection stages, and the strategies adopted to deal with those problems.

CHAPTER 5

Methodology

The study aims to look at the underachievement of children of Caribbean origin in schools. The field work was designed to gain as much information as possible from the subjects under investigation. However, one of the drawbacks for social scientists is the difficulty in obtaining precise information on the topic under investigation. This to some extent will depend on the type of area to be studied, the topic of the investigation and the respondents concerned. One also has to take into account the time and resources available. Due to the fact that some topics may be seen as sensitive and difficult to extract information, the reaction of the respondents must be given careful thought. In order to overcome this, one has to exercise caution in preparing the questions and when approaching the respondents.

The area of study is situated to the West of the Midlands. This seemed very promising, and I was very enthusiastic about embarking on what seemed a very fruitful project. But as I later discovered there were unforeseen problems to be encountered that had not been anticipated before hand. The research began in the Spring of 1985 until the summer of 1986 and has constantly been updated to the present wherever possible. The methods used were interviews which were recorded and questionnaires to be filled out by pupils in their fifth year of schooling. During the first year of the study, seventeen teachers and three lecturers were interviewed They seemed very helpful and cooperative. Statistically, they were unable to give specific information about the school performance of Caribbean children because no records were kept on ethnic performance. The teachers said that they did not separate pupils into ethnic groups as such, because they treat all pupils the same. So this exercise was not forthcoming as they did not have the specific ethnic records to refer to. They however suggested that there were no learning problems with Caribbean children as some of them did well at school. They also suggested that if I needed any further assistance or information they would be glad to help. Some even suggested that I looked around the classrooms or visit the school any time I wanted to. This aspect was very pleasant and prompted me to prepare for the next stage, that of interviewing the children and to ask them to fill out the questionnaires. This the teachers were aware of and gave their approval.

However, during the second year of the study problems gradually emerged. I had prepared 150 questionnaires to be filled out by high school pupils in their fifth year of schooling before they left school in the summer. 50 questionnaires were also prepared for college students which had to be later abandoned as I was not permitted to interview the students. These were to be filled out by whites, Asians and Caribbean pupils. This was so because there were only a few Caribbean pupils now in schools which turned out to be 10 who I had access to both for interviews and the questionnaires. If some schools had not declined this number would have been far greater. Caribbean children were also underrepresented in the interviews and accounted for 10 while Asians were 30 and whites 50. As it happened the teachers strike escalated during that year and this greatly hampered the study in the sense that access to schools became more restricted, as the schools now faced a staff problem. Some of the planned visits had to be rescinded, rescheduled, or shortened. For me the time factor became a pressing problem, because the data had to be collected before the end of the summer term, after which time many of the children would have left school. In the end only 60 questionnaires were actually filled in, because some schools faced a staff shortage and the teachers said that they were having some difficulty in coping with the problem. I had to make the best possible use of the time that was available. The children were very cooperative and helped as best as they could.

Some schools had declined to take part, because as they saw it they were facing problems of their own. Thus some may have used the strike to refrain from taking part. Some also retracted from allowing the children to fill in the questionnaires when they realized that the study was trying to locate race as an issue of underachievement amongst black children. One school where the headmaster was very cooperative the previous year when he was interviewed said he had changed his opinion and would not allow the children to talk about something which they knew nothing about, as it would be asking them to make value judgement. A college principal had also declined for the same purpose. He said the students might say yes to a question when they actually mean no. Hence we have responsible tutors and guardians making value judgements on behalf of their pupils. This would seem a way of undermining their pupils intelligence, as has often been the case where teachers have misjudged their pupil's capability. The majority of the teachers on the whole seemed to be understanding especially those who were in the midst of preparing a multicultural curriculum. Many were also aware that vast changes were required in schools to meet the new technological age, and was preparing for this by regularly consulting with potential employers.

Conclusion

The methodology has given an insight into some of the problems faced by social scientists when embarking upon fieldwork which is a vital aspect of sociological research. Much can be gained in the process especially if the respondents are cooperative. Although there was some reluctance on the part of some teachers to cooperate for the various reasons mentioned, those who cooperated have greatly contributed to the study. It would seem that teachers are governed by certain ideologies which govern their judgement in how they deal with certain issues. It takes great courage for teachers who were socialized into thinking that the black race was genetically inferior to be able to talk about such a topic openly with a view to want to change things. Even within a small area such as Stoke they seem to vary in their outlook, and this will dictate the rate of change they seek within their schools. Their responses and those of the children involved in the study, have provided some useful starting points which helped a great deal in the construction of the book. Having explained the methodology, I will now proceed to give an account of the result of the interviews from the teachers and the children's point of view, and the questionnaires as they have been filled out by the children.

◆

CHAPTER 6

Interviews with Teachers

After some in depth planning the research began in the spring of 1985 until the summer of 1986 and beyond. First, one had to be sure that the questions to be asked about what the teachers thought of the academic performance of Caribbean children in schools were of the right type. As previously discovered questions relating to race and ethnicity are often viewed as sensitive and unnecessary by some teachers and should be left alone. But on the whole, some of the teachers were very understanding and sympathetic especially those who are actively involved in multicultural education. The research involved trying to assess the academic performance and experience of Caribbean children in schools, and their perception of schooling in general. The term ethnic or black may sometimes be used to refer to Caribbean children unless otherwise specified. Though my aim was to concentrate mainly on high schools, it was later decided to start at the nursery level, then through the primary and secondary schools, due to the minute number of Caribbean children in the area. This would also give me an idea of the processes through which the children proceed through school, and their learning potential at an early stage. The schools chosen were mainly in areas where there were a reasonable ethnic population, as they were to be the main focus of the study. I visited 3 nursery schools, 5 primary schools, 7 high schools 2 colleges, the Language Centre, and a school for retarded children on the outskirts of the city. The number of teachers interviewed were 17 and 3 lecturers, most of whom have had contact with children from ethnic minority backgrounds. I will now attempt to explain what was discovered at the different levels using at least 2 examples in each case.

Nursery School 1

After arriving at the school my discussion with the Headmistress began by asking her about the composition of the school, and the percentage of Caribbean children that attended. The school is situated close to dwelling areas, and is beautifully surrounded by trees, its own gardens and play areas securely fenced around by railings so that the children can be allowed to play in safety. As it turned out, there were only 3% of Caribbean children attending the school, over 60% Asians, and 37% whites. At this early stage, there was already an absence of Caribbean pupils, which altered the course of the research. The Headmistress proceeded to talk about problems of language which they were experiencing with Asian children. We discussed whether there was a language barrier facing Caribbean children, and she said there was none whatsoever. There was neither a language nor learning difficulty facing Caribbean children.

Q Are there any specific problems with Caribbean children in schools?

A None whatsoever. But there is a language problem with Asian children when they first start school.

Q Why is this so?

A Because they speak English as a second language. It is rarely used in the home or playground. Many of the mothers do not speak English at all and when the children come to school, they speak no English either. But they soon overcome this, because the language centre provide teachers who come to the school on a half daily basis to assist with the problem. They mainly cater for the under five's in the school because at that age it is considered best not to uproot them from the secure environment of the school to another environment to which they are not accustomed.

The headmistress went on to say that another problem facing the school was that sometimes Asian children are taken back to visit their parents homeland for long periods of time and when they return to the school they may experience some learning difficulty due to the long absence. We are aware that teachers are concerned about absenteeism amongst their pupils, but they should also be aware that it is important to Asian families to retain a close knit family relationship with their grandparents and other relatives. This is part of their cultural heritage which they take pride in maintaining. Although the extended family in the West is not as popular as it used to be, and has to a certain extent declined, it is still very popular in the East and this is a tradition that Asian families try to maintain. The teacher also talked about irregular school attendance by some older Asian girls who probably have to stay at home to help their mothers with looking after the younger children.

Q   Can the parents be persuaded to send their children to school regularly?

A   Well, there is a problem of communication between the school and the home. Many Asian mothers cannot speak English and this seems to isolate them in the home. She said that there was a need for them to be educated enough so that they can communicate more effectively with the teachers about their children's needs and educational requirements. The headmistress outlined that there was a need for mothers to be consulted about issues like the importance of regular attendance at school and in some cases, dietary requirements. Just then the health nurse came in the room and joined in the conversation.

The nurse said that she was glad to be visiting that afternoon, because she found the conversation very interesting. She said that matters relating to dietary requirements and health matters need to be explained to the mothers, as they are so important to the welfare of their children. She too stressed the need for interpreters which would allow for better communication between parents, the school and the health centre in the interest of the children.

Conclusion

Referring to the conversation that took place, and what the headmistress had outlined, a great deal about the performance of children could not be explained at nursery level, because the children were too young for any future projections to be made about their academic ability, as they were only between the ages of 3 and 5 years old. There was neither a learning nor language difficulty with Caribbean children. However, the Head's main concern was about communication problems that existed between the home and the school. If this problem could be solved, it would allow for greater and more effective understanding between parents and teachers. It would give them greater freedom to liaise with the parents and to discuss their children's needs. This would explain that there is a need for teachers of minority languages to be employed in schools to help the teachers with their daily tasks of interpreting the needs of minority children. If there is a lack of liaison between the home and the school, the parents will not know how well or badly their children are doing at school, and if left until later, this can have serious consequences for the children's educational and other welfare issues. The Local Education Authority has been slow in responding to minority issues, and has only started gathering statistics on minority issues since the later part of the 1980s. While in places like London, Bradford and Birmingham etc., those issues are more readily dealt with, probably because of the larger number of black residents, and greater parental pressure on the authorities for change.

Nursery School 2

After making an appointment with the headmistress, I arrived at the school as planned. I took a check list of questions to make sure that there were sufficient items to be discussed. The headmistress was very enthusiastic and very much in control of the situation. She knew that the topic was based on ethnic issues, and as it happened, she had previously been on a race awareness course which she found very interesting. I asked her about the ethnic minority children at the school, and whether or not she was experiencing any difficulties with them. She said that all was well, and that the children were happy at school. There were no children of Caribbean origin at the school at the time, but there was about 70% Asian children in that school.

Again the topic of language seemed paramount. The headmistress said that most Asian children speak no English at all when they first start school, because in the home they speak their mother tongue, which meant that most mothers are unable to help their children with lessons in English. She said those mothers who speak English are able to pass on the skills to their children, but very often others are unable to do so.

Q How do you deal with communication problems?

A The language teachers help up a great deal, and the children who speak dual languages often help us to interpret other children's comments, and sometimes those of the parents.

The headmistress went on to say that such reciprocity creates an atmosphere that is pleasant and acceptable to all concerned. It also helps to break down some of the barriers that would otherwise exist. The school operates on a flexi-basis, which allow the parents to visit the school in the mornings and afternoons to talk to the teachers about any problems that they may have concerning their children. She said that as a means of creating good community relations, parents are allowed to go on school trips with them. This will reduce the barriers that would otherwise cause friction between parents and teachers, and the children. The headmistress also spoke of absenteeism and lateness amongst some Asian children. But she said she had overcome this by gently persuading the parents about the importance of regular attendance and punctuality whilst the children are at school. Sometimes she tells the parents that if they are not there on time, she will come to their homes and fetch them herself, and this often works.

Q How do they respond?

A Very well, because they often cooperate. This kind of rapport can only lead to good relationships and better understanding between people of different groups.

The headmistress said that one worrying aspect was that if a child was suffering from any defects such as hearing or speech, it may not be recognized early enough, so that immediate therapy can be administered. That could cause problems when the child goes to the next school where the demands are greater.

Q What about the children's learning ability generally?

A It is difficult to comment at this stage. So much depends on the amount of time they spend here, and that is causing some difficulty at the moment.

This difficulty was one of accommodation. Children are admitted at the nursery at the age of three, but due to it being a small nursery, very often they are nearly four and a half years before they can be admitted. This gives them only six months before they go on to primary school. She said that this was inadequate to equip them sufficiently for the next stage, because the classes will be larger, and they will probably have fewer teachers. There will also be less possibility of a close teacher/pupil relationship. She suggested that a good start at the nursery is important as it helps them to become familiar with different concepts in preparation for primary school, but unfortunately this is not the case. She said that at this stage, it is important to them to become familiar with concepts and sentence structure, because if they miss out on this vital stage, later on they may have difficulty in catching up, and some things will go over their heads without them being able to grasp it.

Q How do you deal with racism?

A There is no racial problem here. We have a good mix of children, and the teachers and everyone get on well with each other. They all play happily together. When they are older it may manifest itself.

Q Why is this so?

A It may be due in part to parental influence, racist remarks in the street or the media. This may in part be based on certain socio-economic groups who think that other groups who are physically different to themselves are taking their jobs or are living off the Welfare State. It is very easy for certain groups to get stereotyped and labelled in this way. When this happens, they become visible scapegoats, because someone must take the blame. I think much prejudice developed in the USA, where the poor whites projected their own inadequacies and failures on to black groups, due to their own socio-economic conditions.

But there was no mention of the covert racism on which Britain thrives, as she gave the impression that all was well, and racism was another country's problem. Even though she admitted that during New Commonwealth migration to Britain, she asked why were all these people coming here. Here we have an educated teacher who was totally unaware of Britain's post-war prosperity, and hence a need for manual labour to rebuild the country, and to meet the needs of industrial expansion that occurred at the time.

I asked her whether or not she thought that books contributed to racism. Her reply was that books are constantly changing and in time they will reflect normal situations of both blacks and whites instead of singling out and emphasizing on blacks as inferior, they will be more positive in their attitudes. She also emphasized their tendencies to reflect white middle class values, images and attitudes. She pointed out the fact that no equal references are made to reflect the positions of blacks in society, nor to show any of them in positions of authority. This will make it difficult for black children to want to do anything positive. She emphasized that there is a need for more positive points to be made about the ability and capabilities of blacks so that they will be viewed in a more positive light. She however suggested that a great deal will depend on whether or not some parents know about the education system sufficiently, in order to make the best out of it to help their children. She said that some parents may be too tired to help especially if they are working, but professional people who are fluent in English, and help their children, those children are often at an advantage from the word go. She said that the progress a child makes at school will largely depend on his/her experience from home, and that a limited home experience will give the child a weak starting point at school. Under those circumstances, only the very clever ones will quickly excel and make progress.

Judging from those comments, it would appear that teachers have certain expectations of children and place them in certain categories as soon as they start school. The very bright ones will be seen as worthy of being given the attention they need, and this will help them get along even quicker, while the less bright ones may suffer as a result of not being given equal attention. This may not be deliberate on the part of some teachers, but it is said to happen. The same applies when children are streamed. The top streams work hard and achieve good results, probably because they are expected to do well, whilst in the lower streams there is less motivation to do well, because they see themselves as less capable, and may not work as hard as they should. They are also encouraged less by their teachers, and this may also demotivate them. As Coard (1971), Stone (1981), Taylor (1983) have pointed out, teachers have certain expectations of their pupils, and those who fit into the most favourable categories will exceed over and above the rest provided they have the ability to do well.

Many of the teachers whom I interviewed mentioned that ability and academic success go hand in hand. This may be a valid point, but success at school can take different forms, eg. some children may be bright when they first start school but may then start to lag behind after a while for various reasons, while others may not be very bright to begin with, but may make progress as they go along. Some may find the school's environment too restrictive and this may determine how well they perform. If teachers judged each child on merit rather than on preconceived ideas which they take to the school with them, each child would have a better chance of being successful at school. One cannot say that at the nursery level there is no racism, but there is a possibility that it is less noticeable at this stage, and a great deal will depend on the teachers attitudes towards the children.

Primary School 1

Similar procedures were used in the primary schools, but as the children were older some of the questions had to be altered accordingly. The school had a population of less than 200, of which only about 4 were of Caribbean origin. I told the headmaster that the research was about children in the area, but mainly Caribbean children in schools, as I was looking at their academic performance and their perceptions of schooling. Also if the schools were experiencing any difficulties with black children that required any special help.

Q Are there any language problems facing Caribbean children?

A None whatsoever, but we do have a language problem regarding Asian children.

Q How do you overcome this?

A We allow parents to come into the school with toddlers of pre-school age, so that they can become familiar with the surroundings and the school environment before they actually start school. A language teacher also visits the school on a one day a week basis to help those children who are experiencing difficulty with language. The school is also trying to adapt a multi-ethnic education approach which involves introducing a variety of cultures into the school.

Q How is this done?

A If a child of ethnic origin goes away on holiday to their parents country of origin, we ask them to bring something back, and whatever item it is, will be discussed in the class. We also, try to make the children understand why other people may dress differently, or eat different food. Asians are particularly demonstrative of this, as at the moment they account for the greater number of ethnics in the school.

Q Are children taught anything about the geography and history of places like the Caribbean, Asia and Africa which would help them to understand better why other people's lifestyles are different?

A At this age children are not interested in learning about far away places, because it may only confuse them. When they reach secondary school they may have a choice because they may have more subjects to choose from, and they may also have a better understanding of other places. Another implication is that due to the ethnic diversity, it would be difficult to cater for the needs of all minorities. We try to deal with those issues by gradually introducing into the classroom aspects relating to other cultures. We also have a Parent Association, where parents are persuaded to attend meetings and take part in the discussions. However, probably due to certain cultural traditions, Asian mothers seem to be restricted to the home. There also appears to be a language barrier, which makes it difficult for them to fully partake in what is going on around them.

The headmaster further suggested that it is important for the home environment to be of a certain standard. For instance overcrowded homes or noisy environments would not be ideal for children who want to proceed. The right atmosphere must be created. He said they do not hold back any child, regardless of origin. All children are encouraged and stretched to the limit. It is possible that specially gifted children are not held back in some cases in this area, especially if their parents take an active part in ensuring that they get the best out of schooling. But the statement does imply that teachers do seem to have a psychologically inbuilt assumption about home conditions and home backgrounds which could inadvertently affect children's progress at school, especially the ones who need special encouragement. It is possible that the type of interaction that they create, will not be beneficial to those children, and they are the ones who are likely to fail at school. If teachers do not create the right kind of atmosphere to make all pupils feel welcome and valued, regardless of their home backgrounds, there is likely to be mistrust and hostility between pupil and teacher which will result in children losing interest in their lessons rather than actively participating.

Q How do you deal with racism?

A We have not experienced it here. It is something that is probably learned in the home or other children unintentionally making certain remarks.

Q Do you think that books create racism?

A I do not think that there is any discrimination as far as books are concerned. If children's attention are brought to something specific, then they are bound to take notice of something that they may not have previously thought about.

Q But what about the racist contents that are found in books that children read daily such as Noddy?

A This does not incite children to be racist. Books are chosen according to the ages of children, and unless it was distasteful for a particular age group, then it would not be wise to ban it. We also have to think of budgeting. Books are not easily replaced. But they are constantly changing, and in time publishers will put things right.

Conclusion

Should any headmaster be looking to the publishers to put things right, or should that begin in the schools by looking at their books and the teaching materials to see if they are being fair to all the children in their care?

It would appear that as far as racism is concerned, some teachers do not admit that it exists, but neither can they ignore it. Although the headmaster seems to be making some changes in the school to cater for multi-ethnic education, he is prepared to do so in his own time. Though he stated that there was no racism in his school, he accepted the fact that changes are a crucial factor in avoiding any future conflict within the school, and this he was prepared to do without a great deal of hesitation.

Judging from the discussion, and the changes that the headmaster is implementing, there is an indication that he seems liberal in his outlook and is prepared to do whatever is necessary to foster good race relations within the school. The fact that ethnic cultures have already been introduced, and ethnic parents are allowed to take their pre-school toddlers at certain times, is an indication of the headmaster's good intentions to foster good race relations in the school. This may indicate that schools vary in terms of teacher's attitudes and location of schools, and probably what the headmaster considers to be a problem or lack of it. If teachers are prepared to admit that they are having problems where racism is concerned, and are prepared to request help, many problems facing minority children could be dealt with more adequately, and sooner rather than later.

Primary School 2

Like most of the other schools so far mentioned, this school is situated in the neighbourhood. This makes it ideal for young children who live locally, and do not have to travel a far distance to school. This school is fairly large and although the number of Caribbean children have declined over the years, there is still about 2.5% attending this school. The Asian population is about 37.5%. This is a significant change, because just over a decade ago there would have been a large proportion of Caribbean children attending there. The headmaster put this down to geographic mobility amongst Caribbean youths.

Q Could you comment on the academic performance of Caribbean children?

A Their academic performance is good, especially when they are willing to take part in a lesson. They can be very enthusiastic, but there are occasions when some may think that there is a colour problem and this makes it difficult for them to partake, because they may display a feeling of pessimism which they project as a guard. This can pose some difficulty for the teachers concerned to know which is the best way to help such pupils.

Q Do you think that an ethnic centre that provides advice on such matters would help?

A Yes, it would be helpful. Very often the child may be suffering from problems arising at home, or emotional instability. This does not relate only to black children, but also to the white working class children who may be suffering from some form of social deprivation.

Here the headmaster does not want to be seen to be addressing only black issues, but has linked social deprivation with issues relating to the white working class, many of who are said to be suffering from some form of social deprivation. The headmaster suggested that home background was very important, and that performance and background go hand in hand. He said that children from deprived homes may lack those basic skills in early reading and writing. He said that if those early skills are missing, to a certain extent it will impede their performance when they enter school. Equally, he said if they have poor or outdated material at home it will not help in improving their standards later. He said that in the case of black children, they need someone whom they can relate to, eg. black teachers who are more representative of them and with whom they will feel more valued. They need people like those who will be able to channel them in the right direction and help them to develop their abilities. He said that although at times teachers may want to help particular pupils, it is sometimes difficult to get through to them and know exactly what is affecting them and how they could be helped. This was one way in which he saw that any deep-rooted problems could be solved.

During the interview the headmaster also suggested that teachers may not always have the time to devote to particular pupils, however much they may be willing to help, due to them having to cope with fairly large classes. Some classes had well over 30 pupils, which left very little time for individual help on a large scale. He said this could only be solved if the classes were much smaller where teachers would have more time to spend with individual pupils.

Q   What is it that inspires a child to do well at school?

A   Achievement to a large extent will depend on the ability of the child. This does not however rule out the possibility that children require help from adults especially parents and teachers.

He also emphasized that it is important for value to be placed on other cultures in terms of type of clothes, food, houses, with an explanation as to why that was the case. He said this was a necessary part of curriculum changes, that he was in the process of introducing gradually. The deputy head joined in the conversation as we discussed ethnic issues. She said that no child should be made to feel inferior through media presentation which depicts their homeland as mud huts, poverty, disease, and people in rags. She pointed out that it is no wonder that many children deny any knowledge of their ancestral homeland because it makes them feel inferior. She supported the idea of a restructured curriculum which would enlighten other pupils as to why other people's cultures are different, and their adaptation to different types of climates. She said it was necessary that the types of inferiority fostered in ethnic people should be erased by changing the meaning of words that have been so structured in society as a means of condemning them. She spoke of 19th century literature as a typical example of such misconception and the denial of the rights of black people.

In a personal communication, Freeman (1984) who carried out a research on racism locally for a dissertation told me that some teachers were uncooperative during her interviews about racism. They did not want to know about it. She spoke about the damaging effects of stereotyping on the black races throughout history. She pointed out that text books in particular set out to teach religious doctrines, nationalism, social and moral ethics as a form of socialization, and those values were internalized throughout history. She suggested that Singh (1973) demonstrated how subtle distortions and stereotypes played a direct part in forming children's attitudes to themselves and to others. This can be seen in Milner's study and the dolls test where the majority of children chose white dolls because they thought they were more beautiful than the darker ones. B. Dixon (1977) looked at the use of the English language and how certain words denote good or evil. He noted that in most terms blackness signified evil, while white signified good. Those distortions have governed people's way of thinking since 16th century when the word 'blackamoor' first appeared in the English dictionary as a derogatory description of black people.

Husband (1982, p41) gave an account of the first encounter of English voyagers to the West Coast of Africa in (1550). These voyagers set out with the idea of meeting people similar to themselves, but were surprised when they met people of very different characteristics to themselves. The English thought they were unchristian and had very peculiar habits when compared to themselves. Hence blackness became a theme for European writers in which every description of the African meant baseness, dirty, foul, disastrous, wicked etc. Whiteness on the other hand meant purity, virtue, beauty, angelic etc. These myths were to govern the way people thought and acted for many centuries later. Authors have written that many blacks suffer from self-inflicting hatred, but have not confirmed that it is a result of the myths and falsehoods in European literature. By the same token, many blacks still foster the idea that whiteness is good and blackness is bad. Such distorted views of colour gradations continue to dominate people's whole outlook on life. Twitchin and Demuth argued that ethno-centricism has strong tendencies in any group who feel that their way of doing things is the right way. They suggested that it is because people are conditioned in their upbringing to think in a certain way. Ossie Davies (1967) in the USA identified 60 synonyms that signified whiteness as favourable and blackness as unfavourable and another 20 that related to race. He made the following quotation:

"The English language is my enemy. Any creature good or bad, white or black, Jew or Gentile, who has the English language for purposes of communication, is willing to force the black child into 60 ways to despise himself, and the white child 60 ways to aid and abet him in the crime."

(O. Davies: 1967).

The passage demonstrates how everyday use of language can create racism in an indirect form, knowing or unknowingly e.g., black-ice, blackleg, black cloud, blackmail, all of which have the meaning of something that is considered to be bad or horrid.

Q   How do you deal with racism?

A   It is not present in this school. We view all children in the same light. Ethnic children do perform very well. No one is held back and this can be seen in the performance of some ethnics. However, at the infant level and up to about the age of eleven, teachers can cope with ethnics, but as they get older and go higher up it becomes more difficult, because no one is able to give instructions on problems that may arise, and to advice teachers on how to do this.

Q What measures are being taken to get parents more involved in their children's education?

A Parents are encouraged to attend services and PTA meetings. This is intended to encourage a better racial mix, and as a means of breaking down any racial barriers that may exist between different racial groups. We are considering more ways that may be beneficial.

Conclusion

This particular school has not been known to foster nor encourage racism. One could therefore say that the headmaster was doing all he could to encourage good race relations between groups. The area has always had ethnic children and there has never been any racial tension between groups. The teachers have always been very good with ethnic children, so there could be no real reason to think that they encouraged racism within the school. The headmaster commented on the good pass rates of ethnic children which is a good indication of their dedication to their pupils. The children with high ability are especially encouraged to keep up their high standards of work, whilst the lesser ability ones are given every possible help that the teachers can give. This applies to black and white children alike. But as the headmaster said, due to large classes, very often they are unable to help each individual child as they would like to do. But there was no hint of racism amongst the teachers at this school, as the success rate for ethnic children was very good and could be commended. Although the number of Caribbean children at this school have declined over the years, there is now a large number of Asian children now attending the school and the headmaster is doing everything he can to cater for their needs. This involves, encouraging the parents to attend the school whenever possible, and invite parents to attend various types of activities which seem to be working out well. It would appear that schools vary in their attitudes towards minority children. This will be dependent on the headmasters/mistresses outlook, and that of the rest of the staff and their perceptions of ethnic children. I would therefore comment that not all schools have racist teachers, and the reason could well be that some teachers are very liberal in their outlook, and are not misguided by European literature and history which subjugated blacks as inferior.

Secondary Schools

This section will look at secondary schools and the attitudes and perceptions of teachers towards children of Caribbean origin. At this stage it would be expected that teachers would be accustomed to dealing with black children, and would be able to comment positively on their academic ability. I interviewed 17 teachers and heads, and 3 lecturers. The response was good as they freely spoke to me about what they thought of the academic abilities of Caribbean children. This is an account of the interviews with headteachers.

School 1

Seven secondary schools were visited, and as I discovered there were only a few children of Caribbean origin who were still at school. This made it difficult for me to quantitatively measure their academic success. There were no records kept by the schools on their examination pass rates, but the teachers gave me whatever help they could. I spoke mainly to the heads or deputy heads. They could see no reason why Caribbean children should be academically different to other groups. In fact they said that they were just as capable as any other group in being successful at school. One headmaster said they had good potential, but for some reason some of the Caribbean boys did not seem to use their capabilities as well as they should. However, he did say that some of the girls were hard working and had achieved some good results. When asked about the number of Caribbean children in the school, it only amounted to 0.71%, a very small number indeed when compared to a few years previously.

Q   Do you keep any record of ethnic performance?

A   No. We do not keep a check as such, because our duties are to integrate children, so we treat them all alike. But we have discovered that ethnic children do work hard of which the Chinese are the hardest working group. Even if they come to school with a limited amount of knowledge, within a short space of time they excel and surpass the others. They are a very dedicated group. I have since discovered on a BBC TV Programme 15.9.91, that in Japan education is very highly valued, and children spend long hours at school. They also work very hard at home because to fail at school is not acceptable, so schooling is modelled on succeeding educationally.

The deputy head intervened and said that children of Caribbean origin are capable and work hard, but very often they do not push themselves forward enough and by so doing, they often lag behind. She said if only they would apply themselves more, they would be high achievers. She said that from the 3rd year to the 5th year they are in the higher classes, but some of them tend not to excel. The Head was asked how children were placed for examinations. The reply was that there are policies regarding examinations. It states that for any pupil to sit GCE they must satisfy the criteria set by the examination board, and must have at least a certain guarantee of passing the examination. It is on that basis that pupils are placed in the groups that are best suitable to them, or if there is a good chance that they will pass the type of exams that they enter for. They stressed that exams are based on capability and that pupils must be dedicated and hard working, with a view to passing those exams which they take. The interview was well demonstrated by both Head and Deputy, but there was a tendency that they were defending a European view on what should be taught in schools, with the intention that other cultures were not as important because it is in Britain that the children have to live.

Q   How are children with learning difficulties catered for?

A   The school has a remedial class for such children, who are of no specific group. It is more of an individual problem such as broken homes, homes with no proper working facilities, or language problems in the case of some Asian children. But on the whole it is mainly the 'lazy' children who are placed in remedial classes. The length of time may vary according to individual, but every effort is made to ensure that a satisfactory progress is made.

Q Are there any behavioural problem with Caribbean children?

A Not more than is found among white children. Such a problem is displayed by both black and white children alike, and is not confined to any particular group. The headmaster commented, "I've found that Caribbean parents are strict disciplinarians who believe that caning is good for their children but I can't see this to be a necessity, because in the school they are not seen as a problem, and do not appear to be in need of any special discipline."

Q Do Caribbean children do more sport than other children?

A No, they are very good at sport, but they are not forced to do anything against their will. They are capable of combining sport with academic work.

Could the teachers openly admit that they encouraged black children into sport? Several black children seemed to think that this was the case, in that if they were good at sport this was very much recognised by the teachers and encouraged, whilst their academic work did not seem to matter as far as the teachers were concerned. This would give a broad view that teachers do tend to unwittingly steer Caribbean children into sport; because not only is it good for the image of the school, but it is also something that teachers think they can do naturally. Cashmore (1982, pp4, 104, 106) interviewed a number of black sportsmen and sportswomen about their interests and experiences of going into sport. He found that many were disillusioned by achieving little at school and saw no promise of improvement. They consistently underachieved when compared to whites and Asians. Many of the interviewees suggested that their teachers did not seem to care about their academic work, as long as they did well in sport. Some suggested that if they did nor cooperate, they would be ostracised by their teachers. As a result, the academic work of many was neglected because of the long hours they spent on the sports field. Some would even be taken out of their lessons to compete in games, and if they were good they were made to concentrate on sport. One respondent told Cashmore that 'it is as though the teachers expect you to fail, and you begin to believe it yourself and do fail.' He believed that this is one of the important reasons why black children are continually underqualified academically.

Some ex-pupils of Caribbean origin suggested that some parents could have been more helpful in offering them advice. But it would appear that some of the parents were of the opinion that everything concerning school should be left to the teachers as they do in the Caribbean. Some had no idea of the differences in the Caribbean school system and the British school system. Bushell (1973) as quoted in Rampton, suggested that some Caribbean parents do not seem to regard the importance of stimulation by conversation or the use of toys during infancy. But maybe Bushell has not looked into the fact that some Caribbean parents do buy toys for their children, but in some homes frequent conversation about school work may be lacking, due to the above mentioned factors. Rutter and Miller (1972) discovered that there was less conversation between some Caribbean parents and children. A further study by Rutter in (1975) showed similar results, there were fewer interactions in general between some Caribbean families. The authors had not taken into account the fact that most of the migrants to this country have to work long and unsocial hours doing shift work, and bring up their families without any help from the extended family. This puts additional strain on their energy and resources, as the social services do not help them or provide any facilities for them. It is not that some of those parents do not want to interact with their children but their circumstances may not allow them to do so. This is where sociologists tend to draw inferences without the facts, because they are not aware of the situation and how certain families may be affected.

However, this is not the case with all Caribbean families. Some do take the time to offer advice to their children. Those who have been successful have high regard for their parents and the moral support which they gave them. This could in part derive from the fact that those parents may be better educated, and therefore their aspirations for their children were paramount. They were better equipped to get what they wanted out of the education system and used it to their full advantage. The parents who visit the school regularly and discuss their children's progress with the teachers will stand a better chance of getting full cooperation from the teachers than those who visit occasionally.

Some of the teachers thought that discipline in the Caribbean homes were harsh, strict, and repressive, as opposed to school discipline which they saw as self-discipline, understanding, tolerance, and informality. Most Caribbean parents believe that caning is good for the child. The parents therefore blame the school for not imposing such discipline which will instil good behaviour in the child. Some parents also see corporal punishment as a form of learning motivation that will make the children work harder at their lessons. Such conflicting views between teachers and some Caribbean parents, could in part encourage some children to underachieve due to a lack of understanding between parents and teachers as to what good discipline ought to be. Some parents think that such a 'soft approach' by teachers is not helping their children, but the teachers also have to try and restore a balance between themselves and the pupils concerned. Whereas it would have been acceptable for teachers in the Caribbean to use whatever method that was necessary to deal with learning and behavioural problems, the black youths in this country would have a different conception on corporal punishment and would feel that white teachers are deliberately singling them out for punishment. Teachers had to try to avoid such conflicts. This type of problem does not occur in the Caribbean because children know their place when they go to school, so they adhere to the discipline set by the school. Dhondy et al (1982) sums up the situation that existed in some classrooms in some London boroughs. She noted that in one of the schools where she taught the most prominent topic of conversation in the staff room was about black kids. It was at a time when schools were beginning to merge, and there were constant disruption, especially in the lower classes where the children were almost exclusively black. The authors pointed out that the teachers did not know how to deal with them and most of the lesson time would be spent trying to maintain order. Such disorderliness obviously had a stigmatising effect on black children throughout most of the country, but this effect was greatest where there were large numbers of Caribbean children in schools. They were immediately seen as threatening the established order of the British school system. If teachers could not maintain discipline in their schools, who else could? This was a fear many teachers had of Caribbean children and many blamed them for disruptions in schools.

In such cases where teachers had no prior training or experience to deal with problems relating to black children, the Local Education Authorities and the DES were probably at fault for not making an attempt to recruiting black teachers to help black children settle in schools. This probably would have had a more calming and stimulating influence on the children to see people who look more like themselves as role models, rather than someone distinctly different to themselves to whom they could not relate. Even adults sometimes have this problem of associating with or accepting others, but we very often think that children should automatically adapt to whatever the situation may be. At one of the schools where I did my research, I was asked by a little black girl as I entered the school, "Are you coming to work here?" When I said no, she looked very disappointed. Others did not openly ask the same question, but it could be interpreted that they felt the same way. Those who were asked if they would like to have ethnic teachers, all said yes, it would greatly help them. This shows that the Education Authorities have ignored the needs of black children in schools by firstly depriving them of their own history and culture, and secondly, for failing to provide them with role models who could be of invaluable help to them.

The training of minority teachers should now be a priority for policy makers in education, so that black children can have someone to relate to, and not feel alienated in a society in which they are part of.

School 2

The procedures were very similar as with school 1. There was a dramatic decline in the number of Caribbean children in schools at all levels. Whereas they usually form about 7% of the school's population, there was now only about 3% in some cases. The headmaster said that the reason for the decline was that the bulk of the 1960s-70s Caribbean pupils had gone through the system, and that it might be another decade or so before another generation fill that vacuum. He said that there was a changing pattern, because whereas Caribbeans settled in the area first, many have now left and have been replaced by Asians which is a more recent group.

Q   What would you say about the academic performance of Caribbean children in schools?

A   Well, what myself and some of my staff have found, perhaps this is too general a statement, but Caribbean girls are hard working and are very keen to get on. But with the boys, some are more hard core, and although they have the ability, never seem to use it. You may have a situation where say there are 20 Caribbean lads, you only need a few of them not doing anything and the rest will follow.

The head also said that not all of them were like that, some do well, but others seem reluctant to use their ability. He put it down to lack of motivation. But what causes a lack of motivation? Could it be that these boys needed some encouragement to be motivated? The headmaster said that this type of behaviour could in part be due to them harbouring resentment due to a lack of opportunities for young blacks, hence they portray an attitude which makes it look as if they don't care. The headmaster went on to say that there are those who are very good and will work to the best of their abilities, while others will not work. He said he did not think that it was lack of parental support because very often parents have come to him and have expressed their wishes for their children to do well. But some of the children seem to go contrary and do not seem to have any interest in their lessons. The situation seemed a complex one. Those children may consider themselves as victims of racism in society, which makes it difficult for them to choose anything constructive on which to build their future on. They may think they are wasting their time in trying to achieve qualifications which will not help them in the long run. So rather than spend a lot of time studying hard they might as well not make things too difficult for themselves.

I asked the headmaster if he thought that peer group influence affected school performance. He said that in his experience it has. He told me of a lad who was at school a few years ago who was a real leader. He had such a powerful influence on the others that even people who were more intelligent than himself looked up to him. He said that between 14-16 years of age peer group influence can be more influential than even parents or anyone else. This will lead to a situation where some people will work hard while others can't be bothered to do anything. I asked him whether or not schools are in a position to change the situation. He said that they were looking closely at the courses they offer. Some high schools were now offering (TVEI) Technical and Vocational Educational Initiative. It is more a vocational based course. There is now a demand for technological subjects, and he intended to work towards those courses as it might help solve some of the problems. He spoke of the competition that now exists for jobs of which academic qualifications are no longer the only answer. He said people may have to move to where the jobs are, but in this area they tend not to move because Stoke seems a very insular place. But that may be his opinion of the area, because people have always moved out of the area in search of better opportunities. The Evening Sentinel (29.8.87) showed that by the early part of 1988, about 9,000 people left the area due to the effects of the recession. Prior to that time, many Caribbeans have moved to more prosperous areas to find better employment and better paid jobs.

On the topic of jobs the head said that there was a lot of biases in the job market and employers are in a position to select the best, so he emphasized to his 5th year pupils the importance of being punctual at all times. He said about 50% of school leavers in Stoke now go on to Youth Training Schemes, which gave them some experience from which employers can assess their ability, as in some cases they are not looking for academic qualifications alone, they may want some practical experience also. There is also a course called prevocational education which is aimed at the 16 plus and offers a certificate at the end of it. We talked about the changes that were taking place within education and society and how schools will have to respond to meet those changes. He was aware that schools would need time and resources to cater for those changes, but was of the opinion that in time those challenges would be met, in order to cater for the needs of a changing society.

Q How are children selected for the type of examinations they take?

A Normally, they go in for the type of exams that balance with their ability. If they have the ability, they go in for O levels. There is no restriction with anyone. "If they are a borderline case, we see the parents and if they say O level, we put them in for O level. What they achieve is up to them as every one will be given the same chance. Within the framework of the school we don't say because he is Asian he is only doing this or that. The only thing with some Asians is the language problem. Even though some have been born here, their parents don't speak English at home, and this creates a language problem. With the West Indians, there is no such problem because they speak English. They may have a dialect but this is no problem, and they go in for the courses that commensurate with their ability. But I do get the feeling that some West Indian boys do not achieve what they should achieve.

The Head said that this was probably his own personal opinion, but he was of the impression that things are difficult enough for those Caribbean boys already and they did not want to make it more difficult for themselves. He said that they may from time to time listen to the media or read the newspapers and see how difficult it is for blacks in this country and this may affect the way they think and act. Although there may be some validity in the statement, why is it that Caribbean girls do not seem to be affected in the same way? This statement would seem to suggest that teachers may view Caribbean boys as threatening and aggressive, and as a result tend not to encourage them in their school work. This will only exacerbate the situation, because the boys may think that the teachers are not concerned about their welfare, and may develop an attitude accordingly. Could it be that Caribbean girls are more determined to get on and will persevere no matter what the outcome? As several studies show, teachers are more likely to pick on Caribbean boys than girls, and this can lead to a great deal of resentment on the part of the boys concerned.

The Head said that he and his staff were of the opinion that in the West Indian homes it seems to be the mothers who visit the school, and in the Asian homes, it was the fathers who visited. He said that was not so for everyone, but that was what he and his staff found generally. This led them to believe that the mothers were the strength in the West Indian homes, while for the Asians it was the opposite. They thought that this was probably why Caribbean girls did better than boys, because of the stronger matriarchal ties. This shows how stereotypes are perpetuated and believed by teachers, educationists and researchers, and how they take these preconceived ideas to their work. It was probably the case that the mothers may have more time to visit the schools because the fathers may be working on that particular occasion. In a BBCTV Programme on 15.9.91. it showed that in Japan it is mainly the mothers who visit the schools to discuss their children's progress with the teachers, because presumably the fathers were at work. And yet the Japanese are not seen as coming from loose knit backgrounds. So why is it always assumed that it is the strong matriarchal ties which cause Caribbean girls to do better at school than the boys? It is also the case that mothers are usually the ones to guide the children educationally, like taking them to school, seeing to their school uniform, looking after them when they are ill, etc. So if it is because the mothers visit the school they were of the opinion that West Indians were mother centred, what about when other single mothers have to visit the school, do they draw the same conclusion? In all homes fathers take the least interest in those issues, and yet Caribbean fathers are singled out as uncaring in their children's education. The majority are just as eager to see their children do well educationally because they know that a good education may put them in better position in life by enhancing their job prospects.

I asked him if there were any behavioural problems with Caribbean children. He said "We don't have any more problems with West Indians or Asians, than we do with other groups. In any group there will be behavioural problems no matter who they are. It is just that where there are small groups if there are two or three with behavioural problems it will be magnified more than it is for the majority". He said that over the last few years problems in schools have got greater, but that's to do with all kinds of circumstances outside the school, such as one parent families, unemployment and divorce, all of which have now become a fact, and that's how society was now developing. He said that Caribbean boys should not give up trying, but may be they think that they have less of a chance than anyone else and that will make it difficult for them to apply themselves.

Conclusion

From the interview the headmaster seemed on the one hand to be authentic, and on the other patronizing. There seemed to be some doubt as to whether or not he could adequately cope with the situation facing Caribbean boys. He did give the impression that he understood their problems, but he certainly could not empathise. He said that he was from a working class background and had to struggle to overcome all the odds, so Caribbean boys were in a position to do the same. He had not taken into account the fact that not only were those boys from a different culture, but they were also of a different race, which is a very prominent feature in their everyday encounter with society. This puts them at odds in the way they are seen and treated by others. Whereas he can disguise his working class origin, these boys cannot disguise their physical characteristics. This he had not taken into account because his colour does not affect him in any way. His background he can disguise now that he is a headmaster. His experience does not allow him to think and act in the same way as Caribbean boys do. It appeared to be that the boys needed help from their teachers with reassurance and advice to use and develop their talents. But having failed to get the support they needed, they probably felt that they could not be bothered to work hard. This may have prompted them to drift from their schoolwork, and develop an interest in peer group setting which will give them the support they need. This may not necessarily be in academic terms, but they are aware of each other's social needs, and will thrive to achieve this end. If teachers do not show the same interest in their welfare, they may easily lose interest in their schooling. Teachers are looked upon as second guardians by some pupils, so they have to show a willingness to help them in whatever way they can by encouraging their pupils to trust them. If this kind of mutual trust is missing, very often talented children will end up wasting very valuable time and talent, and instead of being high achievers, will lose out and become underachievers. A female pupil who attended that school told me that she was of the opinion that teachers did not know how to adequately deal with Caribbean children, because if it was raining and they congregated in the corridor, they were made to move along, but if it was a group of white children, no one would bother them. It seems to be the case that if black children are seen to congregate in numbers, they are immediately seen as a threat to the established order of society. If they are split up then they cannot cause too many problems, so they must not be given the chance to form groups. A black female student told me that at high school she used to sit next to her cousin and the teacher separated them. This made things difficult for her as there were only a few black pupils at the school. I am of the opinion that although sometimes teachers may mean well and may like to think that they are fair to all their pupils, unfortunately sometimes this is not the case in reality. It could well be that in the past, for instance during the 1960s to the early 1980s, most teachers could not adequately cater for the needs and well-being of Caribbean children. But perhaps they did not want to admit to such a failure in not being able to control a particular group of children who were seen as strange and different to them. To save themselves any embarrassment Caribbean children were allocated to lower streams, where the fault would be pointed at them rather than to the authorities.

Some teachers may not be intentionally racist, but may lack the necessary expertise and tact that is required to deal adequately with ethnic minority children. This was pointed out to me by a headmaster who said that very often teachers may want to help ethnic children, but for some unknown reason, they cannot get through to them. Some black children may see teachers as representatives of a dominant white culture, which is in a sense alien to them, and may find it difficult to trust their teachers, and hence, have difficulty in partaking in their lessons as they would wish. Equally, if they are not encouraged by their teachers to partake in the lessons as a means of developing their talents, they may see the school as an alien place to be, and as a result may lose interest altogether. In order to overcome this problem, there should be more black teachers employed in schools and colleges, so that black children can have someone with whom they can identify with, and look to as role models. Several black children have also commented on the issue, and likewise some white teachers seem to think this is a good idea. But the government has made no attempt to encourage the training of black teachers as a positive input to help black children overcome their difficulties. In my opinion they may be discouraged from doing so rather than being encouraged. This is due to the fact that several black applicants told me that they have been turned down at interviewing institutions. The police force is trying to redress this balance by actively advertising to encourage young blacks to join the force. But the education system seems adamant in encouraging such a move. Is this to be viewed as another form of discrimination in the education system, that blacks are not capable of instructing the nation's youngsters to take their places in society? Or is it also the case that black teachers will educate black pupils over and above their academic ability because of an awareness of the problems which they face? It is only when black children see a mix of black and white teachers in schools, that they will feel that they are adequately being catered for, or rather when white teachers begin to perceive them as individuals with ability and learning potential as they view any other pupil. Until LEAS, teachers and educationists redress this balance, it will be difficult for black children to be fully integrated in the school system.

◆

CHAPTER 7

The Children's Experiences and Perceptions of School

This chapter will look at how the children in the study perceived school and their experiences of schooling. Questionnaires were designed and administered for this purpose, followed by interviews. The formula Chi-Square was applied to test the relationship between variables. A detailed analysis has been made and variables have been cross-tabulated where necessary for analytical purposes. The children said that their careers would be determined by the level of qualifications they hoped to acquire, or their interest in a particular type of occupation. I also wanted to know how many were aiming to go to college and where possible, into higher education. This would give me an idea of how much value they place on education, and how enthusiastic they were in making use of the education system. It was hypothesised that those who have positive attitudes towards school and have the support of their teachers and their parents, would be more likely to want to pursue further education. This may not necessarily be by social class, as the area of study is traditionally a working class area.

The result of the questionnaires and the answers given at the interviews showed that the children had positive attitudes toward school. As was hypothesised, success at school was found to have a bearing on how the children perceived school. They were enthusiastic about doing well at school in order to gain some qualifications which they saw as a vital necessity in their search for work. For example as a contrast, children who play truant or show a lack of interest in their lessons are not likely to be successful at school. The reason for truancy is not quite known, but some children would put this down to boredom and a lack of interest in school work. The 'lads' in Willis' (1977) study did not see school as being of particular interest to them. Instead of fully partaking in the school's values, they rejected them and adopted their own values which made them feel worthwhile. These 'lads' were of working class backgrounds, and may have internalized certain working class values which were meaningful to them. To them, being tough is how real men should be, while the 'pen pushers' were seen as sissies. They may have adopted this type of attitude as a way of getting back at the teachers for their being too authoritarian, because they did not like the authoritarian attitude of the teachers, nor how they were treated like children. Some of the children whom I interviewed seem to think that they should be treated more like adults, or at least individuals who should be allowed to express their own views, rather than constantly being told what to do by their teachers as some of the lads expressed to Willis. Although the children in my study were also of working class background, they did not display these characteristics, but some were of the opinion that they should be treated more like adults by their teachers. In time some children do develop an anti-school attitude if they think that their teachers are not cooperative with them. They do look to their teachers to set an example for them to follow and if teachers fail to recognize this, it can lead to hostility and resentment between teachers and their pupils. This might have been the case with some Caribbean children and their teachers. If teachers fail to recognize their true potential they may not get the help and attention they may need in order to develop their personalities and attitudes towards school and society as a whole. If children feel that the schools have failed them, they are more likely to develop anti-school attitudes, rather than those who see the school as providing them with the skills and knowledge that will help them later on in life. It is the duty of the school to provide pastoral care for their pupils, and to help them to overcome any difficulties that they may be undergoing during their adolescence. If their confidence in themselves and the school is dampened because of uncaring teachers, they will react in ways which they think will protect them against other uncertainties by becoming hostile to school.

The children in my study did not have those types of attitudes, but they were eager to do well at school, with the hope that by getting a good education, it will help them to get better jobs. Even though Stoke is heavily industrialized, this did not deter the children from believing that qualifications are important, and that it can enhance their job prospects. Caribbean and white children seem to have similar aspirations in that they go in for the type of occupations to commensurate with the types of qualifications that they hoped to acquire. The Asian boys were somewhat different in their outlook. Although they were mainly of Pakistani origin and from working class backgrounds, and some of the fathers were unemployed through redundancy, some still aspired to go into the higher professions. Their determination seemed overwhelming, in that they did not seem likely to be deterred by anything other than if they got low examination grades. Whereas the Asian girls just either wanted to get a job locally, or were unsure of what they really wanted to do. This was probably due to restrictions within the home which do not affect the Asian boys in the same way. Caribbean girls had positive ideas and wanted to go into computing, secretarial, nursing or social work. Overwhelmingly, this seems to be in line with traditionally female occupations, but none of them wanted to go into the factories like their parents did. This is a vast improvement in that they were not prepared to settle for the menial type of jobs that was available to migrants in the 1950s-60s. Caribbean boys were a little less sure about what was available to them, and this was probably to do with the fact that Caribbean boys may not get the type of help that they need from their teachers. But they said that their examination results would help them to decide their future occupations. The following tables will give an indication of those children who said that they wanted to continue further and higher education.

No. of pupils who were aiming to go into
Higher Occupations for schools A, B, C, and D.

Table 7
School A

	Whites	Asians	Caribbeans	Total
Males	0	3	0	3
Females	1	1	0	2
Total (N)	1	4	0	5

Table 8
School B

	Whites	Asians	Caribbeans	Total
Males	1	1	1	3
Females	2	1	1	4
Total (N)	3	2	2	7

Table 9
School C

	Whites	Asians	Caribbeans	Total
Males	1	3	0	4
Females	0	0	0	0
Total (N)	1	3	0	4

Table 10
School D

	Whites	Asians	Caribbeans	Total
Males	0	5	3	8
Females	0	0	0	0
Total (N)	0	5	3	8

Table 11
Overall total for each group

	Whites	Asians	Caribbeans	Total
Males	2	12	4	18
	(11.1%)	(66.7%)	(22.2%)	(100%)
Females	3	2	1	6
	(50%)	(33.3%)	(16.6%)	(100%)
Total (N)	5	14	5	24
	(20.8%)	(58.3%)	(20.8%)	(100%)

Expected Occupation of Respondents

The result of the data showed that Asian boys were more likely to want to go into the professions. Out of a total of 24 pupils who wanted to choose a professional career, Asian males were the most prominent group that accounted for 66.7%, followed by Caribbean males 22.2%, and white males accounting for 11.1%. White females took precedence over other groups accounting for 50%, 16.6% Caribbeans, and Asian females, 33.3%. The discrepancies can be explained in a number of ways eg. In some cases there were no Caribbean pupils that were representative of the sample, as in some cases there were none in some schools. Some Asian girls tended not to pursue further and higher education due in part to cultural and religious reasons, and family loyalty. Traditionally, after they leave school some get married, some go to work locally, while others remain at home to help with the younger siblings and housework or help with their parents business. But there was an Asian girl age 15 who said that she wanted to be a nursery teacher. When I asked her why, she said she's got a little nephew and she likes looking after him because he makes her laugh. Having had the experience of looking after a young nephew who she found to be amusing may have inspired her to want to choose a career in looking after young children.

Q Will you be going to college to do a course in nursery teaching?

A No.

Q Why?

A I don't really like school that much.

Q How are you going to qualify as a nursery teacher?

A I do childcare as one of my subjects, so I hope that will help.

Q What do your parents think about this?

A They say it is alright.

We discussed the subjects which she was taking, and whether or not they included science subjects. She said that she did a general combined science including biology but nothing like physics or chemistry as she didn't like those subjects. I asked her if many girls were taking up science. She said the number was still very small, and girls still seemed to opt for things like cooking, sewing, and things like that, because they are meant to do cooking, aren't they? I asked her if that was what she believed. She said yes, because that is what girls want to do and they are expected to do so. I discovered that many Asian girls are still of the opinion that it is alright for women to stay at home and do the housework and look after the children. Based on those expectations, they may find it difficult to want to do anything different to what they are already accustomed. They think that women should stay at home and take care of the housework and family. Many women today still think along those lines. I asked her if her parents visited the school to discuss her progress with the teachers. She said, not really, because it is too far and they usually stay in to look after the smaller children. When asked whether or not she went out a lot, she said no, she liked to stay home and watch TV. The boys have much more free time, but she didn't mind staying at home. On the whole girls tend to be more home-centred than boys, and as a result some may want to go out less.

Another Asian girl aged 15 said she wanted to be a business woman. When asked why, she said that the family owns several businesses. She has also done some training in manufacturing and retail at school and likes it very much, and that is why she wanted to continue in the field of business. It is also the case that there was not likely to be any conflict between herself and her parents because she was not expected to go away to college to pursue her career, an idea that many Asian parents are against. As she would be joining the family business it was greatly approved by her parents. She said that in time she would get married to someone chosen for her by her parents which is the custom which they are used to.

Q Will you be going to college to do further training in business management?

A I don't know because for us Asian girls it's difficult for us to go to college and a lot depends on what my father decides.

Q Do you think he will change his mind later?

A When the time comes he might, but he won't let me go to a further education college, because he says he has seen the state of girls there, and he definitely would not let me go to one.

Q What about a sixth form college, would he send you to one?

A I don't know because my cousin went there and left after a few weeks because of her father, and she was quite good. It can be hard for Asian girls. Boys have much more freedom. Girls get married fairly quickly, and the husbands don't allow their wives certain freedom, that's how things work for us. But I told my father that I won't get married quickly, and he seems to understand. I used to find it hard to take at the beginning, but I got used to it, like father deciding most things for us.

The above statement shows that many Asian girls seem to be under some restraint in not being able to choose for themselves what they want to do especially in furthering their education. I was told that many Asian girls have wasted their talents in this way, by not being allowed to go to college to take up a career. Although it is now understood that some Asian parents are now allowing their daughters to take up some form of further education, it would appear that the majority are still confined in the home where their parents make the decisions for them. Caribbean girls are much freer to chose what they want to do, although very often their parents help them to make their decisions, but this is not enforced upon them. When I asked the pupil about her relationship with her teachers, she said that it was very good and the teachers were very nice to her and they explained things if she did not understand. She was taking a mixture of CSEs and O level examinations. This pupil appeared to be very intelligent and had a clear idea of what she wanted to do. Could this be one of the reasons why she got a lot of help from her teachers? As studies have shown, and many children in my research have suggested that teachers are inclined to concentrate mainly on the bright pupils and on those taking examinations.

I am trying to establish whether or not there is a similarity between the different groups and the type of careers they intend to pursue. I am however aware that the study can only claim to show attitudes and expectations as the children saw it, and not the actual behaviour of the different groups involved, due to the conditions under which the study was carried out, i.e. in a classroom setting. Under normal circumstances they may have been freer to express their views, and to talk more freely, but although they seemed relaxed and at ease, maybe they had deep underlying feelings of anyone else other than the researcher getting hold of what they had to say, even though they were assured that everything they said would be confidential. Those ex-pupils whom I interviewed who had already left school, seemed more open and relaxed, because they knew that there would be no repercussions on their part, so they spoke with a more open mind and said what they wanted to say.

The result of the test showed that there was no difference between the groups and future career prospects. The pupils tend to choose their particular careers to commensurate with their abilities, and depending on whether their examination grades were good. Many were still undecided about the type of career they would choose until they got their examination results. If they got good grades at O level, many were planning to go on to college to do A levels and possibly to university. If the grades were not so good, many were planning to go to college to re-take their O levels. This confirms the importance pupils are now placing on examination qualifications.

Information about College

Chi-Square test was used to determine where pupils got their information about college. I wanted to know who was the most helpful in giving advice to pupils. Was it the teachers, parents, careers advisers, or was it from advertisement. Most of the pupils who answered that question said that the school supplied the most information about college. It appeared that the parents gave very little help on this. Only 3 out of the 60 who answered said that the home supplied them with information about college. A further 4 did not answer. Careers advisers seemed to be the next most helpful as 21 pupils suggested, while 2 said advertisements. According to the results, it could well be that parents have very little knowledge about the various stages of their children's education. Could it be that some parents are not very familiar with the education system, and therefore leave their children's progress to the teachers who they see as the experts, whilst they keep a low profile on the matter. This is the case with most Caribbean parents, and it would appear that some working class parents are in a similar situation. Some of the pupils admitted that their parents visited the school only on open evenings, while a few did not bother at all. But all the Caribbean parents visited at least once a year.

Taking into account the fact that the open evening is only once a year when parents are allowed to look around the classrooms at their children's work and other exhibitions, this might leave very little time for them to have a good discussion with the teachers. They may as a result leave the school thinking that all is well and their children are doing fine without actually thinking about their future careers. As Douglas (1964) noticed, middle class parents take an active interest in visiting their children's school whenever it is necessary to talk to the heads and teachers, so that they can be kept up to date with their children's progress. It is also a middle class philosophy to plan for the future of their children, which is done well in advance. I have tried not to discuss class in detail, as it is not the main theme of the study, but neither can it be omitted, because of the structure of society and the hierarchical divisions in terms of wealth, education, income, background and power.

Haralambos and Heald (1980 p209) pointed out that teachers have tremendous power in awarding grades and assessing students, and we need to look at the procedures that guides these processes. As Becker discovered in a study conducted at a Chicago high school, teachers tend to classify and evaluate students in terms of the ideal pupil. Those pupils who are closest to this ideal, are from non-manual backgrounds. Those from the lower working class origins are farthest from this ideal. Their behaviour may be perceived by teachers as a lack of interest and motivation, uncontrollable and unrestrained. By drawing such inferences, there is the likelihood of conflict and misunderstanding which reduces the chances of effective interaction between teachers and some lower class groups. Cicourel and Kituse investigated the effects of counsellors in order to gain an understanding in their role in allocating students on courses in preparation for college entry. They found that although grades and IQ tests were claimed to be the main deciding factors, the students social classes were the most important influence on the way the evaluation was done. Even when students from different social class backgrounds were found to have similar academic records, those from middle and upper class backgrounds were perceived by counsellors as natural college prospects, and would be placed on higher level courses. These findings merely reflect the effects of power and social class backgrounds on the academic achievement of pupils. The higher the educational levels of parents, the more likely they are to keep in close contact with the school and to exploit the availability of scarce resources. This idea has not yet filtered through to many working class parents, and as a result, they are unable to take full advantage of the education system. There is now a variety of courses at colleges, which allow school-leavers to go on courses which are not based specifically on academic qualifications, but provide some work experience which act as a preliminary base when school-leavers go to seek employment.

Table 12

Do you expect to go to college?

	Yes	No	Don't know	Total
Girls	20	12	1	33
	60.6%	36.3%	3%	100%
Boys	13	11	1	25
	52%	44%	4%	100%
Total (N)	33	23	2	58

Table 13

Where did you get information about colleges?

	School	Home	Careers Adv.	Advert	Total
Girls	20	1	11	0	32
	62.5%	3.1%	34.3%	0.0%	100%
Boys	11	2	10	1	24
	45.8.%	8.3%	41.6%	4%	100%
Total (N)	31	3	21	1	56

When Chi-Square was calculated to determine whether or not more middle class children went on to college than working class children, it showed that there was no difference between class background and those children intending to go college. It would be expected that more children from middle class background were intending to go on to college, but there was no correlation when the test was applied. An explanation would probably be that the area of study is almost predominantly working class, so the number of middle class children would be very small. The sample would have to be representative of both classes before this could be determined.

Table 14

Do you think that more middle class children go on to college than working class children?

	Yes	No	Total
Girls	14	18	32
	43.7%	56.2%	100%
Boys	10	15	25
	40%	60%	100%
Total (N)	24	33	57

Of the questionnaires 3 were missing values. The result of the remaining 57 with 1 (d.f.) when chi-square was calculated was 0.7760. A figure as high as that suggests that there is no correlation between children who expect to go to college and class background. This was the children's perception of the situation. According to their parents occupations which were mainly manual work, there were hardly any whose parents were in white collar jobs. Therefore there would be too few middle class children in the sample to validate such statements. But on the whole, it would appear that due to the current recession, it is more difficult to obtain jobs, and this situation has forced many young people to continue their education rather than to seek work. Many youngsters are now attending college who might otherwise have gone to work. On offer at colleges are a number of courses, many of which are non-academic, and can be pursued as leisure courses, or to gain work experience. Howle for the Evening Sentinel (18.9.91) reported that more teenagers are now staying on in further education in Staffordshire than ever before. He found that over 52% of 16 year-olds carried on their education compared to 44% in 1983. Mike Tappin of the County Economic Development suggested that this was a great improvement as when he came to the county in 1974, he was shocked to discover that only 29% in Stoke-on-Trent stayed on in further education. He suggested that this figure is now around 40% which was encouraging to know that attitudes towards education and training were gradually changing.

Class was used as a variable to determine the type of exams that students sat, eg. whether it was GCE, CSE or none. When the test was applied there was no significance. But according to the calculated results, there was some variation between examination by class, and examination by sex. There were 52% girls and 47% boys taking GCE, while 37% girls and 62% boys were taking CSEs. On the other hand, when calculated by sex, there were 70.6% girls, and 29.4% boys taking GCE, while 51.4% girls and 48.6% boys were taking CSE. Table 15 shows the result of the type of exam the pupils were expecting to take.

Table 15

What type of exams will you be taking?

	GCE	CSE	None	Total
Girls	9	13	1	23
	39.1%	56.5%	4.3%	100%
Boys	8	22	3	33
	24.2%	66.6%	9.0%	100%
Total (N)	17	35	4	56

The figures in table 15 are the result of Chi-Square calculated when class was used as a variable, and how the children answered the question. The table shows that some bias may exist within the schools whereby teachers treat pupils differently in terms of gender and class, which can be seen in the type of exams they take. It could well be that girls are naturally brighter or work harder, in which case they would get favoured into taking O level examinations as teachers can use their influence in determining who takes what type of examinations. Chi-Square was used to determine whether or not performance at school was linked to home background. The result showed that there was a direct correlation between performance and home background. With 2 d.f. there was a significance level of 0.01 which signifies that if the survey was carried out for the whole of the population, it would be at the 99 per cent confidence limit.

Chi-Square was used to determine who had the most influence on pupils over their choice of careers. It was discovered that parents had the most influence over career choices. This was at the 97% confidence limit. It is well documented that in homes where parents take an interest in their children's school work, they are more likely to succeed at school. The children in the interviews said that if their parents advised and encouraged them, they tended to work better than if no advice was given by their parents. We could therefore say that there is a link between performance at school and the amount of help that they get at home from their parents. It could therefore be concluded that children from middle class homes are more likely to succeed at school compared to working class children who may possess similar ability but may not get the same amount of help at home. They are therefore at a disadvantage, because they cannot successfully compete with children from more affluent home backgrounds. This may be so as children who go to school with early reading and writing skills always have a head start over and above those without those skills. Many teachers have suggested that this is the case because they do not have the same starting and finishing points in the education system as children from affluent homes. Middle class children can choose from a variety of options such as private schools, independent and boarding schools.

The availability of private schooling is denied to or is beyond the means of most working class children. The parents cannot afford to buy the type of education that they would like for their children. I interviewed two Caribbean families who sent their children to private schools. Everything was fine when they could afford the fees, but as the fees started to escalate, they could no longer afford to pay and had to withdraw the children and send them to state schools. I asked them why did they choose private education when there were some good state schools that offered free education. They said that at private schools the classes are smaller and the children get more individual attention which enhanced their learning ability. The parents also hoped that private schools would provide an avenue for the children on the job market. The fact that they had to withdraw their children due to economic circumstances, is an indication that even if more working class parents wanted to educate their children privately, the fees would be beyond their means. We could say that one of the disadvantages in education is the inability of many lower class parents to buy the type of education that they would like their children to have.

I interviewed a black student of Caribbean origin who received private education. Both of her parents were teachers and offered her tremendous support without which she said she would not have made it through the education system. She said that when her mother tried to get her into the local primary school the headmistress told her that she would send her a letter of acceptance, but she did not write to her mother as she said she would. So her mother decided to send her to a public school instead. She said that she experienced discrimination in a variety of ways. She did a joint project with a white pupil and the white pupil got higher marks than she did. When it was time for them to take the 11 plus exams, about half the total number of pupils failed including herself. Several of the children appealed and won, but she lost her appeal, even though some of those who won were not as bright as she was. Her mother was by now annoyed and sent her to another private school. At this school she achieved eight O levels, while some of those who had won their appeal at 11 plus, only achieved between four to six passes, and some gained none at all. Her English and Maths teachers tried to discourage her from taking those subjects because they did not think she could cope with them. She insisted on doing them and passed the exams. If the other girls did extra homework the headmistress would mark it but if she did any it would not get marked. She said that when she did her A level music, she was often ridiculed by the teacher who often shouted at her and made her feel like a dunce. She said she would often go home in tears and wanted to give up music but her parents decided to pay five pounds per week for extra tuition which enabled her to continue. Some of the girls were rather unfriendly towards her and often talked about primitive tribes in Africa. She said she wanted to be a lawyer, but her teachers tried to encourage her to do psychology instead. Her parents insisted that she did a law degree in which she was successful.

After assessing the experiences of Caribbean students in educational institutions and others not here mentioned, there is no doubt that most British institutions do foster institutionalized racism. This can be linked to 19th century European literature and the ideologies which were accepted as the correct forms of teaching and learning processes. As Foster Carter et al argued in 'Sociology New Directions' (1985), in Britain it is hardly likely that racial prejudice is exclusively the property of a few bigots. We have to look at the culture and history of that society, and see how the media transmits negative racial stereotypes (T. Bilton et al: p43). The authors went on to argue that prejudice then became enshrined within popular cultural traditions and the dominant social institutions. These institutions then transmit mistaken notions about the attributes and capabilities of other racial groups. It then becomes difficult for individuals so enmeshed with those ideas to think otherwise.

Several ex-black pupils told me that in the past, careers advisers tended to divert them from their intended career choices to something much lower than their capabilities. Because of such misguided effort on the part of some careers advisers, black students who have successfully made it through the system have emphasized the fact that it is very important for parents to take an active role in helping their children through the education system, otherwise they would not have made it. They stressed that if parents do not become involved, it is likely that many black children will become disillusioned and grow up to be dissatisfied adults in a society where black minorities face much greater problems than the white indigenous people. The students' own experiences show that whether black children attend public, private or state schools, they are likely to encounter some form of racial discrimination, whether it be from the staff or fellow students. I spoke to another black female student who was from Africa. Her father was a doctor and she had done most of her schooling in Europe. She was at college doing her A levels after gaining 9 O levels. She said that some of the lecturers were somewhat hostile towards her, and some of the girls were very unfriendly. Racism would seem to be a problem throughout European societies. But most of the indigenous people seem to think that it is correct in all its forms, and there is nothing to be rectified. I must however add that it is not just black people who face racial discrimination in the education system. Jews, Gypsies, Italians etc are likely to be singled out, partly because they are seen as different. According to the media reports, Italian children at school are told by other school mates to 'go home'. Gypsies are teased on a regular basis and called terrible names too. But black pupils are particularly vulnerable, because their physical characteristics do not allow them to take on any form of disguise, and hence they become especially susceptible to misguided forms of discrimination. Although physical features are not the only types of racial discrimination, it does play a major role, due to 19th century ideologies about the baseness of blackness, and the stigma attached to being black. This has meant that many people will try and avoid using the term black to describe themselves, because it is a European terminology that was created to discredit the black races to make them feel inferior.

Interaction in the Home

Chi-Square was used to determine the amount of conversation between parents and children in the home.

Table 16

Do you talk to your parents?

	Often	Not often	Never	Total
Girls	22	9	0	31
	71.0%	29.0%	0.0%	100%
Boys	11	16	1	28
	39.2%	57.1%	3.6%	100%
Total (N)	33	25	1	59

Chi-Square calculated with 2 (d.f.), showed a significance level of 0.03. This is at the confidence limit of 97%, and would have been representative if the sample was taken for the entire population. Statistically, the table shows that more girls than boys converse with their parents in the home and account for 71.0% compared to 39.2% of boys. To a lesser extent, 57.1% of boys and 29.% of girls have fewer conversation with their parents. Only one boy did not seem to have any form of conversation in the home. According to the results of Chi-square calculated, orientation to school is closely linked with the amount of interaction that takes place in the home. Where conversation is frequent in the home, those children are more likely to succeed at school because their parents will have a much clearer idea of what they want to do and how to go about helping them in their choice of careers. Crooks points out in Black Sportsmen by Cashmore, that for many Caribbean parents, "children are to be seen and not heard", a saying that many parents were brought up believing themselves. They tried to instil those same values in their children without realizing that societies were rapidly changing, and that children were after all individuals in their own rights. He suggested that some parents don't listen to what the children say about the classroom. You can read books, study hard, and work hard, but don't hold any arguments with your parents, they can be very strict. But parental guide can take different forms. Probably, by sending their children to school regularly, buying their uniform, making sure they wear clean clothes, some parents may think that they are encouraging their children in that way. Having done their part, they may be of the opinion that teachers should play their role by educating their children in the best possible way. Teachers on the other hand may think that Caribbean parents are not doing enough, so why should they bother if the parents do not care? This kind of silent interaction could lead to all sorts of unforeseen problems in schools. A Caribbean boy whom I interviewed said that no matter how good his grades were, his father's reply would be, "you will have to do better next time." The father did not take the time to listen and then give his opinion. This is why it is important for parents to listen to their children before making remarks which may discourage them. The boy said that he had a lot of encouragement from the headmaster which helped him tremendously. This shows how a lack of proper interaction between parents, children and the school can lead to confusion and conflict in the home and at school. Crooks suggested that the gap between parents, children and teachers are responsible for some of the problems facing some Caribbean children. But he has failed to point out that such gaps can also exist between black or white pupils and their parents and teachers, and that teachers could do more to involve Caribbean parents in the schools. In the past, many failed to do so, as they may have thought that black parents were incapable of helping with their children's schoolwork.

Many researchers have discovered that teachers tend to assess pupils in different categories in terms of the ideal pupil, the well dressed pupil, the well behaved etc., and on those premises base their judgements and opinions about them. Sharpe and Green (1975, p70) looked at the perspective some teachers hold of their pupils. They spoke of a Mrs. Carpenter whose view of some of her pupils were that they were thick, disturbed, insecure and probably of low intelligence and achievement potential. Out of a class of 36 pupils the teacher felt that only 3 were normal in terms of social and emotional adjustment, and were achieving up to and beyond her expectations. On that basis her pupils were sorted, assessed and categorised. She blamed the home for offering little in the way of encouragement. Hence she held a low expectation for their future and welfare. Lacey (1977) found that teachers take certain attitudes with them to the classroom on which they base their interpretation of particular pupils as soon as they came into contact with them. Some of the white pupils whom I interviewed said that middle class and the brighter children always seem to get more attention from teachers. As a result the less bright ones who really need help may be left to struggle on their own, in which case they may come to dislike schools for not offering them support. Some said that they found some subjects boring because the teachers do not try to make them interesting, and so they found understanding and partaking in those lessons difficult.

In Principles of Teaching Method, A. Pincent (1969, p534) suggested that part of effective teaching conduct is that teachers should establish a vital personal contact with their pupils. This would create a form of community feeling and interest between teacher and pupil. He suggested that this aspect of social contact is the foundation for good motivation. It will inspire in the pupil the will to work hard and to succeed. But according to some of the pupils whom I interviewed this was not the case. When asked on the questionnaire, "Could teachers be more helpful to their pupils." And if the answer was yes, What could be done: Out of 60 questionnaires, 41 said yes, teachers could be more helpful to their pupils and explain things to them better. It would appear that teachers expect children to be able to understand difficult concepts without giving them any help for clarity. This shows that teachers are not aware that they could try to understand their pupils better and help them more where necessary. As Pinsent argued, teachers should maintain effective intellectual contact with their pupils which includes the following:

1. Being aware of their degree of maturity and general intelligence.
2. Knowing about their aptitudes and interests.
3. Being aware of their mental background and their intellectual difficulties.
4. Having a knowledge of their immediate local environment, and cultural factors relating to this.

Pinsent stated that teachers should infer their pupils state of mind and difficulties they may have in understanding certain concepts. It would assume that this is something that teachers do not take into consideration. Many ex-pupils told me that if they asked the teacher to explain something that they did not understand, they would be ignored and would be afraid to ask any further questions. Those are the children who are likely to become withdrawn from the lessons without further participation. It has been well documented that teacher expectation can have positive effects on children's behaviour and learning abilities. H. Miller in Social Foundations of Education (1978, p270) argued that in the USA the impact of the teacher involves much more subtle variables than those ordinarily studied. He suggested that the most popular explanation is the achievement differences between white middle class students and those from lower class minority groups which is manifested in the hypothesis of the 'self-fulfilling prophesy' or the 'pigmalion effect'. He asserts that teachers prophesying low achievement levels for minority pupils actively help them to underachieve by communicating to them a sense of inevitable failure. Brophy and Good in H. Miller, discovered during their study on teacher behaviour that teachers paid more attention to, and interacted more with high expectancy students. They found that these students were praised more often for correct answers and criticised less for incorrect answers. They were also given more cues to help find the correct answers to a problem. The authors conducted another study of nine classrooms and found no such behaviour in teacher attitude. But in fact they compensated by more frequently interacting with the lower ability range by initiating work related roles with them. (H. Miller: p275). He argued that unless theorists can establish whether or not there is a link between the way teachers interact and behave with different students from whom they expect good or bad performance, there might be a danger that self-fulfilling prophesy hypothesis might fall apart. This was said in relation to controversies that emerged after the Rosenthal and Jacobson's study in 1968, (in H. Miller: p274) when they handed teachers lists of children chosen at random whom they predicted would make progress during the school year. At the end of the year they found that the IQ scores of the younger pupils had improved, but not that of the older ones as they predicted. The study provoked severe criticisms, and most similar attempts at such a replication in the USA had failed.

Some studies in Britain tend to support the view that interaction between teacher and pupil will determine how well pupils do at school. In the case of Caribbean pupils, especially in the early 1960s, it could be assumed that because of previous stereotypes and a lack of previous contact with black children, most teachers would have negative views of black pupils. As Taylor (1981, p195) pointed out, the situation regarding Caribbean children is a complex one. As well as teacher expectation, there is also a question of teacher attitude in general toward minority pupils. According to Taylor this area of study has been little explored in this country when compared to the USA probably because of its sensitivity, and the idea surrounding the issue that there is no need for this kind of research in Britain. The local authorities may not have realised that some teachers may have been racist and could have extended prejudiced attitudes towards black children.

A study carried out by Allen and Smith (1975) was designed to test teacher attitudes and opinions on the academic and social behaviour of Caribbean children. 510 teachers in 25 primary and secondary schools were consulted. The result showed that most teachers strongly indicated unfavourable opinions against Caribbean pupils. Taylor (1983, p195) suggested that some of the comments they made on the questionnaires also indicated large scale stereotyping of Caribbean pupils. Tomlinson (1979) also found evidence of stereotyping of Caribbean pupils by teachers who were interviewed in connection with an ESN assessment. They elaborated at great length about Caribbean pupils and often had generalized views about them that their learning processes were slower than for Asians and other groups. During my research one of the questions that the pupils answered on the questionnaire and interviews were as follows:

Table 17

Do you think that the learning process for Caribbean children is slower than that of other children?

	Yes	No	Total
Girls	2	26	28
	7.1%	93%	100%
Boys	6	11	17
	35.2%	65%	100%
Total (N)	8	37	45

The response rate was low for this particular question. Perhaps it could be contributed to the fact that not all the children managed to complete the questionnaire due to the time in which they had to fill them in. Some white children may also not have been in any class with Caribbean children, due to their small numbers in school locally, and so could not have responded. Some of the children in the interviews said that they had not been in any classes with Caribbean children, and for that reason they either answered as best as they could, or said that they could not comment. The majority of the children said no, they did not perceive Caribbean children as slower learners than other children. As they saw it, they were just as capable as anyone else. Out of 60 questionnaires, 45 answered as follows: 26 girls and 11 boys said no, against 2 girls and 6 boys who said yes. The result showed that there were still some negative attitudes amongst some white pupils as to how they perceive Caribbean children as academically incapable though this number was very small. It would appear that this belief has a long history in the colonization of blacks as former colonial subjects, and the ruled. It has been mentioned by J. Rex that this could have been the case.

Although these topics are rarely mentioned by sociologists, several studies of this kind have been carried out in the USA in relation to the explanation of poor blacks in ghettoized areas. These topics are more widely studied in the USA partly due to their openness in addressing certain issues, while in Britain it is thought that if certain problems such as racism is ignored it will simply go away. Such racist practices are more covert in Britain, but at the same time very effective in their outcome. Rex and Moore (1974) carried out research on the issue of race relations, and the problems facing blacks in Britain, but they have simply emphasized the fact that blacks are seen as occupying an underclass in the metropolis. But it could now be argued that many young blacks are now establishing themselves as a new up and coming middle class. Many are not prepared to fail where their parents have failed to establish themselves as white collar workers and entrepreneurs. With greater awareness and better educational opportunities, they are making use of the available resources - but to what extent, as there are still limitations.

C. Husband and A. Phizacklea (1986) have gone into further detail about the situation facing blacks in Britain and why this should be so. They argued that the ideological significance of nationalism for members of the working class whom they interviewed, is that to many, the racialization of blacks was based on the notion that they themselves are members of a distinct and separate nation to which the 'coloureds' could never belong by virtue of their race. The authors emphasized that the presence of West Indians reminded the working class of Britain's declining world position both economically and politically. At the same time the concept of race was constantly mediated by politicians and the media which exacerbated the situation and Caribbeans and Asians became scapegoated for the decline in Britain's inability to maintain her Empire. One of Powell's controversial speeches in (1968) was:

"The West Indian or Asian does not by being born in England become an Englishman. In law he becomes a United Kingdom citizen, by birth in fact he is a West Indian or Asian still."

Husband argued that owing to the fact that Powell's (1968) speech, and Nugent and King (1972) on the National Front, and Fielding

(1981), have all made political appeal on the idea of nationalism, they received political support from the working class, which sums up the fact that this is an ideological construction which has considerable significance for the entire nation. He also suggested that since 1945 consecutive governments have made political appeal for support on the basis of the national interest and have been successful. Therefore race became an important part of working class political consciousness.

Nairn (1977) went a step further than Husband and included the English bourgeois. He stated that English nationalism can only be expressed in the negative term of race, due to the origin of the English bourgeois state and the inclusion of the working class (Husband: p293:4). Both authors have emphasized the importance of nationalism to the ideology of race. Although there are several arguments about the origin of race, it would appear to have its roots in the political and capitalist economy where blacks were either used as free or cheap labour for a prosperous economy. As soon as the economy went into decline, their labour was no longer required, hence they became scapegoated and blamed for the economic decline.

Homework and Leisure:

Homework was another significant factor when tested against orientation to school and future job prospects. The result showed a significance level of 95% that the amount of homework that pupils say they do, or the amount of time they spend on homework increased their orientation to school. They also had a clearer idea of what they want to do in the future.

Table 18

How much time do you spend on homework per week (hours)?

Hrs	1	2	3	4	5	0	Tot.
Girls	9%	36.3%	12.1%	24.2%	12.1%	6.0%	100%
Boys	8.0%	48.0%	12.0%	16.0%	4.0%	12.0%	100%
Total	5	24	7	12	5	5	58

When the test was applied it showed that there was no significance between boys and girls and the amount of homework they said they did. This would have been expected because the sexes have differing views about the amount of time spent on homework which will be manifested in the way they choose their future careers. Traditionally, boys were the ones who went on to further and higher education or apprenticeships, while girls participated in household chores, or learning a few skills to fill those roles. However that trend is now changing, and girls are now spending more time on homework than boys as the table shows. At the lower end of the scale where 1 or 2 hours is spent on homework, both sexes spend equal amount of time on homework. But as the number of hours increased, the number of girls seem to double, while that for boys remained low. From this we could say that women's participation in acquiring educational qualifications in order to pursue a career is increasing. Many girls are now realizing the importance of educational qualifications that were previously denied them.

During the interviews, some of those who said they did no homework, expressed their desire to do so if they were given any to do. But some said that their teachers did not give them any homework because this depended on the subject teacher. They thought that probably some subjects were more important, and required additional time. They were of the opinion that additional homework would help their progress. This was so for both boys and girls. On the questionnaire (v29) the children were asked if homework affected their leisure. Chi-square was used to determine whether or not there was an association between the two variables. The result showed that there was a significance. With 1 d.f. this was at the 97% confidence limit that there was an association between homework and leisure. Although most of the children said they did some homework, this was only an average of 3 hours per week, or three quarters of an hour per night. More girls than boys seemed to think that homework did not affect their leisure activities. One reason could be that boys are more accustomed to pursuing outdoor activities while girls tend to be more homecentred, and this will have a bearing on the amount of homework that each group do.

Table 19

Does homework affect your leisure time?

	Yes	No	Total
Girls	10	23	33
	30.3%	70.0%	100%
Boys	14	10	24
	58.3%	41.6%	100%
Total (N)	24	33	57

Out of 60 questionnaires there were 3 missing values, so the total who answered were 57. The next table looks at what the parents want their children to do after leaving school eg. should they go to work, carry on with their education or learn a trade. I wanted to see what their parents response was on the issue and whether or not they favoured their children furthering their education, as the children saw it.

Table 20

What do your parents consider to be the best choice for you when you leave school?

	Work	F. Ed	Trade	Total
Girls	11	20	2	33
	33.3%	60.6%	6.0%	100%
Boys	5	15	4	24
	21.0%	62.5%	17.0%	100%
Total (N)	16	35	6	57

The result showed that the majority of parents want their children to continue their education, but they were the views of the children themselves. Parents are probably aware that educational qualifications are now very important in choosing a career. 20 parents wanted their daughters to go on to further education, and 15 parents want their sons to go on to further education, while a lesser minority want them to go to work. As many parents were denied the chance of a good education, they were probably trying to allow their children to have that chance. Owing to the fact that education has now become a political issue and often makes media headlines, parents are now realizing that they have a choice and the right to choose the type of education that they want their children to have. But no matter how much this is part of a government strategy to give parents the right to choose the type of school they would like to send their children, in reality this is not necessarily the case. This is because there aren't many choices open to working class children as many parents would like. As I have heard on the media, as far as State schools are concerned, if the school of their choice do not have any accommodation left the parents have to look elsewhere. Preference can also be given to children of church going parents over those who do not attend church in the case of Church schools. As sociologists of education have discovered, education is still a class issue and is very much dominated by the middle classes. Hence, choices for many working class parents for their children are very much restricted, despite reforms to give parents a wider choice.

Anthony Heath in "In the Classroom", looks at educational changes throughout the 19th century, and discovered that class inequality has remained unchanged. He argued that there is no doubt that educational standards have risen enormously, but education is still divided by class. Heath drew from Glass's study of (1949) where it was noticed that even before the less able children of affluent parents were able to secure fee paying places at grammar schools, children of poorer parents were kept out. Halsey (1972) found that the social engineering of the 1944 Education Act had no measurable impact on class inequalities. He found that boys who were educated before the Act was enforced, were as divided by social class as those who were educated afterwards. He stated that the economically advanced classes conferred great educational advantages on their children. Thus, the gap between the classes remained constant. Even the re-organization of comprehensive schools that began in the late 1960s, but did not actually reach its height until the mid 1970s, reflected these class differences by means of catchment areas. This is in effect the division between the ex-grammar schools and secondary modern. The point I am trying to make is, that it is hardly possible for some parents to have a choice of schools, because of the hierarchical structure of society and how it operates to ensure that certain groups remain at the top.

Homework facilities in the home:

On the questionnaire (v30) children were asked whether or not they had a quiet room at home in which to do their homework. This would give me an idea of the conditions at home under which children did their homework, and whether or not they took their homework seriously.

Table 21

Have you a quiet room for homework?

	Yes	No	Total
Girls	27	7	34
	79.4%	20.5%	100%
Boys	10	13	23
	43.4%	56.5%	100%
Total (N)	37	20	57

By looking at conditions at home under which pupils work, it is my intention to establish whether or not home circumstances affected their school progress. As Douglas (1964) found that home circumstances can affect school progress, although this was linked to large families. Out of 60 questionnaires that were administered, 55 answered the question. It showed that there was evidence of association between boys and girls and the conditions under which they work at home. 79.4% of girls said they had a quiet room at home in which to do their homework, compared to 43.4% of boys. While those who said no the question was 20.5% girls, and 56.5% boys. As can be seen, less boys seem to work under quiet conditions.

An explanation could be that boys are more likely to be playing their radios, stereo, or watching TV whilst doing their homework. This shows that boys may be better able to cope in noisy conditions whilst maintaining their concentration. But it could well be the case that girls take their homework more seriously than boys, due to their determination to do well academically. They very often see themselves as being at a disadvantage by virtue of their gender. M. Fuller (1987) discovered that this was the case amongst the Caribbean girls whom she studied in London. They were determined to succeed, because they knew that the odds were stacked against them in terms of their race and gender. But as they saw it, this fatalistic view could be overcome with hard work and motivation. Those boys who were highly motivated said that they were not deterred by noise, nor did their schoolwork suffer as a result.

Gender and Expectation

As was traditionally the case, girls had a different perspective towards school. They were expected to get the minimum amount of learning from school while boys were expected to get the maximum benefit. It is also the case that working class boys were not expected to get a great deal either, as school was the preserve of the middle classes. I wanted to assess pupils attitude towards school to see if there are any differences in how boys and girls perceive school. It was hoped that on this basis I would be able to hypothesize whether or not achievement at school was related to how they perceived school. The question was:

Table 22

Do you like being at school?

	Yes	No	Total
Girls	13	20	33
	39.4%	60.6%	100%
Boys	18	6	24
	75%	25%	100%
Total (N)	31	26	57

The test showed a direct relationship between boys and girls and their attitude towards school. With 1d.f. < 0.01, was at the 99% confidence limit that the sample would have been representative if it was taken for the whole of the population. Boys appear to have a more favourable attitude towards school than girls and account for 75.0% compared to 39.4% for girls. Conversely, a far higher proportion of girls said they did not like school, and accounted for 60.6% compared to 25.0% of boys who said no. According to the result, this probably could be explained in a historical context, where traditionally boys (especially the middle classes) had greater access to schooling than girls. J. Mitchell, A. Oakley, and T. Blackstone, in "Rights and Wrongs of Women", looked at the effects of gender differentiations, which poses problems for women. They argued that more women are now dissatisfied with their roles as a reserve army of labour either as unpaid housewives or an unpaid workforce.

I decided to look at the type of subjects that girls follow, to see whether or not they are now breaking with tradition and taking up science based subjects. As it happened, many were still not following subjects such as physics and chemistry, they found them to be boring. But they mainly took biology, a subject that girls are supposed to take. The only exception was, if they were hoping to take up a career in medicine or other related fields, then science subjects would be included. Here are the views of some of the pupils at the interview, which will include boys as well as girls. An Asian girl aged 16 gave the following answers to the questions:

Q What are your views of school?

A I like it very much.

Q What type of exams will you be taking?

A 8 O levels in biology, physics, chemistry, maths, French, English language and literature, and home economics. I want to do medicine or food technology. But I haven't quite made up my mind yet. I hope to go to a sixth form college to do my A levels. I am planning on taking 4 subjects.

Q   Do you expect to go to university?

A   That will depend on my A level grades.

This student had a clear idea of what she wanted to do. She was very enthusiastic about the whole concept of schooling, and she liked everything about school. She said her parents were in the retail business, and they support her in her choice of career. Like most other parents, her parents visited the school on open evenings, but this student had no problem with her schoolwork. She said she got on well with her teachers and communication was fine between them. I asked her if she experienced any form of racism at school. She said not with the teachers, they are very kind to her, but she sometimes got teased and called names by some of the children. I asked her how does she deal with them. She said she just ignored them.

Female pupil age 15 - Caribbean origin:

This is part of the discussion that took place at the interview.

Q   Do you enjoy school?

A   Yes, very much.

Q   What subjects are you taking?

A   English, biology, maths, typing, chemistry, French and geography.

Q   What type of exams will you be taking?

A   O level and 16 plus.

Q   Will you be going to college.

A   Yes, to do a special course in hotel reception, because that is what I want to do.

Q Have you ever thought of going to a polytechnic or university?

A No, but my brother is at one, and my parents wouldn't mind, but I don't know yet.

Q Do you talk to your parents about what you would like to do?

A Yes, they encourage me a lot. They say its best to carry on with my education because jobs are scarce.

Q Have you experienced racism in school?

A Yes.

Q By Whom?

A Not the teachers, it's the children.

Q What do they do?

A They call you wog and nigger.

Q What do you say to them?

A Sometimes I ignore then, sometimes I hit them.

Q Are the teachers helpful?

A Most of them are alright and helpful.

Many of the children said that they did not find the teachers to be overtly racist. They said that most of them were helpful. But it should be noted that in some classes there was only one black child, which meant that it would be unlikely that any teacher would display racist behaviour. As previously mentioned, where there are large numbers of Caribbean children, they are more likely to attract teacher stereotyping because they are more visible. A white girl said that this may not happen in her class, but she has heard that in some classes the teachers just concentrate on the brighter children, or the middle class ones. Several studies have shown this to be so. It would therefore appear that teachers treat children on the basis of what they see as the ideal pupil, by paying the most attention to middle class or the brighter ones who really need less help. While the less bright ones who might be willing to try hard do not get the same level of attention, and as a result will benefit less from their schooling. This is because they have to struggle harder to try to overcome the difficult hurdles that lay ahead, but without much success, as they may not get the help that they need. Many Caribbean children suffer this type of disadvantage and as a result they cannot make the kind of progress that they would like to make whilst at school. The help of the teacher is vital to the development and well-being of their pupils, and if they are denied this help it is likely to lead to disappointment and failure, and possibly their resentment of school. Nash (1973, p30) in Classrooms Observed, suggested that children modify their behaviour in response to the way they are perceived by their teachers eg. If the teacher regard work to be above the pupil, s/he will not make it, and likewise if the pupil believe s/he is capable of little, will have low expectations of themselves and achieve little. He argued that the essential cultural messages of the school are conveyed through a number of interactions between teacher and pupil, and this interaction process has everything to do with the child's status, self-esteem and future aspirations. Teacher perceptions also shape the child's behaviour and learning ability.

Female age 15 - Caribbean origin:

This student wanted to do either secretarial work or drama, but could not quite decide what to do. Although she liked school very much, she said she was not very good at maths, but she was quite good at commerce, business and typing. She said that after she had decided what she does best, she would proceed from there.

Q   Do you enjoy school?

A   Yes, very much.

Q   Are you taking any science subjects such as physics and chemistry?

A   No, but I am quite good at computers. I like it, and later there will be a lot of jobs going in computers.

Q What type of exams will you be taking?

A CSEs likely.

Q Will you be going to college?

A Yes.

Q How much help do you get from your parents?

A They help me a lot.

Q Have you experienced racism in schools?

A I used to get called names by the children, but not so much now.

Q How do you find the teachers?

A They are alright. They help me a lot.

As previously mentioned, pupils tend to choose their careers based on their abilities. This student was expecting to take CSEs, but considered this to be within her scope. She was not aiming for the impossible, but something which she thought was manageable to her.

Male age 14 - Caribbean origin:

Although it was too early to choose a career, this pupil knew that he wanted to do something in engineering. He said that although it was not definite, he was thinking of joining the Royal Air Force probably as a ground staff.

Q Do you like school?

A Yes, I enjoy it.

Q What type of subjects are you taking?

A Physics, chemistry, maths, history, RE, PE, woodwork and graphics.

Q What type of exams will you be taking?

A It might be GCE, but the teachers have not quite decided yet, because by then it might be the new GCSE.

Q Any CSEs?

A No.

Q How do you find your teachers?

A They will help you in some subjects, but it depends on how large the class is.

Q Have you experienced racism in schools?

A Some of the children are. You get a few name calling such as coon or nigger.

Q How do you respond to them?

A I just ignore them.

Q Are the teachers aware of this?

A Well some say if they hear of any name calling, they will deal with those responsible, even if its just to be called fat.

Q Have you thought of going to university or polytechnic?

A I think I would be out of place. I don't think I would fit in. After college I think I would have achieved enough, or maybe I would have to know more about universities.

Some of the answers from this pupil would suggest that many working class parents were not aware of the complex stages of education, and how to guide their children successfully through them. There is a need for parents to have more knowledge about the education system, so that they can fully partake in their children's education. In the TV Documentary 28 UP, middle class children at the age of seven knew which boarding school they would attend, and were aware of the importance of going to university. At the same time many of the working class children had their sights set on particular jobs when they left school. This pupil said that he was quite pleased with his work and found that the teachers encouraged him a lot. He also got a great deal of encouragement from his parents. He usually got from grade A to C plus for his work, and his teachers were pleased with such good standards. The teachers always told the children not to be influenced by anyone else, they should be their own selves, and he found that to be encouraging.

Female age 16 - White:

This student said that she wanted to join the police force. When I asked her why, she said that it looks interesting, and she likes helping people. She thought about going to college, but then discovered that she did not need A levels because in the police force they have their own training schemes. Was she trying to avoid taking her A levels? She said not really, it was just that as she did not need them so it wouldn't be wise spending time taking them.

Q Do you like being at school?

A Yes.

Q What type of exams will you be taking?

A O level history and geography, and CSE English, French and maths.

Q Are you taking any science subjects?

A Biology.

Q Why not chemistry and physics.

A I've failed both exams, and I didn't like the subjects very much.

Q Who influences you most in your choice of career, teachers, friends or parents?

A Parents.

Q Do you talk them often?

A Yes, they help me a great deal.

Q   Do you think there is racism in school?

A   No.

Q   Are children treated differently in school?

A   Yes.

Q   Who are the ones that are treated different?

A   Mainly middle class ones but not in my class. But I've heard that in some classes the teachers just concentrate on the ones in the upper classes, and are not interested in the others.

As can be seen from the interview, there seems to be some element of class differences that operates within the schools as could be expected. Quite a few pupils have commented on this. For this we need to look at teacher perspectives and the expectation they hold of their pupils. The ones who are favoured usually do well, while those who are less favoured, are usually the losers. Until teachers change those attitudes and treat all children the same regardless of their backgrounds or origins, there will always be winners and losers, because some children will be bound to fail at school.

Male age 16 - White:

This pupil did not seem to like school very much, although he was not very keen to leave either. He saw school as being alright, but he was eager to move on to do something else. He was not very academically oriented, and this could have been the reason why he thought it was time for him to leave school.

Q   Do you like being at school?

A   It's alright.

Q   What do you mean?

A   School is alright but I am looking forward to leaving because I think I have had enough schooling.

Q Are you eager to earn your own money?

A I would like to earn my own money, but that's not the main reason. I just want to do something else.

Q Are you taking any exams?

A Yes two CSEs and one City and Guilds.

Q Why aren't you taking any more?

A I didn't do very well in my mock exams. I moved up one class and they expect you to catch up on two years work.

Q What type of work will you be doing when you leave school?

A Painting and decorating or something to do with construction work.

Q How did you choose that particular type of occupation?

A When I did my option I did City and Guilds Construction at college and I found it to be alright, so I decided to do something in that particular line of work.

Q What is your relationship with your teachers?

A Good, especially our careers advice teacher, but I get on with most of them.

Q Why don't you get on with the others?

A Well if there is something I don't know and I ask a particular one, he will say "shut up" and things like that. If you are taking the exam he will help you, but if you are not he will say, 'Well you are not taking the exam'.

It must be rather irritating if a child shows enough interest in a lesson, and asks a question which he does not know, and the teacher tells him to shut up. That will deter him and maybe other children from asking further questions. So as a result, they go through school not knowing something that they really wanted to know. Of course teachers or anyone else are not expected to have an answer for everything, but at least let the child know.

I wanted to see why some children want to leave school, rather than going on to further education. It would appear that the ones who are not academically oriented, are more likely to want to leave school so that they can do something different. This pupil said that he had failed his mock exams, in which case he did not feel capable of carrying on with his schooling. I asked him if his wanting to earn his own money was a factor. He said that money was not a factor why he did not want to carry on, because he had had enough schooling and wanted to do something different. Choice seems very important for some teenagers, in that if they do not consider something to be worthwhile pursuing, they would rather do something that is interesting to them. His parents supported this idea, and wanted him to do what suited him best. I asked him if he had any friends of Caribbean origin. He said yes, there was one at school with whom he played football. He has recently left but will be returning to school to take his exams in maths, English and some others. I asked him if he thought that Caribbean pupils work hard enough at school, and he said they work the same as white kids do, and there was no difference with them academically.

Male age 15 - Asian:

This student was aiming for a career in the medical field either as a doctor or a chemist, but was still undecided which he would opt for. Although he was hoping to do well in his exams, there was still a hint of uncertainty that if the grades were not good enough, this might be a drawback in his choice of career which he hoped very much to pursue. But he seemed very confident that things would work out well for him.

Q   Do you like being at school?

A   Yes.

Q   Have you decided what you would like to do when you leave school?

A Something in the medical field.

Q What type of exams are you taking?

A I hope to do O levels in chemistry, physics, biology, and some CSEs, then I want to go to sixth form college to do some A levels in order to go into medicine.

Q What do your parents think about your choice of career?

A They want me to be a doctor.

Q What type of job do your parents do?

A My father worked in the pottery industry until recently when he was made redundant and my mother is a housewife.

Q Do you think you will get the necessary qualifications to pursue a medical career?

A Yes.

Was this a personal choice that this student wanted to be a doctor or did he already have other relatives in the medical profession? He said it was a personal decision that he made. I asked him about racism in schools whether or not he had experienced any. To which he replied "not much, very little among the children." But he found racism in books offensive and distasteful, and there was a need to get better books in the schools. This shows that the curriculum does not cater adequately for black children, and it is no wonder so many fail the school system. At the same time some teachers seem to think that children do no take notice of racism in books, unless it is pointed out to them. This is a way of ignoring their own prejudices, whilst undermining the intelligence of many of their pupils. Many teachers seem to think that the books which children read do them no harm, unless something is pointed out to them, then their attention will be drawn to it. Yet many black children have told me that those books had offended them to the point of making them feel withdrawn and did not feel like taking part in the lessons. This student seemed very enthusiastic about pursuing a medical career. However, it may not have occurred to him that it can be costly and expensive to pursue certain careers, and this may lead to disappointment if his parents cannot adequately help with the expenses involved, especially where medical and some other professions are concerned. His class background may also act as a barrier into the medical field as can be seen in the education system which selects by class certain pupils for specific professions. This is why children from middle class homes can plan their careers positively and with certainty because they know that their parents will help to support them financially whatever the cost, and there are no barriers to deter them. Many working class children cannot depend on this kind of support, because their parents may not be able to afford the additional cost of financing their studies. This is where the dividing line appears when it comes to giving your child a good education as so much will depend on cost and affordability. Here we find that social class continues to dominate the education system with the middle classes being able to buy their children's education, while for most of the working classes it is a case of depending on State education for their children and this does not carry the same prestige as private education.

Chi-Square tests showed that more boys liked school than girls. This would be expected based on the history of the development of education when girls had less schooling than boys. Some of the comments which the children gave as to why they liked school were very important, because it was from their own experiences and outlook. On the topic of how and why they chose particular occupations, the answers ranged from it was what they liked, or something that they were capable of doing, or something that was manageable to them. For instance, those who were taking 7 or 8 O levels, were confident of going to college to do their A levels. Many of them were also planning that if they got good A level grades, they might consider going to university. On the other hand, of those who were doing fewer O levels or CSEs, some were planning to go to college to do more O levels, then see what the results were in order to make further plans. This shows how important qualifications are for the majority of the pupils tested, and how enthusiastic they were to do well at school.

Conclusion

The study has investigated children's experiences and perceptions of school in an area that is considered to be working class in origin. It found that despite this view, the children had positive attitudes towards school and were eager to do well at school in order to increase their job prospects. This was so for all three groups of pupils studied. I have looked at the situation regarding children's experiences and achievement in schools from a qualitative point of view, using participant observation, interviews, and questionnaires which were administered locally. As it turned out there has been some positive findings which have led me to believe that even though a statistical analysis could not be made, a qualitative explanation can yield positive results. As would be expected, based on certain historical factors and how children were educated before the introduction of compulsory education, boys seemed to value education more than girls. However, girls seem to be catching up on their education, as many were very enthusiastic about school and the choice of having a good career through the opportunities that are now available to women.

It is clear that most of the pupils had positive attitudes toward school, and clear ideas about what they wanted to do in the future. They did not seem deterred by having to work hard at school. They were determined to do their best whilst they were at school in order to secure a worthwhile career for the future. They did not find school to be boring, but only a little repetitive at times, but this did not hinder their determination to work hard towards achieving some form of qualifications which they considered to be important in their search for employment. But most of the children were dissatisfied about certain aspects of schooling. They said their teachers should be more caring, and should explain things to them better. Some also thought that they were being treated too much like little children and should be treated like young adults. They wanted the teachers to provide a more caring atmosphere in the schools and project more warmth and friendliness towards them which would make them feel more at ease. This would also enable them to work better at school. These statements show that teachers need to change their attitudes towards their pupils regardless of their backgrounds, origin and colour.

As far as Caribbean children locally are concerned, they do not appear to be isolated from the school system when compared to Caribbean children elsewhere, this being the views of 7 respondents. Some of the children often reply, "I was the only black child in my class, so I just got on with my work, this did not prevent me from getting on." However, it was also brought to my attention that in the later part of the 1960s-70s, it was noticed that the majority of black children locally were in the lower streams, and the observer who was white, did not know why this was so at the time because racism was not yet seen as a problem in schools, and the term underachievement amongst Caribbean children was not yet apparent. The observer may have therefore thought that this was quite normal in school practices. But now with the introduction of Section 11 teachers into schools to help children mainly with their language problems, more discoveries are being brought to light, in the sense that black children may have been the victims of covert discrimination previously at the local level. This is despite the fact that several teachers have told me they treat all children alike and do not hold any child back. There is now some changes taking place in some schools, because many are now involved in implementing a multicultural curriculum. This is with the intention of catering for ethnic children in schools, as opposed to previously having a Eurocentric curriculum which did a great deal of harm to some black children. The Local Education Authority has recently responded to the need for a multicultural curriculum. But this shows how far behind other authorities it is in catering for ethnic needs. This was not seen as a priority previously, which would create some doubt as to why the authority did not act sooner in catering for ethnic children in schools. Could it be that racism is endemic in the entire country and is manifested in the education system? This is still one of the authorities where there is still an absence of black governors, teachers, educationists and social workers, and no attempt is being made to encourage such a move. Maybe educationists chose to take a negative approach in thinking that they are being fair in their dealings with minorities, but probably they are unaware of their own unconscious racism and prejudices, and how differently they treat minorities. In the past there were many Caribbean children who could have done well at school locally, but they had to go to college to take their O levels which they should have taken at school. They saw it as racism amongst teachers. According to studies carried out elsewhere in the country on the same topic, racism was a possible cause. I have however stressed the impossibility in measuring such a variable. But teachers are trained to accept middle class values, and this they take with them into the classroom. How can they during their first meeting with Caribbean children, readily accept them as achievers based on those values and ideologies which they hold? If they hold low expectations of Caribbean children this will be manifested in the way they interact with them, and this is likely to be internalized by the children concerned. Racism is an intangible variable that cannot be identified as other variables such as class, gender or background, but the consequences can be so insidious that it is even more damaging. If the fault is obscure how can it be rectified? This would require the re-training of teachers on a large scale, and race awareness courses to help right the situation. This would probably help them to abolish some of the previous stereotypes that have governed their way of thinking for decades, and to take a new approach to classroom thinking and assessing children according to their capabilities rather than by race, colour or class. According to Entwistle (1978) the structure of British society is resistant to change. As he saw it, there is an inherent fear amongst those who hold the balance of power that if changes are made too rapidly, this will upset the stability that the country enjoys. In order to protect such cherished values and standards the dominant groups form ideologies which they then transmit to the lower classes mainly in the form of nationalism and superiority. This gives the lower classes pride in defending their country against foreigners for the good of their society. The British education system was founded on a middle class philosophy, and is therefore likely to remain a middle class institution dominated by middle class values. Unless drastic measures are taken to reform the system to enable minority children to be better accommodated, they are likely to remain outside the system which is inevitably divided by class and race.

◆

CHAPTER 8

Summary and Conclusion

During the period of the late 1950s to 1960s when Caribbean children first entered the British school system, teachers were not aware of such matters as racism, ethnic diversity, or the cultural backgrounds of black children. The only knowledge that many had of black people were the derogatory terms that was portrayed in European history and literature that blacks were inferior and hence had a lower intelligence than whites.

Under those circumstances, it would be likely that they would be inclined to treat black children differently than white children. This could probably have been one of the reasons why so many black children failed at school. This later led to the issue of black underachievement in schools which greatly angered many black parents. However, it is likely that in sparsely populated areas where black children are few in number, some teachers may be reluctant to categorise all black children as underachievers. Under those circumstances it could be argued that in a low profile area some schools may be more likely to treat pupils on the basis of ability rather than on colour differences. This is because large numbers of black children tend to attract the stigmatized version of them being seen as troublemakers, and this has to be taken into account. It has been pointed out to me by some black parents and pupils that this seems to be the case. I have used the term 'some schools', because they vary in terms of teacher attitudes. Some teachers seem to be better able to deal with Caribbean children than others. Again this may be based on their ideology and whether or not they possess liberal attitudes.

I spoke to a young Caribbean mother who was having problems with a headmistress over her daughter who was at primary school. She said if there was any misbehaviour at the school, the black child would be the first to be blamed by the teacher who did nothing to find out what the problem was. This is not an isolated case, other black parents have suggested likewise. This type of attitude by teachers could be a hindrance to the achievement of Caribbean children, no matter what area they may live in. Teacher attitudes would seem a very important factor in how they interact with their pupils, and their perceptions of them as potential achievers or failures. Some Caribbean children in the area have achieved well with the help of their teachers. But it could well be that their home environment provided the impetus which was aided by the schools. The parents in this category have told me that they constantly instilled in their children the value of a good education. Some teachers have told me that the child who comes to school equipped with a certain amount of knowledge will excel over and above those who do not possess that knowledge. Such remarks show that some children do start school at an advantage, and those are the ones who are likely to achieve well. Teachers will be more inclined to offer them more help than that given to the less able ones. Several children have suggested that this is the case. If Caribbean children are seen by their teachers as coming from disadvantaged homes, it is likely that they will be seen as underachievers from the very beginning of their schooling, and this will continue throughout their school days.

There is a problem faced by sociologists when carrying out certain types of investigation which requires in-depth information on a specific issue. Racism seems to be one of those topics which rates very unpopular with some teachers and this will make it difficult to gather information on the subject. Some teachers tend to be defensive when such an issue arises, and would rather avoid the subject than to discuss it openly or even admit that racism exists. I have been told by some Caribbean parents that their children had problems with their teachers during the 1960s and 1970s and that certain schools in the area had previously refused to take in black children. They were only admitted after the parents opposed the headmaster's view and insisted that their children be sent to that school. Here we see that blacks are constantly struggling to be accepted by society and even to have their children educated is problematic. How then can teachers say that they are not racist when that is the very attitude they portray to black parents and pupils? They seem to say one thing and then practice another. Dhondy et al (1982) found that this was the case in some London schools where black children were left without any form of proper supervision while the teachers sat in the staff room refusing to teach them.

The children's experiences and perceptions of school indicated that in areas that are sparsely populated, there is the likelihood that given the chance, children will be more inclined to work harder especially if they are encouraged to do so by their teachers and their parents. The fact that they feel less isolated from the school system, they are better able to channel their energies into their work, rather than spending time accounting for misbehaviour or nursing hurtful feelings for constantly being ostracised by their teachers. Their chances of achievement can therefore be rated as better than in densely populated areas where stereotyping may be used as a factor in assessing their abilities. The children will see school more positively, because for them it has a meaning. The majority of the children who took part in the study in all groups said that they liked school because it offered them a base on which to build their future. Their views about school were very positive, and even those who were somewhat reluctant about what they thought of school, said it was better to be at school than to stay at home because although they had to work hard at school, they would get bored at home with nothing to do. They said that school provided them with the knowledge that will equip them to meet other challenges in the outside world. There were hardly any anti-school pupils among those who were interviewed, nor those who took part in the questionnaire. No one actually said that they hated school except for one white boy who said that from the first day he went to nursery school he had always hated school ever since. But despite that, he does not play truant and was prepared to stay on until he finishes school, when he hoped to find a job that he liked doing.

Although most of the children said that they had a good relationship with their teachers, there were some who thought that teachers should be more caring. Two thirds of those who took part in the questionnaires gave different reasons about what they expected from their teachers. Some said that teachers should be more polite and understanding, some said teachers should spend more time with their pupils and the majority said that teachers should explain things better to them. This shows that there appears to be a communication problem with teachers and their pupils, which requires some attention.

This would suggest that the views of children seem a neglected area of study and require more investigation. Some children suggested that they are treated too much like little children rather than like adults, especially in their teens and no one seems to listen to them. They would like to be listened to more in order to give their opinions on matters that concern them. It seemed rather unacceptable that teachers with their skills and knowledge do not take their pupils needs into consideration more fully. A further one third of the pupils who said that teachers should be more helpful, did not give an explanation how this should be done, but expressed their wish for a better understanding from their teachers.

From the various reasons which the children gave about their teachers not being helpful enough, it would appear that children have different needs that are not adequately met by their teachers, nor do teachers try to understand their pupils problems sufficiently. Some of the children are of the opinion that teachers should listen to them more, and try to help them in whatever way they can. As one boy said, it appears that children have no rights at all, as no one is prepared to listen to them. It is often expected that children should show politeness to their teachers at all times, but do teachers do the same to their pupils? One teacher told me that children will react according to how they are treated. If you treat them right, they will never forget, and they will respect you. She said that politeness is a reciprocity and not just a one way process, and children may not take kindly to being shouted at all the time nor to being ignored when they ask for an explanation about something that they do not understand. This seems to be a factor that many children would like to see changed, and a wish that teachers should explain things to them more. According to the statements given by the ethnic children themselves, they did not perceive their teachers as overtly racist, they said that most of them were helpful. But we must remember that there are a great deal of changes that are now taking place in schools, and some teachers are more understanding than they used to be some years ago.

Most Caribbean parents in the study said they were eager for their children to do well at school, but they were not fully aware of the workings of the school, and would like teachers to be more cooperative and let them know how they could help with their children's education. This shows that there is a lack of communication between the home and the school which needs to be rectified. Until black parents are better informed about the school system and are able to take an active role in their children's education, it is likely that black children will be at a disadvantage educationally. Some parents said that they were willing to do this but did not know how to go about it. This is where the schools should play a part in integrating the parents into the school system so that they can play a role in the education of their children. Black and white pupils alike have favourable views about school, and are determined to get as much education as possible which they see as an important aspect for their future well-being.

The Local Education Authority has recently responded to the need for a multicultural curriculum for schools. The purpose of this approach is to enable schools to develop a curriculum that would be more suitable to the needs of all pupils. It aims to introduce a variety of ethnic cultures into schools which will enable teachers and pupils to value ethnic cultures and respect their way of life. But why should it have taken the local authority so long to be implemented? It would appear that the ethnic population in the area were not seen as constituting a problem so the Education Authority did not consider them to be a priority case. If this scheme had been introduced much earlier, it would probably have benefited the fairly large number of Caribbean children who attended schools in the area during the 1970s. Many of those children may have needed some form of special help, but they were not seen as requiring any help so no attention was given to their cause.

The Local Education Authority has been slow in responding to such needs, probably because it was not seen as a pressing issue. To be more than a decade behind other counties in the implementation of multicultural policies would seem to warrant questioning. There should be a monitoring scheme to ensure that those policies are not just read and forgotten, but every effort should be made to monitor its progress and to check its effectiveness. This might help in making teachers more aware of their responsibilities and duties to all their pupils. Very often teachers may like to think that they understand their pupils, but this might not be the case, and problems remain unsolved.

At a local education forum (1991) where minority issues were discussed, it appeared that the whole idea surrounding multicultural education and equal opportunities for minority groups were grossly misunderstood. When the topic of minority governors were raised, there were no proper procedures for appointing them, and no positive action was in progress. When one of the teachers involved in the scheme was asked about such a move, she replied that race did not come into it, they appoint the best suitably qualified person for the job. From their point of view the best qualified person will be a white person. Minority issues are constantly being managed and dictated by white educationists on their terms, while minorities for whom the schemes were designed to help, have no say in matters that concern them. It was also suggested that some colleges have policies on sexual harassment, and more recently the introduction of a policy on racial harassment.

Unless policies are clearly defined and followed through with proper procedures for monitoring to ensure their effectiveness, there is the likelihood that the whole idea surrounding multiculturalism will become decadent. During my interviews with the children who were of various races, colour, and backgrounds, a great deal was discovered about them that teachers were not probably aware of. This is because they may not have taken the time nor the trouble to find out what the children's needs were. As mentioned in chapter 7, most of the children said that they would like their teachers to be more helpful and understanding. They would also like teachers to explain things to them better. I am not saying that all teachers fall into this category, as some are very dedicated and helpful, but teachers should be more aware that their own beliefs and values may not necessarily fit into the classroom in which they teach. There is a need for the re-training of those teachers, and a re-structuring of the curriculum and the classroom from a Eurocentric to a multi-racial where policies are implemented and monitored for their effectiveness. This would ensure that all children feel that they are part of the school's environment, and are able to partake fully in their lessons and other school activities without a feeling of isolation from the school system.

Conclusion

After looking at all the previous evidence by other authors, and subsequent findings which I discovered, it is worth stressing some of the difficulties involved when researching certain sociological topics. By this it is meant that some variables cannot be quantified and have to be carefully examined before a conclusion can be reached.

However, after carefully analysing the topic of underachievement amongst Caribbean children, it remains for me to say that I have to disagree with some of the previous studies which linked underachievement to factors such as the use of Creole, family pathology, matriarchal family, large family etc. Those studies have largely ignored how structures and institutions create racism, and how this may be used as a factor to cause underachievement amongst Caribbean children. It is also worth looking at teacher attitudes and expectations of Caribbean children and interaction within the school, and the effect that this can have on children's achievement. It is very easy to look at factors outside the school, because those variables are observable eg. communities, social class, social deprivation, language, home background and economic factors, which can equally contribute to the hypothesis of the underachievement theory. But if it is found that other crucial explanations are lacking such as classroom procedures and practices, interaction between teacher and pupil, teachers perceptions and evaluations of certain groups of pupils, then it is possible to hold those individuals who run those institutions responsible for the outcome of their institutions. Classroom procedures are closed to the outside world and no one actually knows how decisions are made as to teachers evaluation and assessment of individual pupils. What is it that cause teachers to place some children in O level streams, and others in CSE streams? Can teachers' assessment of their pupils be totally objective and free from bias or prejudice? Why have so many studies shown that Caribbean children were mainly located in the lower streams, or sent to ESN schools?

If teachers had an interest in black children achieving at school, they would make an effort to ensure that they achieve. For instance pupils in upper streams achieve and do very well because they know that they are expected to be achievers. They are also usually encouraged by their teachers and this gives them the impetus to do well. Conversely lower stream pupils underachieve, because they are denied the opportunity to be achievers. As a result they see themselves as failures both in the school and outside of the school. Are these children responsible for the type of education which they receive at school? Good teaching practice will result in good success rates regardless of children's backgrounds or cultural origins, while poor or differentiated teaching practice will result in poor achievement rates.

A recent Government report on Schools on a BBC news report November (1993) showed that nearly one third of school children are not being taught properly. The report puts this down to bad teaching practices, of which the outcome is poor standards of education. It also found that some lessons were badly planned, and that teachers overcompensated for children of disadvantaged backgrounds, and did not encourage them enough. The report stated that the key to high standards of education is good teaching.

P. Ramsden (1992, p268) looked at teaching practice in Higher Education and suggested that to improve teaching, it is important to encourage students to learn, and help teachers to teach. He outlined that the process of teaching and learning should be conceived as imaginative, arduous and pleasurable. But it has to be a reciprocity with teachers and learners taking a delight in the matter. If teachers understand how to help their pupils, they will get a better understanding of how to improve teaching. Ramsden pointed out that bad teaching makes the subject matter monotonous and difficult to grasp, and can make students/pupils frightened and insecure.

During my research many pupils told me that if they did not understand a lesson that was not explained properly, they would feel lost, insecure or even frightened. The matter was even made worse if they asked the teacher a question and did not get a positive response, or being told to shut up. They would become withdrawn and too frightened to ask any further questions. Ramsden suggested that teachers should be prepared to take the initiative especially by listening respectfully to students/pupils in how they can be helped. He suggested that as with bad teaching, so is bad evaluation, and bad educational development, and the end result is bad outcome.

However, there need not be a bad outcome if the teachers are prepared to:

1. **Listen to their pupils/students.**

2. **Show a willingness to help them.**

3. **Treat their pupils/students with respect regardless of their origin or background.**

4. **Treat their pupils alike, so that they all have an equal chance to succeed. This was said to me by many teachers that I interviewed.**

5. **Do not ridicule any pupil in the presence of their mates. As the Rastas at Milltown High suggested, this made them feel low and degraded.**

6. **Encourage pupils/students to learn.**

The study shows that it is not just one level of education where there are difficulties faced by teachers in getting to understand their pupils/students, but at all levels of education. This indicates that what is required is an evaluation of Teacher training methods, and how they can be better trained to meet the needs of all their pupils/students regardless of their class backgrounds or origin.

However, this will be especially so if the pupils are of a different race, due to the added hostility they face in schools and society. Racism would therefore seem a factor for underachievement, but this would require further and more extensive research due to the intangibility of the issue.

◆

Bibliography

Abrahamson, M. (1981) Sociological Theory. Prentice Hall Inc. Cliffs. N.J. USA.

Adler, M. Petch, A. Tweedie, J. (1989) Parental Choice and Educational Policy. Edinburgh Univ. Press.

Alcock, M. (1985) A study of the Staffordshire Education Authority's Response to Multicultural Education in Stoke-on-Trent, with particular reference to Teacher Attitudes in Pre-Secondary Schools. Unpublished M. Ed. Thesis, Univ. of Keele.

Alibhaj, Y. New Society (29.1.88.).

Bagley, C. (1975) Race, Education and Identity. Macmillan, London.

Bagley, C. & Verma, K. (1979) Racial Prejudice, the individual and Society. Saxon House, Farnborough, U.K.

Banks, O. & Finlayson, D. (1973) Success and failure in Secondary Schools. Methuen & Co. Ltd., London.

Banks, J. (ed) (1973) Teaching Ethnic Studies. National Council for Social Studies, Washington, D.C, USA.

Banton, M. (1987) Racial Theories. University Press, Cambridge.

Baker, M. (1981) The New Racism. Junction Books Ltd., London.

Barnes, B. (1974) Scientific Knowledge and Sociological Theory. Routledge & Kegan Paul Ltd., London.

Bassett, G.W. et al. (1978) Individual Differences. Allen & Unwin, Pty Ltd., Australia.

Bastiani, J. (1987) Parents and Teachers. NFER, Nelson Co. Ltd. Berkshire.

Batron, L. & Walker, S. (1983) Race, Class & Education. Croom Helm, Kent.

Becker, H. S. (1986) Writing for Social Scientists. How to start and finish your thesis, book, or article. Chicago, U.P.

Bernstein, B. (1971) Class, Codes and Control. Roudedge & Kegan Paul, London.

Bhat, A. et al. (1988) Britain's Black Population. Gower Publishing Co. Ltd. Herts. Eng.

Bhatnaghar, J. (1970) Immigrants at School. Cornmarket Press, London.

Bhatnaghar, J. (1981) Educating Immigrants. Croom Helm, London.

Bilton, T. et al. (1981) Introducing Sociology. Macmillan Press Ltd., London.

Brakes, M. (1985) Comparative Youth Culture. Routledge & Kegan Paul Plc, London.

Bowles, S. & Gintis, H. (1976) Schooling in Capitalist America. Basic Books, N.Y.

Britain's Black Population. (1980) The Runnymede Trust and the Radical Statistics Race Group. Heinemann Educational Books, London.

Brown, R. (1976) Sociology of Education. Knowledge, Education and Cultural Change. Tavistock Pub. Ltd., London.

Burgess, R. (1986) Sociology Education & Schools. B. T. Batsford, London.

Burroughs, G.E.R. (1971) Design and Analysis in Educational Research. Alden and Mowbray Ltd., Oxford.

Carnoy, M. (1974) Education as Cultural Imperialism, Longman Inc. N.Y.

Cashmore, E. 1982) Black Sportsmen. Foreward G. Crooks. Routledge & Kegan Paul, London.

Cashmore, E. (1979) Rastaman. The Rastafarian Movement in England. Allen & Unwin, London.

Cashmore, E. & Troyna, B. (1982) Black Youth in Crisis. George Allen & Unwin Ltd., Herts. Eng.

Chigwada, R. The Education of Afro-Caribbean Girls: New Society, (4.3.88).

Coard, B. (1971) How the West Indian Child is made Educationally sub-normal by the British School System. New Beacon Books, London.

Cohen, L. & Holliday, M. (1982), Statistics for Social Scientists. Harper & Row Ltd., London.

Cole, M. (1989) Social Contexts of Schooling. Falmer Press, East Sussex.

Coleman, J. (1967) The Adolescent Society. New York Free Press.

Conger, J.J. (1973) Adolescence and Youth. Harper & Row, N.Y.

Commission for Racial Equality. (1978) Five Views of Multicultural Britain. C.R.E. London.

Cropley, A. (1983) The Education of Immigrant Children. Croom Helm, London.

Curran, J. et al. (1977) Mass Communication and Society. Arnold Pub. Co. Ltd. London.

Davies, O L & Goldsmith, P. ed. (1976) Statistical Methods in Research & Production. Longman, London.

Davison, R B. (1966) Black British Immigrants to England. Oxford Univ. Press, London.

D. E. S. (1975) A Language for Life. HMSO, London.

D. E. S. (1971) The Education of Immigrants. H.M.S.O. London.

Dhondy, F. Besse, B. Hassan, L. (1982) The Black Explosion in British Schools. Race Today, London.

Douglas, J W B. (1964) Home and School. MacGibbon & Kee, London.

Edwards, V K. (1979) The West Indian Language Issue in British Schools. Methuen and Co. Ltd., London.

Eggleston, J. et al. (1986) Education for Some. Trentham Books, Stoke-on-Trent, Eng.

Eggleston, J. et al. (1985) The Educational and Vocational Experience of 15-18 year old Young People of Minority Ethnic Groups. (HMSO).

Entwistle, H. (1978) Class, Culture, and Education. Methuen and Co. Ltd., London.

Floud, J E. (1966) Social Class & Educational Opportunity. Heinemann, London.

Foner, N. (1979) Farewell Jamaica, Jamaican Immigrants in London. Harper and Row, N.Y.

Fontani, M. & Weinstein, G. (1968) The Disadvantaged. Harper & Row, N.Y.

Foster, P (1990) Policy and Practice in Multicultural and Anti-racist Education, Routledge.

Fryer, P. (1984) Staying Power, The history of Black People in Britain. Pluto Press. London.

Gaine, C (1987) No Problem Here. A practical approach to Education and Race in White schools. Hutchison, London.

Genovese, E D. (1968) In Red and Black. Marxian explanations in Southern and Afro-American History, Vintage Books, N.Y.

Gibson, A. (1986) The Unequal Struggle. Centre for Caribbean Studies, Caribbean House, London.

Giddens A. (1973) The Class Structure of Advanced Societies. Hutchison & Co. Ltd., London.

Giddens, A. & Held, D. (1982) Class, Power and Conflict, Macmillan Press Ltd., London.

Giglioli, P. (1972) Language and Social Context. Penguin, Harmondsworth.

Giles, R. (1977) The West Indian Experience in London. Heinemann Education Books Ltd., London.

Giles, R. (1971) Multicultural Education. Heinemann Educ. Books Ltd. London.

Goldthorpe, J H. (1980) Social Mobility and Class Structure in Modern Britain. Oxford Univ. Press, N.Y.

Gower G. (1983) The Education of Minority Groups. (OECD) Organization for Economic Cooporation & Development Comparative Studies.

Grace, G. (1978) Teachers, Ideology and Control. Routledge & Kegan Paul, London.

Halsey, A. (1961) Education, Economy and Society. Free Press, New York.

Halsey, A.H. (1961) Ability and Educational Opportunity, (OECD), Organization for Economic Cooperation & Development.

Halsey, A.H. & Goldthorpe, D. (1980) Origins and Destinations, Family, Class and Education in Modern Britain. Oxford University Press, Oxford.

Haralambos, M. (1980) Sociology, Themes and Perspectives. Univ. Tutorial Press Ltd., Slough.

Hargreaves, D.H. (1967) Social Relations in a Secondary School. Kegan Paul, London.

Hayslett, H. T. (1976) Statistics Made Simple. Doubleday & Co. Inc. N.Y.

Hartman, P. & Husband, C. (1974) Racism and the Mass Media. Davis-Poynter, London.

Hill, C. (1969) Immigration and Integration. Pergamon, Oxford.

Hill, D. (1976) Teaching in Multiracial Schools. Methuen, London.

Holly, D. (1967) Education or Domination. Arrow. London.

Husband, C. (1982) Race in Britain. Hutchison, London.

Jackson, B. (1979) Starting School. Croom Helm Ltd., London.

James, A. & Jeffcoate, R. (1976) The School in Multicultural Society. Harper & Row Ltd., London.

Jeffcoate, R. (1984) Ethnic Minorities and Education. Harper & Row, London.

Jeffcoate, R. (1979) Positive Image. Staples Printers, London.

Jones, C. (1977) Immigration and Social Policy in Britain. Tavistock, London.

Johnson, K.R. (1970) Teaching the Culturally Disadvantaged. (S.R.A.) Science Research Associates, Inc. California.

Kapo, R. (1981) A Savage Culture, Namara Group, London.

Keddie, N. (1973) Tinker Taylor, Penguin Books, Harmondsworth.

Khan, N. (1976) The Art Britain Ignores. Commission for Racial Equality, London.

Kirp, D. (1977) Race and Schooling in Britain. Univ. of California, California Press Ltd., London.

Klein, G. (1985) Reading into Racism. Bias in Children's Literature and learning material. Routledge, London.

Knox, F. (1985) Migration to Britain. Theories of Immigration, Unpublished thesis, M.A. Univ. of Keele.

Lacey, C. (1977) The Socialization of Teachers. Methuen, London.

Lawton, D. (1968) Social Class, Language, and Education. Routledge, London.

Lynch, J. (1986) Multicultural Education. Routledge, London.

Mac an Ghaill, M. (1988) Young gifted and Black. OUP, Milton Keynes.

Majoribanks, K. (1976) Ethnic Families and Children's Achievement. Allen & Unwin, Sydney.

Megarry, J. et al (1979) World Year Book of Education, Education of Minorities. Kogan Page Ltd., London.

Miles, R. & Phizacklea, A. (1979) Racism and Political Action in Britain. Routledge & Kegan Paul, London.

Miller, H. (1978) Social Foundations of Education. Hunter College, New York.

Miller, H. (1967) Education for the Disadvantaged. Free Press, Macmillan & Co. USA.

Milner, D. (1983) Children and Race. Penguin, Harmondsworth.

Mirza, H.S. (1992) Young, Female and Black. Routledge.

Montague A. Multicultural Education at Work. New Society, (5.2.88).

Morris D. (1982) The Human Race, Methuen, London.

Morris, D. (1967) The Naked Ape. Cape, London.

Moore, R. (1975) Racism and Black Resistance in Britain. Pluto Press, London.

Mullard, C. (1973) Black Britain. Allen and Unwin, London.

Nash, R. (1973) Classrooms Observed. Routledge & Kegan Paul, London.

Newton, J. (1986) Race and Class in Women's History. Routledge & Kegan Paul, London.

Owens, A. Hurd's New Colour Bar, New Society, (27.11 88).

Palmer, F. (1986) Anti-Racism an assault on Education and value. Sherwood Press, London.

Payne, J. (1967) A Comparative Study of the Mental ability of 7-8 years old British and Non-British Children in a Midland Town. Unpublished Thesis, Univ. of Keele.

Pearson, D. (1981) Race, Class, and Political Activism. Gower Pub. Co., Ltd., London.

Pincent, A. (1969) The Principles of Teaching Method. Harrop & Co., Ltd., London.

Pryce, K. (1979) Endless Pressure, A study of West Indian Lifestyle in Bristol. Penguin, Harmondsworth.

Pursell, C.H. (1977) Education and Inequality. The Free Press, Macmillan Co., Inc. N.Y.

Purvis, J. & Hales, M. (1983) Inequality in Education. Routledge & Kegan Paul, London.

Rampton, A. (1981) West Indian Children in our Schools. HMSO.

Ramsden, P. (1992) Learning to Teach in Higher Education. Routlege, London.

Raynor, J. & Harden, J. (1973) Equality and City Schools. D.o.E. Routledge & O.U.P.

Reedy, S. & Woodward, M. (1980) Family, Work, and Education. Open University Press, Hodder & Stroughton, G.B.

Rex, J. (1986) Race and Ethnicity. Open University Press. Milton Keynes.

Rex, J. (1970) Race Relations and Sociological Theory. Routledge & Kegan Paul, London.

Rex, J. & Tomlinson, S. (1983) Colonial Immigrants in a British City. Routledge & Kegan Paul, London.

Romaine, S. (1988) Pidgin and Creole Languages. Longman Inc. New York.

Rubenstein, D. ed. (1973) Education & Equality. Routledge & Kegan Paul, London.

Sharpe R. & Green A. (1975) Education & Social Control. Routledge, London.

Silver, H. (1973) Equal Opportunity in Education. Methuen, London.

Simon, B. (1971) Intelligence, Psychology, and Education. Lawrence and Wishart, London.

Simon, B. & Taylor, W. (1981) Education in the Eighties. Billing & Son, London.

Smith, D. & Tomlinson, S. (1989) The School Effect. Policy Studies Institute, London.

Stone, M. (1981) The Education of the Black Child. The Myth of Multicultural Education. Fontana, Glasgow.

Smith, T.E. (1981) Commonwealth Migration. Macmillan, London.

Straker-Welds, M. (1984) Education for a Multicultural Society. Bell & Hyman, London.

Stubbs, M. (1976) Language, Schools and Classroom. Methuen London.

Summer, R. & Warburton, F.W. (1972) Achievement in Secondary Schools. J. Garner Ltd., Lancs.

Swann, M. (1985) Education for all. HMSO.

Taylor, M. (1983) Caught Between. NFER- Nelson, Berkshire. U.K.

Taylor, M. & Hegarty, S. (1985) The best of both Worlds. NFER/Nelson Co. Ltd. Berkshire.

The Victoria History of the County of Stafford, VII. (1967) Institute of Historical Research. Oxford Univ. Press.

Thompson, G. (1977) Race Relations. Blackie, Glasgow.

Tierney, J. ed. (1982) Race, Immigration and Schooling. Holt, Rinehart and Winston, Eastbourne.

Tomlinson, S. (1983) Ethnic Minorities in British Schools. Hienemann Education Books Ltd., London.

Troyna, B. & Smith D. (1983) Racism, School and the Labour Market. National Youth Bureau, Leicester.

Troyna, B. & Williams, J. (1986) Racism, Education and the State. Croom Held Ltd., London.

Turner, J.D. (1975) Education and Deprivation. Manchester, Univ. Press.

Verma, G.K & Bagley, C. (1979) Race, Education & Identity. MacMillan, London.

Verma, G.K. & Bagley, C. (1984) Race Relations & Cultural Differences, St. Martin's Press Inc. New York.

Verma, G.K. & Bagley, C. (1975) Race and Education across Cultures, Heinemann, London.

Verma, G & Brandon, A. (1986) Ethnicity & Educational Achievement in British Schools. MacMillan Press Ltd., London.

Walker, R. & Alderman, C. (1975) A Guide to Classroom Observation. Methuen, London.

Wallman, S. (1979) Ethnicity at Work. MacMillan Press, London.

Willey, R. (1984) Race, Equality & Schools. Methuen & Co. Ltd., N.Y. & London.

Willis, P. (1977) Learning to Labour. Saxon House, Teakfield, England.

Woodhead, M. & McGrath, A.(eds) (1988) Family School & Society. Open Univ. Press. G.B.